Poverty

KEY CONCEPTS

Published

Poverty

Ruth Lister

polity

First published in 2004 by Polity Press

Polity Press
65 Bridge Street
Cambridge CB2 1UR, UK.

Polity Press
350 Main Street
Malden, MA 02148, USA

ISBN: 0-7456-2563-0
ISBN: 0-7456-2564-9 (paperback)

A catalogue record for this book is available from the British Library.

Typeset in 10.5 on 12 pt Sabon
by SNP Best-set Typesetter Ltd., Hong Kong
Printed and bound in Great Britain by MPG Books, Bodmin, Cornwall

For further information on Polity, visit our website: www.polity.co.uk

To J. with love and thanks

Contents

Preface

As I explain in the Introduction, my understanding of poverty has been shaped in part by my experience with the Child Poverty Action Group and more recently as a member of the Commission on Poverty, Participation and Power. Over these years, I have been privileged to learn from people – with and without experience of poverty – too numerous to name. However, before acknowledging those who have directly assisted me with this book, I do wish to pay tribute to Professor Peter Townsend. He has been an influence on my own career; but more importantly his lifetime's commitment to the anti-poverty cause continues to be an inspiration to many.

In writing this book, I was fortunate to be able to employ Jan Flaherty as a part-time research assistant for a year. I am grateful to her for the excellent assistance she provided and also subsequently for her insights when commenting on the draft text. I am grateful too to a number of friends and colleagues who have commented on the text. Fran Bennett, Jim Kincaid and Adrian Sinfield gave generously of their time to read the whole draft. John Clarke and David Taylor commented on all or part of chapter 6. Advice on particular chapters from Dennis Smith, Peter Golding and Mike Pickering – all colleagues in the Department of Social Sciences – was testimony to how much I have gained from working in this collegial, interdisciplinary department. I thank all these colleagues and friends for their feedback, even though I have not been able always to do it full justice, largely because of space constraints. I would also like to thank Andrew Arden, Saul Becker and Jane Lewis for their encouragement and wise counsel at a moment of crisis and Louise Knight, my editor at Polity, for her patient and good-natured support.

Ruth Lister

Abbreviations

APPGP	All-Party Parliamentary Group on Poverty
BSAS	British Social Attitudes Survey
CASE	Centre for Analysis of Social Exclusion
CEC	Commission of the European Communities
CESCR	Committee on Economic, Social and Cultural Rights
CoPPP	Commission on Poverty, Participation and Power
CPAG	Child Poverty Action Group
DfID	Department for International Development
DSS	Department of Social Security
DWP	Department for Work and Pensions
EAPN	European Anti Poverty Network
EC	European Commission
EOC	Equal Opportunities Commission
EU	European Union
IDS	Institute of Development Studies
IEA	Institute of Economic Affairs
ILC	International Longevity Center
ILO	International Labour Organisation
IMF	International Monetary Fund
IPPR	Institute for Public Policy Research
JRF	Joseph Rowntree Foundation
ODI	Overseas Development Institute
OECD	Organization for Economic Co-operation and Development

OHCHR	Office of the High Commissioner for Human Rights
PIU	Performance and Innovation Unit
PSE (Survey)	Poverty and Social Exclusion (Survey)
SCCD	Standing Conference on Community Development
SEU	Social Exclusion Unit
SOSTRIS	Social Strategies in Risk Society
STICERD	Suntory and Toyota International Centres for Economics and Related Disciplines
UKCAP	UK Coalition against Poverty
UN	United Nations
UNDP	United Nations Development Programme
UNICEF	United Nations Children's Fund

List of Figures

Introduction

The need to lend a voice to suffering is a condition of all truth.

Adorno, 1973: 17–18

At the start of the twenty-first century, almost half the world's people suffer in a state of 'deep poverty amid plenty', measured (somewhat arbitrarily) as an income of less than $2 a day (World Bank, 2001: 3). Deep poverty is not just a phenomenon of the global 'South' but exists also within the affluent 'North'. In the US, the official poverty rate is over one in ten. In the EU, the latest figures indicate 15 per cent live below the (higher) poverty threshold. In the UK, the proportion is even larger: over a fifth of the population, including more than a quarter of children, compared with one in seven in 1979 of both children and adults.[1]

Poverty as a material reality disfigures and constrains the lives of millions of women, men and children and its persistence diminishes those among the non-poor who acquiesce in or help sustain it. It is therefore not surprising that many who write about poverty emphasize the word's moral and political claims:

> If the term 'poverty' carries with it the implication and moral imperative that something should be done about it, then the study of poverty is only ultimately justifiable if it influences

individual and social attitudes and actions. This must be borne in mind constantly if discussion on the definition of poverty is to avoid becoming an academic debate worthy of Nero – a semantic and statistical squabble that is parasitic, voyeuristic and utterly unconstructive and which treats 'the poor' as passive objects for attention, whether benign or malevolent – a discussion that is part of the problem rather than part of the solution. (Piachaud, 1987: 161)

I write this book with that warning ringing in my ears. There are also ethical issues involved when writing a book about poverty from a position of relative affluence. These include the danger of silencing and treating as objects those with the everyday experience of poverty who are rarely in a position to have their thoughts published. It is therefore important to acknowledge that, in addition to traditional forms of expertise associated with those who theorize and research poverty, there is a different form of expertise born of experience.

My aim is to draw on both forms of expertise. Moreover, my own understanding of poverty derives not just from the academic literature but from sixteen years working with the Child Poverty Action Group, a campaigning charity; from participatory research with Peter Beresford; and from my membership of an independent Commission on Poverty, Participation and Power, half of whose members had direct experience of poverty. The last experience involved 'an extraordinary journey' in enhanced comprehension, as those of us without direct experience of poverty learned from those who live it daily (CoPPP, 2000: v; del Tufo and Gaster, 2002).

The importance of incorporating the perspectives of those with experience of poverty into the theorization of and research into poverty, through participatory methods, tends to be recognized more in the context of poverty in the South than the North. The use of such an approach in the South has provided new insights into what poverty means and feels like for those experiencing it. The results also offer important lessons for poverty analysis in the North, which is the main focus of this book, at a time when globalization means that the causes of poverty are increasingly common to both (Townsend, 1993; Townsend and Gordon, 2002). Breaking down the intellectual barriers between South and North could do much to enrich and revitalize thinking about poverty (Maxwell, 2000).

While I write from a UK perspective, I will attempt to apply these lessons from the South to my own analysis. I will also be referring to material from the wider continent of Europe and from the US. Nevertheless, it has to be remembered that what it means to be poor can be very different in different societies, not just as between North and South but also, for instance, as between the US and Scandinavia. Socio-economic structural and cultural contexts shape the experiences and understandings of poverty. Thus 'poverty is at the same time culture-bound and universal' (Øyen, 1996: 4).

Concepts, Definitions and Measures

This means that there is no single concept of poverty that stands outside history and culture. It is a construction of specific societies. Moreover, different groups within a society may construct it in different ways. Because of the moral imperative of poverty and its implications for the distribution of resources both within and between societies, it is a political concept. As such it is highly contested. Concepts of poverty have practical effects. They carry implicit explanations which, in turn, underpin policy prescriptions. The emphasis placed upon socio-economic structural conditions, power relationships, culture and individual behaviour varies. The policies developed to tackle poverty reflect dominant conceptualizations. In practice, concepts are mediated by definitions and measures and it is important to differentiate between the three, as they are frequently conflated. Thus, for instance, 'concept' and 'definition' are often used interchangeably. A clearer separation between the three terms helps to avoid confusion and unnecessary polarization between broader and narrower notions of poverty.

Concepts: the meanings of poverty

Concepts of poverty operate at a fairly general level. They provide the framework within which definitions and measurements are developed. In essence, they are about the meanings of poverty – both to those who experience it and to different groups in society. An example would be a 'lack of basic security', understood as 'the absence of one or more factors that enable individuals and families to assume basic responsibilities and to enjoy fundamental rights' (Wresinski Report, 1987, cited in Spicker, 1999: 153).

A study of concepts of poverty also embraces how people talk about and visualize poverty: 'discourses of poverty' as articulated through language and images. These discourses are constructed in different fora, most notably politics, academia and the media. Each of these influences the ways in which poverty is understood by the wider society. In general, it is the understandings held by more powerful groups, rather than by those who experience poverty, which are reflected in dominant conceptualizations. However, this may be changing in the international development context, if powerful bodies such as the World Bank are genuine in their claims to be taking on board the meanings of poverty for those who experience it.

Definitions: distinguishing poverty from non-poverty

Definitions of poverty (should) provide a more precise statement of what distinguishes the state of poverty and of being poor from that of not being in poverty/poor. The following examples, taken from the British Social Attitudes Survey, are designed to assess the extent to which the general public subscribes to 'absolute' or 'relative' definitions of poverty (discussed in chapter 1). Is poverty where someone has 'enough to buy the things they really need, but not enough to buy the things most people take for granted' or where they do not have 'enough to eat and live without getting into debt' (Hills, 2001)?

Following Peter Townsend's path-breaking work (e.g. 1979), poverty researchers commonly define poverty in relative terms, as having insufficient resources to meet socially recognized needs and to participate in the wider society (as reflected in the first BSAS statement). However, as we shall see in chapter 1, definitions differ not just according to the absolute–relative yardstick but also in their breadth. Thus, in practice, there is sometimes a degree of overlap between definitions and concepts. For example, broader definitions like those deployed by some UN bodies incorporate notions such as a violation of basic rights and human dignity that are not unique to the state of being poor but are associated with it. Such 'definitions' are perhaps better understood as conceptualizations. Other 'definitions', such as those sometimes deployed by the UK Government, are more akin to descriptions, listing a number of aspects such as 'lack of income and access to good quality health, education and housing, and the quality of the local environment' (DSS, 1999: 23).

Measures: operationalizing definitions

Measures of poverty represent ways of operationalizing definitions so that we can identify and count those defined as poor and gauge the depth of their poverty. Official measures of poverty tend to use income levels while one-off surveys tend to deploy indicators of living standards and of different forms of deprivation. Examples of such indicators are whether someone does not have and is unable to afford two meals a day or is unable to visit friends and family because of lack of resources. Increasingly, it is argued that a rounded measure of poverty needs to combine both income and living standards (see chapter 2). The case is also being made for listening to what people in poverty themselves think are the best measurement indicators (Bennett and Roche, 2000; Galloway, 2002).

As figure 0.1 shows, the movement from concepts to measures involves a steady narrowing of focus. To move straight to definitions and measures without first considering the broader concepts can result in losing sight of wider meanings and their implications for definitions and measures. In particular, it can exclude the understandings of poverty derived from qualitative and participatory approaches. These frequently highlight aspects of poverty that lie outside definitions focused on income and material living standards and that can be difficult to measure in surveys designed to monitor trends over time and between countries (Baulch,

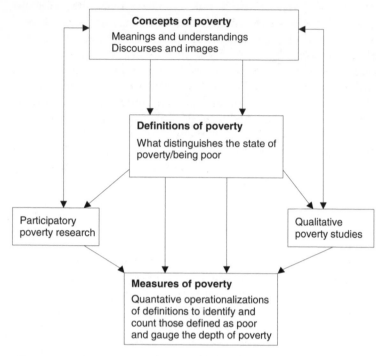

Figure 0.1 The relationship between concepts, definitions and measures of poverty

1996b; Chambers, 1997). Likewise, starting at the bottom with measures can encourage confusion between measures and definitions, so that arguments about competing definitions of poverty often turn out to be about competing measures. The measure of 60 per cent of median income used by the EU and the UK Government is frequently referred to as a definition. The result of treating it as such is an attenuated and highly limited technical definition, which is constrained by limitations of methodology and available data. Measurement is then in danger of becoming a substitute for analysis (McGee and Brock, 2001).

In both cases, omitting the conceptual level can encourage a myopic, technocratic approach that, in its preoccupation with measuring poverty's extent and depth, overlooks how it is experienced and understood. As Else Øyen argues, some of the energy devoted to 'measurement research' could profitably be channelled to trying to achieve greater 'poverty understanding' in terms of what it means to be poor (1996: 10). If we are to achieve greater understanding, we must pay adequate attention to the conceptual level.

What is at issue here is the non-material as well as the material manifestations of poverty. Poverty has to be understood not just as a disadvantaged and insecure economic *condition* but also as a shameful and corrosive social *relation* (Jones and Novak, 1999). This perspective has been illuminated in particular by the participatory approaches developed in the South. Such approaches highlight non-material aspects of poverty such as: lack of voice; disrespect, humiliation and an assault on dignity and self-esteem; shame and stigma; powerlessness; denial of rights and diminished citizenship. These represent what I shall call the 'relational/symbolic' aspects of poverty. They exemplify what Nancy Fraser terms 'symbolic injustice', 'rooted in social patterns of representation, interpretation and communication' (1997: 14). In other words, they stem from people in poverty's everyday interactions with the wider society and from the way they are talked about and treated by politicians, officials, the media and other influential bodies. Terms such as the 'the poor' and 'poor people' can themselves be experienced as dehumanizing and 'Othering' (chapter 5). They are therefore avoided here except where appropriate to the context, when they are placed in inverted commas.

As Caroline Moser (1998) observes, some of the development literature sets up a dichotomy between 'conventional', 'objective', 'technocratic' approaches that reduce poverty to measurable income and consumption on the one hand and participatory 'subjective' approaches grounded in the understandings of people in poverty on the other. While at one level the two approaches reflect different philosophical underpinnings (Shaffer, 1996), arguably they offer complementary rather than incompatible research agendas (see chapter 2). Bob Baulch (1996b) reaches a similar conclusion. He uses the image of a pyramid to schematize these different approaches. The apex of the pyramid focuses on private consumption or income. Moving down, the pyramid broadens out to embrace access to public resources and amenities and also to assets (including human capital such as education). The base widens further to include 'dignity' and 'autonomy', which 'are stressed by local people in participatory poverty assessments'. As Baulch points out, the last two 'challenge the hierarchy implicit' in the pyramid itself (1996a: 3).

Given the hierarchical nature of the pyramid image, figure 0.2 proposes an alternative 'poverty wheel' to represent a relationship of parity and interdependence between the material and the relational/symbolic aspects of poverty. Within the wheel, the material core of poverty represents the hub. This core is referred to as 'unacceptable hardship' in an alternative schema, developed by Spicker (1999: 159). The rim of the wheel represents the relational/symbolic aspects of poverty as experienced by those living in unacceptable material hardship. Both hub and rim are shaped by social and cultural relations. Thus, material needs at the hub are socially and culturally defined and they are mediated and interpreted at the relational/symbolic rim, which itself revolves in the sphere of the social and cultural.

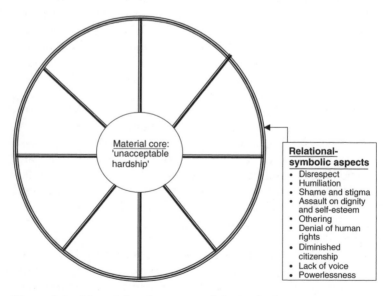

Figure 0.2   Material and non-material wheel of poverty

Chapters and Themes

This is a book about the concept of poverty. Where appropriate, general reference is made to debates about causes and policy responses. Although these are not the book's main focus, it is important to bear in mind the interconnections between explanations, policy responses and concepts, definitions and measures.[2] The book's structure mirrors the move from the material hub to the relational/symbolic rim. It starts, in chapter 1, with definitions of poverty, which are the bread and butter of many textbooks on the subject, but nevertheless raise some tricky questions. The chapter considers the current state of the debate and locates what is a relatively narrow approach to definition within a broader social scientific literature. The operationalization of definitions is the subject of chapter 2, which gives a flavour of the increasingly sophisticated literature on measurement.

Chapter 3 looks at the structural inequalities that frame, shape and interact with poverty. In addition to the more general context of socio-economic polarization that exists both globally and within many societies, it details how poverty is both a gendered and a racialized phenomenon. It also looks at how disability and age interact with poverty and at how poverty is experienced at the level of the individual, household and wider community. Analysis of socio-economic polarization focuses on vertical hierarchical relations of inequality between those at the top and bottom of society. In contrast, the increasingly influential concept of social exclusion constructs a dichotomous horizontal relationship between those inside and outside of society's mainstream.

Chapter 4 is devoted to the concept of social exclusion, which is now a well-established element in discourses about poverty. It is, though, highly contested. The chapter provides an overview of the growing literature on social exclusion and the controversies it has generated. It will consider what, if anything, it adds as an alternative to the concept of poverty and its potential as a lens through which to illuminate previously somewhat neglected aspects of poverty. As well as the relationship between the material and the relational/symbolic, these include issues of dynamics, processes and agency elaborated in later chapters.

Social exclusion can be understood both as a phenomenon and as a discourse. Discourses of poverty are the subject of chapter 5. It represents a further shift of focus towards the relational/symbolic through a concern with how 'the poor' are represented in political and academic discourses and media images. It discusses the language of poverty, and its historical associations, together with contemporary discourses of the 'underclass' and 'dependency culture'. It argues that such discourses serve to 'Other' and stereotype 'the poor' and emphasizes the importance of language and image both to how those in poverty are perceived and treated by the wider society and to how they may perceive themselves.

The cultural meanings created by such discourses create the context within which people in poverty exercise their agency as social actors. These meanings all too often label 'the poor' as passive, be it in the role of benign 'victim' or malign 'welfare dependant'. Within the structural framework developed in chapter 3, chapter 6 in contrast draws on contemporary sociological and international development theory as well as poverty research to explore how people in poverty can be characterized as actors in their own lives, exercising agency, including political agency. This then leads into chapter 7. Here, the focus is on human rights, citizenship, voice and power. One of the most striking developments in the contemporary politics of poverty is the growing demands for poverty to be understood as powerlessness and a denial of fundamental rights and for the voices of those in poverty to be heard in public debates.

The Conclusion draws out a number of key themes. They point to a conceptualization of poverty that gives due regard to four key aspects: its relational/symbolic/cultural and discursive facets as well as its material core; the agency of those living in poverty (within structural constraints); the importance of process and dynamics as well as outcomes; and, underpinning each of these, the perspectives and views of those with experience of poverty. Such a conceptualization, it is argued, could help to overcome the false dichotomy between the material/socio-economic and the symbolic/cultural, and underpin a combined politics of redistribution and recognition. More generally, it aims to integrate the, all too often marginalized, concerns of those in poverty into wider political and theoretical debates about citizenship and democracy and to locate the analysis of poverty within a broader social scientific framework.

1
Defining Poverty

The concept of poverty is translated into policy through a more precise set of definitions and measures. While, as argued in the Introduction, it is important not to confuse definitions and measures, some of the issues raised straddle the two and loop back into conceptualizations. Definitions are the subject of this first chapter; measures are dealt with in the second. After a general discussion of different approaches to defining poverty, chapter 1 looks at the traditional opposition between 'absolute' and 'relative' definitions and at alternative formulations that attempt to reconcile the two.

Approaches to Defining Poverty

How we define poverty is critical to political, policy and academic debates about the concept. It is bound up with explanations and has implications for solutions. Value judgements are involved. Definition thus has to be understood as a political as well as a social scientific act and as such has often been the source of controversy. There is no single 'correct' definition. However, as we shall see, most researchers now accept that any definition has to be understood, at least in part, in relation to particular social, cultural and historical contexts. This has implications for studies that attempt to compare poverty in very different kinds of society.

Broad or narrow?

Definitions vary according to their narrowness or breadth, that is in terms of: whether they are confined to the material core; the nature of that material core; and whether they embrace also relational/symbolic factors associated with poverty, as identified in the Introduction. Nolan and Whelan are among those who argue for a definition towards the narrower end of the scale on the grounds that too broad a definition runs the danger of losing sight of the distinctive 'core notion of poverty' (1996: 193). Following Townsend, they define poverty in terms of the inability to participate in society (which is broader than more 'absolute' definitions confined to subsistence needs), but emphasize that what is distinctive is the 'inability to participate owing to lack of resources' (1996: 188). This confines their definition 'to those areas of life where consumption or participation are determined primarily by command over financial resources' (1996: 193; Veit-Wilson, 1998, 2004).

By implication they exclude non-material elements found in broad UN definitions, for example: 'lack of participation in decision-making', 'a violation of human dignity', 'powerlessness' and 'susceptibility to violence' (cited in Langmore, 2000: 37). Similarly, they exclude some of the non-material aspects emphasized by people in poverty themselves, such as lack of voice, respect and self-esteem, isolation and humiliation (UKCAP, 1997; Galloway, 2002). Given that, as argued in the Introduction, the function of a definition is to differentiate the condition defined (poverty) from other conditions (non-poverty), it makes sense to pitch the *definition* of poverty towards the narrower end of the spectrum. Aspects such as 'lack of participation in decision-making', 'susceptibility to violence' and 'humiliation' are not unique to the condition of poverty; they are also associated with other conditions such as being Black in a White-dominated society. However, in order not to lose sight of the condition's wider meanings and of the interpenetration of the material and the relational/symbolic, it is important that definitions of poverty are not divorced from wider *conceptualizations* such as that developed in subsequent chapters.

Income or living standards?

Another source of variation in definitions of poverty, reflected in the literature on measurement, lies in whether they are rooted in conceptualizations that are concerned with, on the one hand, a person's material resources, especially income, and, on the other, with actual outcomes in terms of living standards and activities (Nolan and Whelan, 1996). As Stein Ringen puts it, 'in the first case, poverty is defined indirectly through the determinants of way of life, in the second case, directly by way of life' (1987: 146). In practice, these two approaches are often treated as complementary (as in Nolan and Whelan's definition above and Townsend's below). Indeed, Ringen's own definition is not unusual in combining the two: 'a low standard of living, meaning deprivation in way of life because of insufficient resources to avoid such deprivation' (1987: 146). Put simply, someone is ' "poor" when they have both a low standard of living and a low income' (Gordon et al., 2000b: 91).

A. B. Atkinson makes a related, but more fundamental, distinction between a concern with standard of living and a concern with a citizen's *'right* to a minimum level of resources' (1989: 12, emphasis added). The former is more common in the literature and as the basis for empirical research. The latter might be said to be implicit in measures of poverty based on the numbers falling below a certain point in the income scale or the level of income provided by a country's social assistance scheme (see chapter 2). While the 'right to a minimum level of resources' has not been widely adopted as an explicit definition of poverty, it does have a value as one element in a broader conceptualization of poverty. It means that people 'are entitled, as citizens, to a minimum income, the disposal of which is a matter for them' and which 'may be regarded as a pre-requisite for participation in a particular society, as a guarantee of "positive freedom" ' (A. B. Atkinson, 1990: 8). As we shall see in chapter 7, poverty is increasingly being conceptualized as a denial of human and citizenship rights.

The conceptualization of poverty in this way is also helpful from the perspective of understanding and combating women's poverty. Following Atkinson, Stephen Jenkins suggests that a feminist concept of poverty can be described in terms of an '*individual* right to a minimum degree of potential economic independence' (1991: 464, emphasis added; see chapter 3 below). Although the feminist definition propounded by Millar and Glendinning is not couched in the language of rights, it focuses on the individual's capacity to be self-supporting on the grounds that 'people who are financially dependent upon others must be considered vulnerable to poverty' (1992: 9). The notion of vulnerability is helpful to understanding the situation of women without an independent income who nevertheless enjoy a comfortable standard of living.

Income or capabilities?

So far, I have outlined a focused approach to defining poverty in terms of an inability to participate in society, involving both a low income and a low standard of living. The work of Amartya Sen offers an alternative perspective on the role of low income in the definition of poverty. It has been hugely influential within the international development context, contributing to a paradigm shift in the meaning of development away from economic growth and GDP to a focus on 'poverty as a denial of choices and opportunities for living a tolerable life' (UNDP, 1997: 2; Vizard, 2001). The human poverty and development indices published in the annual UNDP Human Development Report reflect Sen's approach. Although its initial impact on thinking and research about poverty in the North was less marked, increasingly Sen's ideas are percolating through. His approach offers insights that are helpful to poverty's broader conceptualization in the North. It also, as we shall see below, throws light on the absolute–relative question.

Sen takes a step backwards from both income and living standards to ask why they matter. His answer is that they don't matter in their own right, for they are simply instrumental to what really matters, namely the kind of life that a person is able to lead and the choices and opportunities open to her in leading that life. At the heart of his approach is an understanding of living as involving 'being and doing'. Sen uses two key terms to express this idea: 'functionings' and 'capabilities'. 'Functionings' refer to what a person actually manages to do or be; they range from elementary nourishment to more sophisticated levels such as participation in the life of the community and the achievement of self-respect. 'Capabilities' denote what a person *can* do or be, that is, the range of choices that are open to her. Critical here is the freedom people enjoy 'to choose between different ways of living that they can have reason to value' (Sen, 1990: 114).

Money, Sen argues, is just a means to an end and the goods and services or 'commodities' it buys are simply particular ways of achieving functionings (1985a, 1992, 1999). The role of money in achieving functionings depends on the extent to which goods and services are commodified (i.e. are exchanged for money), so will vary between societies. Moreover, the relationship between money and capabilities/functionings depends in part on how the former is converted into the latter by individuals. This can vary according to personal factors such as age, sex, pregnancy, health, disability or even metabolic rate and body size, which can affect the level and nature of a person's needs. For instance, the capability to function of a disabled person may be lower than that of a non-disabled person even if the former's income is higher than the latter's. This is because of the costs associated with the additional needs disabled people may have to meet in order to achieve similar functionings to non-disabled. Sen's argument is that poverty should therefore be defined in terms not of income and actual living standards but of capability failure: 'the failure of basic capabilities to reach certain minimally acceptable levels' (1992: 109).

There are thus two main planks to the case Sen makes against defining poverty in terms of low income or material resources. The narrower one, concerning the differences in the ability of people to convert income into capabilities, is addressed by Nolan and Whelan. They point out that, as Sen concedes, it is possible to take some account of such interpersonal factors in the setting of income poverty lines. However, on the basis of their own research they conclude that, other than in the case of disability, 'it is not clear that interpersonal variation is so pronounced as to pose a major problem' (1996: 184). Moreover, there is a danger that too great an emphasis on physical factors that affect the conversion of income into capabilities could encourage a narrow focus on physical needs and their physiological rather than social construction (see below).

The more fundamental plank concerns the relationship between low income and a person's ability to live the kind of life she or he values. Sen's formulation of this relationship is helpful in a number of ways. It reminds us that income is a means to an end rather than an end in itself. It focuses on the individual, thereby rendering gender inequalities more easily visible (Jackson, 1998; Razavi, 2000). It also constructs human beings as people with agency for whom the freedom to be able to make choices about what they want to be and do and about how they deploy the resources available to them is of fundamental importance (see chapter 6).

What is at issue is 'a life that is worthy of the dignity of the human being' (Nussbaum, 2000: 5). In effect, capability theorists focus on the positive – of the kind of life we want people to be able to achieve in order to 'flourish' (Nussbaum, 1995: see also Pogge, 2002) – rather than the negative – of the lack of material resources that can prevent them from achieving it. In doing so, they usefully integrate poverty into the wider concerns of the population as a whole and into a wider social scientific literature, rather than ghettoizing it in a separate box. In the context of the South this is reflected in ideas of 'human development' and 'well-being' (UNDP, 1997, 2003; Narayan et al., 2000). Indeed, the concept of 'well-being' is gaining currency in the North also, where a similar approach can be discerned in the notions of 'quality of life' and 'social quality'. These too involve 'a shift of perspective from negative to positive' (Baars et al., 1997: 302). Both Sen and Martha Nussbaum have made the link between their capabilities approach and the notions of 'well-being' and 'quality of life', 'to be assessed', Sen suggests, 'in terms of the capability to achieve valuable functionings' (1993: 31). They point to the strong parallels between their own work and the 'level of living' surveys conducted by Scandinavian social scientists (Nussbaum and Sen, 1993). Motivated by a broader concern with inequality rather than poverty, these focus on how individuals as 'active beings' are able to use their resources (material and non-material) to 'control and consciously direct [their] living conditions' (Erikson, 1993: 73; see chapter 6 below).

Parallels can also be drawn with the concept of 'social quality' developed more recently by European social scientists (Beck et al., 1997, 2001). However, looking at the notion of capability-failure through the lens of social quality helps to illuminate not just the strengths of the notion's positive focus but also its weaknesses as a *definition* of poverty. Social quality is defined as 'the extent to which citizens [and other residents] are able to participate in the social and economic life of their communities under conditions which enhance their well-being and individual potential' (Beck et al., 2001: 7). Although poverty is 'central to the concept of social quality' and its reduction would represent an indicator of social quality, it is only one of a number of conditions that serve to diminish social quality and cannot serve as the sole measuring rod (Beck et al., 1997: 11; 2001). Moreover, the opposite of well-being is ill-being which may, or may not, be associated with poverty (Baulch, 1996b; Bradshaw, 2002)

The problem with defining poverty as capability-failure is that it is in effect conflating a wider condition – be it capabilities, quality of life, well-being or social quality – with what is conventionally understood as one aspect of that condition, namely being in poverty or not. If the two are treated as synonymous, it becomes impossible to separate out poverty as conventionally understood from other conditions that serve to undermine capabilities, well-being or social quality. Sen himself acknowledges that 'the perspective of capability-poverty does not involve any denial of the sensible view that low income is clearly' a major factor in poverty, 'since lack of income can be a principal reason for a person's capability deprivation' (1999: 87). He also makes clear that low income is not the only influence on capabilities. The question then arises as to whether it makes sense to describe as poverty a situation of capability deprivation that has nothing to do with low income. For example, if a wealthy person's ability to be and do is constrained by serious illness, it is confusing to call this a state of poverty.

One way to get round this is to distinguish between the related notions of 'capability' and 'income poverty' – that is, 'poverty as capability inadequacy' and 'poverty as lowness of income', as Sen himself does on occasion (1999: 90). The UNDP similarly distinguishes capability-based 'human' poverty from 'income' poverty (1997, 2003). However, such formulations still involve an elastic use of the term 'poverty' to embrace situations which might not involve lack of material resources at all. It might therefore make more sense to talk of 'capability deprivation', as Sen sometimes does (see 1999: 20), so that poverty can retain the more focused meaning discussed above. Alternatively, Karel Van den Bosch suggests a definition of poverty 'as a situation where people lack the economic resources to realize a set of basic functionings' (2001: 1). This ties capability deprivation firmly to income poverty.

While income is, as Sen rightly points out, a means and not an end, the symbolic and actual significance of money – and lack of it – in commodified, wage-based societies should not be underestimated. As Karl Marx understood, money may be instrumental but it is also inseparable from the power that it confers: 'I can carry [money] around with me in my pocket as the universal social power ... Money puts social power as a thing into the hands of the private person, who as such uses this power' (1987: 431–2).

One danger of downplaying income when defining poverty is that it can be used to justify a policy stance opposed to raising the incomes of those in poverty. It has been argued, for instance, that a capability approach 'requires a change in public policy focus from the reduction of monetary inequalities to the reduction of inequalities in "capabilities"' (Raveaud and Salais, 2001: 61; Williams and Windebank, 2003). This was, in effect, the stance adopted initially by the UK New Labour government. Instead of 'cash handouts', it promised 'hand-ups' – 'opportunity' through education and paid work. Its subsequent anti-poverty policy, in fact, combined a strong emphasis on investment in education, skills, health and public services with some benefit improvements. Although New Labour's policy documents do not refer explicitly to Sen's capability approach, Anthony Giddens, frequently described as Tony Blair's 'guru', makes the link.[1] He suggests that the approach 'provides a solid philosophical grounding for meritocratic policies, and one that dovetails well with the emphasis of the new social democracy upon investing in education and skills' (2002: 39). Although this is an interpretation that Sen himself might not necessarily endorse, for those who still believe in the importance of a more equitable distribution of income and resources to tackling poverty, it serves as a warning. Valuable as the notion of 'capability deprivation' is to the conceptualization of poverty, it should complement rather than supplant more conventional, resource-based, definitions.

Moreover, it is important to locate a capabilities approach, with its focus on individual agency, firmly within a broader structural analysis (see chapters 3 and 6) in order to avoid Townsend's stricture that it 'represents a sophisticated adaptation of the individualism which is rooted in neo-classical economics' (1993: 136). Neither capabilities nor functionings are free-floating, but are shaped by structural positioning and also by welfare institutions and levels of collective provision (Raveaud and Salais, 2001; Veit-Wilson, 2004). These also impact on the ability to convert material resources into functionings. The capability framework is thus able to accommodate the structural constraints and opportunities faced by individuals (Robeyns, 2000), even though it does not address inequalities as such (Phillips, 2001).

To conclude this section, I have explained how, on the one hand, Sen's capability approach can enhance our understanding of poverty but why, on the other, it does not constitute a definition of poverty and why it needs to be deployed with caution. We shall return to Sen's work in the next section in the context of the distinction made between 'absolute' and 'relative' poverty.

Beyond the Absolute–Relative Dichotomy

'Absolute' and 'relative' poverty

This distinction has been central to post-war debates about how to define poverty. Definitions deployed in the late nineteenth and early twentieth century by Charles Booth and Seebohm Rowntree, the pioneers of modern poverty research, were supposedly 'absolute' in the sense that poverty was said to be understood as lacking sufficient money to meet basic physical needs. At its most basic, absolute poverty is defined in terms of survival; more commonly it refers to subsistence, linked to a basic standard of physical capacity necessary for production (paid work) and reproduction (the bearing and nurturing of children). Nutrition is central to such definitions: 'an absolute standard means one defined by reference to the actual needs of the poor and not by reference to the expenditure of those who are not poor. A family is poor if it cannot afford to eat' (Joseph and Sumption, 1979: 27).

Implicit in this statement is a rejection of the alternative 'relative' definition, developed by Townsend and articulated most fully in his monumental *Poverty in the United Kingdom*. Townsend criticizes the narrow subsistence notion of needs, divorced from their social context, upon which absolute definitions of poverty were based. According to his alternative, relative, definition:

> Individuals, families and groups in the population can be said to be in poverty when they lack the resources to obtain the types of diet, participate in the activities and have the living conditions and amenities which are customary, or are at least widely encouraged or approved, in the societies to which they belong. Their resources are so seriously below those commanded by the average individual or family that they are, in effect, excluded from ordinary living patterns and activities. (1979: 31)

The European Commission's definition, adopted in 1984, is similar in tone: 'The poor shall be taken to mean persons, families and groups of persons whose resources (material, cultural and social) are so limited as to exclude them from the minimum acceptable way of life in the Member State in which they live.' Unlike Townsend's, though, it does not spell out explicitly the dimension of *social participation*, which is key to the concept of 'relative deprivation' upon which his definition of poverty is built. Relative deprivation occurs when people 'cannot obtain, at all or sufficiently, the condition of life – that is, the diets, amenities, standards and services – which allow them to play the roles, participate in the relationships and follow the customary behaviour which is expected of them by virtue of their membership of society' (Townsend, 1993: 36).

Relative deprivation is thus a multi-dimensional concept, embracing 'all of the major spheres of life' (1993: 36). Where relative deprivation occurs because of lack of material resources, people can be said to be in poverty. In line with our earlier discussion on the relationship between income and living standards, Townsend emphasizes the need to distinguish between the two: deprivation 'turns on the level of conditions or activities experienced', poverty 'on the incomes and other resources directly available' (1987: 140). He also draws a distinction between 'material' and 'social' deprivation. The former refers to material goods and amenities; the latter to 'ordinary social customs, activities and relationships' (1987: 127). He further differentiates his use of the term to denote 'objective' *'conditions* of deprivation relative to others' from its deployment by W. G. Runciman to denote 'subjective' *'feelings* of deprivation relative to others' (1979: 47, emphasis in original).

The notion of 'relative', which links the concepts of relative poverty and deprivation, needs unpacking, as it embraces a number of different meanings. Broadly these fall into two, interrelated, categories concerning, first, the nature of the *comparisons* to be made in judging whether poverty exists and, second, the nature of human *needs*. We will look at each in turn. The essence of the *comparative* element of relative poverty lies in the idea that it is only possible to judge whether or not someone is in relative poverty in relation to other people living in the same society at the same point in history. This breaks down into three elements: the historical, the cross-national and the intra-national. It is common for those who lived through the terrible hardship of 1930s Britain to claim that 'real' poverty no longer exists. From the perspective of an understanding of poverty as relative, such a comparison is misplaced for it says nothing about what people need to live a decent life in the early twenty-first century. Within shorter time-scales, at a time of a steady rise in general living standards and rapid technological change 'we constantly manufacture new forms of poverty as we drive forward the living standards of the majority without thinking what we are doing to those who cannot keep pace'

(Donnison, 1982: 226). Examples range from expensive forms of heating and inaccessible supermarkets to the spread of new technologies such as personal computers. This has implications for the measures used to monitor trends in poverty (see chapter 2).

Another common response to claims that poverty is prevalent in the rich countries of the North is to point to the deep poverty experienced by millions in the South. Again, the comparison is unhelpful to an understanding of what poverty means for those who live in the former and who face the demands, expectations and costs of living in an affluent consumer society. However, it does open up wider questions of global comparators between the South and the North. In a globalized world, in which countries are more closely bound together through trading systems, electronic communications and cultural networks and diaspora, it may increasingly become 'necessary to accept the relativity of need to the world's as well as to national resources' (Townsend, 1987: 99). This places the issue of poverty in the South firmly in the context of global inequalities.

The final comparative element of relative poverty places poverty in the context of inequality *within* societies. The act of comparison – be it between those on lower and higher incomes, women and men, minority and majority ethnic groups – inevitably highlights any inequalities of material resources that may exist between the groups being compared. This is not, however, to say that relative poverty and inequality are synonymous, as is sometimes claimed. Inequality is concerned solely with the comparison between groups. Relative poverty adds to that comparison the notion of the incapacity to meet certain needs, broadly defined to include participation in society. It is logically conceivable, though unlikely, that a society could be very unequal but without poverty, if all its members had the resources necessary to participate fully in that society.

Understanding needs

Underlying the various comparative dimensions of the notion of relative poverty is a particular understanding of human needs. How needs are understood is critical both to the absolute–relative poverty dichotomy and to the ways in which the debate has moved beyond that dichotomy.

A helpful definition of human needs, which emphasizes the social and psychological, is provided by John Veit-Wilson:

> the full range of intangible and material resources that are required over time to achieve the production, maintenance and reproduction of the fully autonomous, fully participating adult human in the particular society to which he or she belongs. . . . Material resources may support the physical organism but it is the full range of social and psychological resources which are required for the experience of humanity. (1999: 85)

Elsewhere, he defines the adequacy of such resources 'in terms of acquiring and maintaining dignity and being able to take a respectable and recognised part in one's own society' (Veit-Wilson, 1994: 14). Human needs are thus located at both the material hub and the relational/symbolic rim of the poverty wheel described in the Introduction. The importance of the theorization of human needs to social policy has been recognized in recent years. A key issue of relevance to definitions of poverty is whether it is possible to identify needs as an 'objective fact' or whether they have to be understood as 'socially constructed', that is, as a product of a (contested) process of interpretation and labelling. A related question, discussed below, is whether there exist 'universal' needs that we share as human beings or whether all needs are conditioned by social, historical and cultural context.

Townsend's (1979) exposition of the nature of needs places him firmly in the latter camp. Human beings are social as well as physical beings; in addition to physiological requirements our needs reflect a range of social expectations and responsibilities, and also the dictates of laws. Research in the UK suggests that the general population subscribes to just such an understanding of needs. In addition to items connected with basic nutrition, clothing and shelter, well over half of those questioned in the 1999 British Poverty and Social Exclusion (PSE) Survey and in a follow-up Northern Ireland Study defined as necessities items such as a refrigerator, washing machine and telephone and activities such as celebrations on special occasions, visiting friends or family and a hobby or leisure pastime (Gordon et al., 2000a; Hillyard et al., 2003). While more 'luxury' items such as videos and home computers were considered necessities by only a minority, the proportion defining them so had increased since a similar survey in 1990.

The other element of Townsend's argument is that even physiological needs, such as for nutrition, cannot be divorced from social, historical and cultural context:

> The amount and cost of the food which is eaten depends on the social roles people play and the dietary customs observed as well as the kinds of foods made available socially through production and availability in markets. In short, food in all kinds of society is 'socialised'.... The specification of the costs of meeting minimum dietary needs in any society is as problematic as the specification of the costs of fulfilling the entire roles, participative relationships and customs enjoined of a people. (1993: 31)

More recent work on 'food poverty' within industrialized societies throws further light on the significance of the fact that people consume 'food not nutrients' (Dowler and Leather, 2000: 208). Dowler and Leather maintain that 'food is an expression of who a person is, what they are worth, and of their ability to provide for basic needs' (2000: 200). Shopping around for cheap food (often in expensive and inadequately stocked local shops); the attempt to maintain conventional eating patterns, particularly where there are children; the risks of experimenting with new diets when there is no margin for error or waste, if family members reject them; and the inability to enjoy eating as a social activity are all examples of how, for people in poverty, food represents a social as well as a physiological need (Dowler et al., 2001).

As Townsend (1979) acknowledges in a footnote, his conceptualization of need is not new, but, he maintains, the implications had not been fully articulated previously. Indeed, he (together with many other contemporary scholars) cites the economist Adam Smith who, in the late eighteenth century, wrote:

> By necessaries, I understand not only the commodities which are indispensably necessary for the support of life but whatever the custom of the country renders it indecent for creditable people, even of the lowest order, to be without. A linen shirt, for example, is strictly speaking not a necessity of life. . . . But in the present time . . . a creditable day labourer would be ashamed to appear in public without a linen shirt. (1776: 691)

The other example Smith gave was leather shoes; had he been writing today, he might have substituted designer trainers, particularly in the case of 'creditable' young people. The social and cultural conditioning of needs is more pronounced in the context of a modern consumer society. When people are defined increasingly by what they have, 'the poor . . . are re-cast as "flawed consumers"' (Bauman, 1998: 2). Commercial pressures, often targeted through television advertising at children and young people, contribute to 'a common culture of acquisition', which makes it that much harder for parents in poverty to meet their children's needs (Middleton et al., 1994: 5). When brand and label take on more significance than the item itself, meeting the most basic needs for clothing and shoes cannot be achieved cheaply (Farrell and O'Connor, 2003). Yet, the cost of failure can be shame, humiliation, bullying and ostracism for children and young people (see chapters 3 and 5).

Jock Young (1999) describes a bifurcated process of 'cultural inclusion' and 'structural exclusion', in which the delights of mass culture are dangled in front of those without the means to enjoy them. Although most immediate in the wealthy, industrialized societies of the North, globalization means that the process is no longer confined to these societies. Marshall Wolfe observes that 'people throughout the world are now exposed to messages concerning diversified and continually changing norms for consumption' and that even the most extreme forms of poverty 'are being penetrated in incongruous ways by elements of the consumer culture' (1995: 90–1).

Rereading Rowntree and the implications for the notion of absolute poverty

One implication of an understanding of even the most basic physiological needs as socially conditioned is that the conventional notion of absolute poverty falls apart (Ringen, 1987). A number of scholars have questioned the previous conventional wisdom that Booth and Rowntree established an absolute subsistence definition of poverty, which was subsequently challenged by Townsend's relativist approach. In other words, the argument goes, the standard account of the paradigm shift in thinking – from an absolute to a relative definition – that took place during the second half of the twentieth century turns out to be a myth, based on a misreading of these pioneers.

Rowntree had an enormous influence on the study of poverty, which is still felt today (Bradshaw, 2000a). The most detailed rereading of Rowntree can be found in Veit-Wilson's 'rehabilitation' (1986), although elements of his thesis appear in J. C. Kincaid's earlier study (1973). Veit-Wilson argues that the distinction Rowntree drew between 'primary' and 'secondary' poverty and his use of a subsistence standard, based on 'merely physical efficiency', to measure the former have been widely misunderstood. Rowntree did not, himself, believe that only those living in subsistence 'primary poverty' were poor. However, he used this standard as a device to convince the wider society that a significant number of those in poverty could not meet their basic physical, never mind their social, needs. Therefore 'the life-style of the poor was at least in part caused by low income and not by improvidence', as was widely believed (1986: 69).

In one of his later works, Rowntree's response to the question 'why do poor people spend their inadequate incomes on social recreational activities instead of food?' revealed his understanding that basic needs are social and not just physical:

> The explanation is that working people are just as human as those with more money. They cannot live on a 'fodder basis'. They crave for relaxation and recreation just as the rest of us do. But . . . they can only get these things by going short of

something which is essential to physical fitness, and so they
go short. (1937: 126–7, cited in Veit-Wilson, 1986: 85)

Moreover, the very subsistence level used to measure
'primary' poverty included in its list of necessities tea, which
has no nutritional value, but is socially and psychologically
important in Britain (Ringen, 1987). Indeed, Townsend
himself uses the example of tea to illustrate how items
deemed to be necessities can derive from social and psychological rather than physical needs (1979: 50). In his later
surveys, Rowntree also adjusted his list of commodities in
recognition of changing social norms and rising living standards. Earlier, Booth had likewise defined poverty in relation
to customary living standards. Thus, while neither Rowntree
nor Booth developed a notion of relative poverty of the detail
and sophistication of that expounded by Townsend, it is more
accurate to describe Townsend as building on their work
rather than overturning it.

The reconciliation of absolute and relative

Having seen how even supposedly absolute definitions of
poverty involve an element of relativity we turn to the other
source of challenge to the absolute–relative dichotomy. This
lies not in a denial of absolute poverty but in a reformula-
tion of its relationship to relative poverty so as to integrate
the two into one framework in place of two competing definitions. Such a framework, it is argued, can then be applied
to both richer and poorer countries. Of particular significance
here is Sen's work, discussed earlier, and its deployment by
Doyal and Gough in the construction of their influential
theory of human needs. An alternative attempt at combining
absolute and relative within one framework can be found in
the Copenhagen Declaration on Social Development, agreed
at the 1995 UN World Summit on Social Development. We
will look at each in turn.

Sen and the 'absolutist core'   One criticism made of a purely
relativist definition of poverty was that its application to
countries where the great majority had insufficient resources
for an adequate life would mean that only those at the very

bottom would be classified as poor (albeit not in a global context). On its own, it therefore fails to capture the nature of much of the poverty experienced in the South. Sen's contribution has addressed this dilemma in a way which 'reconciles the notions of absolute and relative poverty' (UNDP, 1997: 16). In a controversial paper, he argued that the notion of relative poverty augments rather than displaces that of absolute poverty. There is, he contended, an 'irreducible absolutist core in the idea of poverty', the most obvious manifestation of which is starvation and malnutrition (1983: 159). This absolute core operates in the space of capabilities but frequently takes 'a relative form in the space of commodities' (1983: 161). In other words, what one is able to do or be is a question of universal *absolutes*, whereas the goods needed to translate this ability into actual being and doing take us into the sphere of *relativities*, because the things that people need to do or be vary according to cultural and historical context.

Sen gave the example of Adam Smith's labourer to demonstrate the nature of *relative* poverty. Indeed, he acknowledged that in terms of the 'commodity' of the linen shirt poverty takes a relative form, involving the dictates of custom and comparison with the situation of others. However, in terms of 'capabilities' there is, he contended, an *absolute* requirement of the avoidance of shame: 'not so much having equal shame as others, but just not being ashamed, absolutely' (1983: 161). Following his introduction of the notion of 'functionings', Sen elaborated the relativist side of the argument: the amount needed to buy the commodities necessary to achieve the functioning of appearing in public without shame varies according to the wealth of the country (1992, 1999). His overall conclusion was that

> there is no conflict between the irreducible absolutist element in the notion of poverty (related to capabilities and the standard of living) and the 'thoroughgoing relativity' to which Peter Townsend refers, if the latter is interpreted as applying to commodities and resources ... When Townsend estimates the resources required for being able to 'participate in the activities of the community', he is in fact estimating the varying resource requirements of fulfilling the same absolute need. (1983: 161)

Townsend disagreed and there ensued a debate (summarized in Townsend, 1993), which is generally viewed as having generated more heat than light. At times, it appeared as though they were arguing past each other. Part of the problem lay in different meanings given to the terms 'absolute' and 'relative'. Thus, for example, in response to Townsend's accusation that he was perpetuating a narrow subsistence conception of poverty, dominated by nutritional requirements, Sen made clear that his use of the term 'absolute' differs from its conventional, subsistence, meaning. It is about lacking the basic opportunity to be or do in vital ways, regardless of comparisons:

> The characteristic feature of 'absoluteness' is neither constancy over time, nor invariance between different societies, nor concentration merely on food and nutrition. It is an approach of judging a person's deprivation in absolute terms ... rather than in purely *relative* terms vis-à-vis the levels enjoyed by others in the society. (1985b: 673, emphasis in original)

Had the protagonists separated out and made explicit the different meanings of 'relative' (i.e. as involving various kinds of comparison and as an understanding of needs as socially constructed), they might have avoided arguing at cross-purposes. As it was, Sen was arguing mainly against a purely relativist approach, which, in its use of comparison and on its own, he maintained conflated poverty and inequality (although Townsend himself was, in fact, careful to distinguish the two). He contended that Townsend was wrong in asserting 'the untenability of the idea of absolute needs' (Sen, 1983: 161). Yet, as an aside, he also expressed agreement with Townsend's view of the social nature of needs (Sen, 1985b). This notion of needs was, though, at the heart of Townsend's own argument. In particular, his view, explored above, that even the most basic physical needs are socially determined, was crucial to his rejection of the idea of an 'absolutist core'. Thus he asked, 'are not nutritional requirements dependent upon the work roles exacted of people at different points in history and different cultures?' and 'isn't the idea of "shelter" relative not just to climate and temperature but to what society makes of what shelter is for?' (1993: 135).

Doyal and Gough's translation into a theory of human needs
This is where Doyal and Gough's theory of human needs offers a path out of the thicket of confusion, even though it is not a theory of poverty as such. Doyal and Gough (1991: 156–9) articulate a universalistic understanding of human needs, sensitive to social, cultural and historical context, which draws on and makes more concrete Sen's capability framework. They make the case for a universal conceptualization of basic human needs as 'the universal pre-requisites for successful . . . participation in a social form of life' (Gough, 1992: 8). These pre-requisites are identified as 'physical health' (sufficient for social participation) and 'autonomy of agency' or 'the capacity to make informed choices about what should be done and how to go about doing it' (Gough, 1992: 9).

These pre-requisite needs are close to Sen's capabilities and functionings, although they do not embrace his requirement of the avoidance of shame. They are universal, Doyal and Gough contend, because they are necessary in any culture before any individual can participate effectively to achieve any other valued goals. They are, though, very general and thus not a very helpful guide to social policies. They do not tell us what is required to satisfy those basic needs. Doyal and Gough therefore add a further layer of 'intermediate' needs, defined as 'those characteristics of need satisfiers which everywhere contribute to improved physical health and autonomy' (Gough, 1992: 11). Examples given are: adequate nutritional food and water; adequate protective housing; economic security; and basic education. These intermediate needs provide 'the crucial bridge between universal basic needs and socially relative satisfiers' of them (Doyal and Gough, 1991: 157). These 'socially relative satisfiers' refer to the actual commodities through which these needs are met, which clearly vary according to time and place. They may also vary between groups within a society. The significance of this in increasingly diverse societies has perhaps not been adequately addressed in conceptualizations of relative deprivation, which appear to assume an undifferentiated society with shared cultural norms (Parekh, 2000).

In Sen's framework, intermediate needs link the absolute core in the space of capabilities with the commodities through which these capabilities are transformed into actual doing and being (functionings) within a particular, relative, context. Arguably, a tiered conceptualization of needs, such as Doyal and Gough's, provides the underpinning for Sen's claim that his absolutist core is reconcilable with Townsend's relativism. Indeed, Townsend himself would appear to have subsequently accepted this in a public international statement on poverty that he has promoted. This asserts: 'absolute or basic material and social needs across societies are the same, even when they have to be satisfied differently according to institutions, culture and location' (cited in Townsend and Gordon, 2000: 17).

The Copenhagen Declaration   Moreover, Townsend has now championed a two-part definition of poverty, which emerged from the 1995 UN Copenhagen Summit. This offers a rather different way of combining absolute and relative notions of poverty, even though it shares with Sen's a definition of 'absolute' which 'is neither constant over time nor invariant between societies' (Gordon, 2000: 51). Absolute poverty is characterized as 'severe deprivation of basic human needs, including food, safe drinking water, sanitation facilities, health, shelter, education and information' and is related to 'access to social services' as well as income (UN, 1995: para. 19). It is distinguished from, but is also part of, a much broader notion of 'overall poverty' that refers to 'the total number of people living in poverty in a country' (Langmore, 2000: 36). The definition of 'overall poverty' is, in fact, as much a conceptualization, expressed through a list of manifestations of poverty. These range from 'lack of income and productive resources sufficient to ensure sustainable livelihoods' through 'increased morbidity and mortality from illness' to 'social discrimination and exclusion' and 'lack of participation in decision-making and in civil, social and cultural life' (UN, 1995: para. 19).

Townsend and colleagues in the Townsend Centre for International Poverty Research have adopted this two-level definition on the grounds that it 'was designed to bridge industrialised and developing countries and to afford a basis for cross-national measurement' that would, it was believed, be acceptable to all governments (Gordon et al., 2000b: 86).

(This is despite his earlier rejection of any notion of absolute poverty and of the basic human needs approach, reflected in the absolute definition.) Although this definition was endorsed by many European social scientists in the public statement promulgated by Townsend and has been applied in a range of studies conducted by the Townsend Centre, its wider impact on thinking and policy has hitherto been fairly limited.

Public perceptions and political functions

The various articulations and re-articulations of the notions of and relationship between 'absolute' and 'relative' serve to illustrate that they represent different constructions of poverty, based on different understandings of human needs, rather than two distinct realities. As such, these notions still serve a political function. They are also used to try to make sense of public perceptions of poverty, which will themselves reflect a mixture of academic and political definitions, percolated through the media, as well as personal experience and observation.

UK research suggests that, at one level, there is still a distinction in many people's minds between poverty as an absolute subsistence-oriented and as a more relativist phenomenon, although the distinction is not necessarily that clear-cut. The annual British Social Attitudes Survey has consistently found only about a quarter of the population willing to subscribe to a thoroughgoing relativist definition of poverty as someone having 'enough to buy the things they really needed, but not enough to buy the things most people take for granted'; at least nine out of ten, by contrast, accept that 'not enough to eat and live without getting into debt' constitutes poverty. Around three-fifths also agree that those who have 'enough to eat and live, but not enough to buy other things they needed' are living in poverty (Hills, 2001).

This last formulation, of course, begs the question of what constitutes 'other things they needed' and can be read in two ways. Dean with Melrose label it as 'a breadline definition' and conclude that the 'popular preference therefore is for "hard-nosed" definitions' (1999: 36). In contrast, John Hills suggests that other BSAS findings indicate that people have 'in mind a poverty line which rises in real terms in some way over time'. This, he argues, implies 'some form of relative definition', which goes beyond mere subsistence (2001: 4, 8, 10). As indicated earlier, support for this view comes from the PSE Survey where substantial majorities identified 'social customs, obligations and activities...as among the top necessities of life' (Gordon et al., 2000a: 16).

Qualitative focus group research with people with experience of poverty points to a complexity of views that is not adequately captured in simple, dichotomous terms of either 'absolute' or 'relative'. Instead, people are able to subscribe to elements of both simultaneously:

> Although when asked, some participants subscribed to a relative definition, *all* the groups tended towards an absolute definition of poverty. They thought that it was of a different kind and magnitude to poverty experienced in the Third World and that the kind of poverty they associated with the South was 'real' poverty. Interestingly, when talking about poverty generally and talking about their own experience, as opposed to definitions as such, participants tended to see poverty in more relative terms. Furthermore, when we asked people to define poverty in their own words, their definitions tended to be idiosyncratic and personal [such as 'apologizing for having a decent lawnmower' and 'when I've got to avoid the charity box that I'd want to put in']. (Beresford et al., 1999: 176, 61–2, emphasis in original)

To understand the heat generated by the absolute–relative debate, it is important to remember my earlier point about the political implications of poverty definitions and the moral imperative implied by the term. The terms do not simply act as descriptors of poverty but also signify opposing political positions: absolutist definitions are traditionally associated with the political 'right' and relativist with the 'left'. As David Green argues, 'the manner in which a writer defines poverty reflects his [sic] underlying assumptions about the human condition and his preferred role for government' (1998: 12).

If poverty is defined in narrow, absolutist terms, the role ascribed to government and the resource implications for the policies needed to eradicate it are considerably more limited than if it is defined to take account of social needs and obligations and the living standards the wider society takes for granted. Thus, Rowntree's subsistence standard was taken at face value and was incorporated into the post-war social security system as justification for setting benefits at subsistence level (Kincaid, 1973; Veit-Wilson, 1986). Townsend's defence of his relativist position against Sen's critique was in part fired by his belief (disputed by Sen) that the latter's position 'opens the door to a tough state interpretation of subsistence rations' (1993: 132). Conversely, the idea of relative poverty has been attacked from the right as a political weapon wielded by the left in order to inflate the numbers counted as poor and to foster envy of the rich, by conflating it with inequality, thereby justifying more extensive state action (Dennis, 1997; Green, 1998). Yet, some who subscribe to a relativist definition have warned that, politically, it may rob poverty of some of the moral force of a starker definition, thereby making it easier for politicians to dismiss its importance (Saunders et al., 2002). The fear is that emphasis on poverty's relative nature serves to obscure the ways in which, as we shall see in chapter 3, it can still mean very real hardship and suffering even in wealthy societies.

Conclusion

These debates underline how the issue of definitions cannot be divorced from the political use to which they are put. Moreover, implicit in definitions are explanations of poverty and its distribution, which generally reflect individualistic or structural perspectives. The former attribute the main responsibility for poverty to the 'the poor' themselves; the latter point to how economic, social and political structures and processes – from the global to the local – create and perpetuate poverty.[2] Together, explanations, definitions (and their translation into measurements) and broader conceptualizations combine to shape policy responses to the phenomenon called 'poverty'.

The phenomenon of poverty has to be understood both as a painful reality experienced by millions of human beings and as a construction of competing conceptualizations, definitions and measures. The category of 'the poor' and what we describe as 'poverty' is thus, at one level, an artefact. How we approach the question of definition has important implications for policy and for the treatment of those categorized as 'poor' more generally. The approach favoured here is unambiguously relative, but acknowledges the existence of universal absolute needs. The point is that these can only be satisfied in particular historical and cultural contexts. In this way, we are able to transcend a rather sterile debate between absolute and relative definitions.

Although I have argued for a focused material definition of poverty in order not to lose sight of what is unique to the phenomenon, this must be set within the broader conceptualization articulated in the Introduction and developed in later chapters. Moreover, such a definition needs to be understood within a wider social scientific framework concerning 'well-being', 'capabilities', 'human flourishing', 'quality of life' and 'social quality' so as not to ghettoize poverty in a residual category of little or no apparent import to the wider society.

2
Measuring Poverty

Definitions of poverty are operationalized through measures. Chapter 2 discusses the 'why and how', 'what' and 'who' questions that emerge from the increasingly sophisticated literature on poverty measurement.[1] The choice of measure depends in part on the broader conceptualization, the definition that is being operationalized and on why a researcher wants to measure poverty. However, in practice questions of resources and feasibility mean that measures are but proxies that generally reflect only imperfectly conceptualizations, definitions and aims. Moreover, sometimes the quantification of poverty is divorced from any prior explicit conceptualization or definition.

'Why?' and 'How?' Questions

Ultimately the sole valid justification for measuring poverty stems from the moral and political imperative that action should be taken to eliminate it. Evidence is sought to persuade governments and/or the wider population of the case for action. To this end, information is needed on the extent and severity of poverty and how it affects different groups. Cross-national comparisons and monitoring over time help assess the effectiveness of policies and the impact of social and economic trends. Different measurements can produce different results. Indeed, a comparison of three commonly used measures found remarkably little overlap between those identified as poor on each measure (Bradshaw and Finch, 2003). This means that what may appear to be merely technical questions can have significant political and policy implications. The choices made, especially by governments, may reflect political as much as social scientific considerations (Veit-Wilson, 2004). Although too often overlooked, value judgements are embedded in technical decisions.

While, therefore, there is considerable debate about the relative advantages of particular measurement tools, the need for such tools as an aid to policy tends to be taken for granted in the North and by global institutions such as the World Bank. Some in the development field, however, adopt a more critical stance. Measurement generally implies quantification, which is seen as delivering 'objective facts'. These then become *the* reality despite all the problems associated with measurement. But this measurable 'reality', it is argued, may not be what matters most (Øyen, 1996; Chambers, 1997). The 'hegemony of the measurable' can suppress other forms of 'poverty knowledge' and 'alternative narratives of poverty', better tapped through qualitative, participatory approaches (McGee and Brock, 2001: 4, 35). Qualitative research, more generally, can uncover meanings and provide insights into the experience of poverty that have implications for the development of policy. The challenge to the 'hegemony of the measurable' is important for the broad conceptualization of poverty adopted here and also acts as a salutary reminder that measurements are technical artefacts. Nevertheless it does not obviate the need for quantitative measures, which operationalize more focused definitions for policy purposes. Moreover, quantitative poverty research itself can be informed by participatory methods.

'What?' Questions

Measuring poverty involves two, overlapping, sets of 'what' questions concerning first the indicators of poverty and second the standard (often called the poverty line) against which the indicators are to be assessed (Nolan and Whelan, 1996).

The indicators of poverty

The central issue here is the role of *income*. Should poverty be measured in terms of income, of living standards/consumption or of expenditure? And if the answer is, at least in part, income, should it be confined to actual income or also embrace a wider array of material resources and assets?

The choice between income or living standards stems from the definitional distinction between 'direct' and 'indirect' definitions of poverty discussed earlier. However, as Ringen (1987) pointed out in the 1980s, mainstream poverty research at that time tended to deploy an *indirect* income measure to operationalize a *direct* living standards definition. Where this happens, income is being used, illegitimately, as a proxy for consumption or living standards. Yet a growing body of research suggests that low income may be an imperfect indicator of deprivation of living standards (Nolan and Whelan, 1996; Barnes et al., 2002). Even in a study that found a strong association between an income measure of poverty and an index of hardship, two out of five families in income poverty 'did *not* register on the hardship index' (Vegeris and Perry, 2003: 142, emphasis in original). The disparity may be particularly marked when income is measured at the level of the household and living standards or well-being at the level of the individual, with gendered implications (Payne, 1991).

More generally, people may have a low standard of living for reasons other than current low income. Or, when on a low income, they may avoid or reduce deprivation by various means: running down savings; getting into debt; getting help from charity or family; begging or stealing. A measure of living standards alone would not capture the underlying income poverty experienced in such situations and would gloss over the costs of some of these coping strategies to the individuals involved. Alternatively, when income rises after a spell of poverty, living standards may not rise commensurately where that income is needed to pay off debts. Conversely, where income fluctuates or employment is intermittent, some of it may be saved against an expected further spell of low income. Thus there is a growing consensus that, where living standards are part of the definition of poverty, both direct and indirect measures are needed. This is reflected in the British Government's decision to adopt a 'tiered' measure of child poverty which incorporates both low-income indicators on their own and an indicator that combines material deprivation and low income 'as an additional gauge of living standards' (DWP, 2003e: 12).

There are also a number of technical problems involved in arriving at an accurate measure of income, including possible under-reporting and fluctuations over time. Some suggest therefore that *expenditure* may be preferable to current income both as a more reliable measure of 'normal' income and also as a better proxy for living standards. But expenditure has its own problems, including its lumpy nature (because of occasional large purchases) and its elision of borrowing and saving. Also, from the perspective of individuals rather than households, the expenditure of one person, for example the mother, may improve the living standards of others in the household rather than her own. An attempt to compare and combine the two suggests that 'income and expenditure measures of poverty are tapping quite different dimensions of economic well-being' (Saunders et al., 2002: 230). While neither income nor expenditure measures are perfect, the former are more commonly used in poverty research.

Income, however, though crucial in monetized economies, on its own may represent a rather narrow indicator of the material resources available to individuals. Townsend (1979) therefore, emphasizes the need to attempt to measure the total material resources which are distributed unequally in society, difficult though that may be. In addition to cash income, he identifies four other types of resources: capital assets; value of employer welfare benefits; value of public services; private income in kind. The importance of various kinds of resources is likely to differ for men and women (Ruspini, 2001; Millar, 2003). The significance of capital 'assets' has been acknowledged recently in ideas for 'assets-based welfare', designed to help and encourage people on low incomes to accumulate financial assets. Broader notions of assets and resources are discussed in chapter 6.

The conversion of resources into living standards involves *time* – often women's time (see chapter 3). The, until recently, 'forgotten dimension of time' is also implicit more generally in some of these measurement issues (Walker with Ashworth, 1994: 1). The period over which resources, and particularly income, are measured may affect the outcome. The shorter the period the more important is the distinction between income and consumption (Bradbury et al., 2001). The longer the period, the lower the measured rate of poverty is likely to be because 'temporary mismatches between income and needs' are ironed out (Walker with Ashworth, 1994: 13). Moreover, longitudinal research captures better than snapshot surveys the relationship between income and living standards. When low income is measured longitudinally over a period of years, as a measure of 'persistent poverty', the association with deprivation indicators is stronger than when current low income alone is measured (Whelan et al., 2003). Longitudinal data have also revealed an association between persistent and severe child poverty and income volatility (Adelman et al., 2003).

The poverty standard

In order to translate indicators of poverty into an estimate of the poverty rate, they have to be assessed against a standard, commonly called the 'poverty line', which represents a threshold below which people are counted as 'poor'. There are a number of different approaches to setting this line. These can loosely be divided into those that are criticized as 'arbitrary' (unrelated to criteria of need or deprivation) and those that purport to be 'scientific'. The latter, which are grounded in either expert or more democratic estimates of needs, are discussed below under 'who' questions. 'Arbitrary' approaches commonly underpin official poverty estimates because of their relative simplicity and their suitability for international comparisons. The main examples are: the minimum income levels set under social assistance schemes; a percentage of average incomes, typically now in Europe 60 per cent of the median (i.e. mid-point, which is less sensitive to a few very high incomes than the average/mean previously used); and the World Bank's (much criticized) $1, $2 or $4 a day. The numbers counted are very sensitive to the level chosen.

The time dimension also affects the poverty line. When it is being used to monitor change over time, once the line is set it can be fixed at that level in real terms or it can be linked to increases in average incomes or modified regularly in line with changing expectations. The first is sometimes called an 'absolute' poverty line and the second two 'relative'. The UK Government uses both what it calls 'absolute' and 'relative' versions of its measure of low income, which, as a proportion of median income, is itself a relative standard. This is confusing. A relative standard and moving line are more suitable operationalizations of a relative definition. Nevertheless, such a line can create paradoxes. For example, in a country where average income was falling, this might not count as an increase in poverty, even if those at the bottom were finding it harder to make ends meet. Just such a situation was experienced in some of the transitional economies of central and eastern Europe in the early 1990s (UNICEF, 2000).

Poverty lines are most commonly used to estimate the numbers and composition of 'the poor' (the 'headcount') and policy is then directed to bringing as many as possible up to the line. However, they tell us nothing about the depth or intensity of poverty, that is, the extent to which people's incomes fall below the poverty line. 'Poverty gap' measures have been devised, but are less frequently used than headcount measures. Yet the two can produce divergent pictures of poverty trends (Osberg, 2002; Kuchler and Goebel, 2003). They can also point to different policy priorities, as the groups whose average income falls furthest below the poverty line may not form the largest groups in the headcount (Adelman, 2000). Similarly, policies that are successful in bringing those just below the poverty line up to it (thereby reducing the headcount) may not be the best way of helping those furthest below it (thereby closing the poverty gap).

This is one of the criticisms made by those who question the very construction of poverty lines. At the heart of such criticisms is the question as to whether there exists a clear threshold which neatly divides 'the poor' from 'the non-poor' or whether the relationship between the two is better understood as a continuum, with gradations among those measured as 'poor' as well as among those measured as 'non-poor'. The debate continues, with both sides pointing to evidence in favour of their position. The issues raised are political as well as scientific, because poverty thresholds are, in part, political constructs. Some who dispute the empirical validity of a clear poverty threshold nevertheless acknowledge its political value as a yardstick against which to judge government action. Others argue that preoccupation with the poverty line distracts attention both from an analytical definition of poverty and from the significant number living just above any poverty line whose situation may be little different from those on or just below it (Novak, 2001; O'Connor, 2001).

'Who?' Questions

Who decides?

Veit-Wilson makes the point that what distinguishes different approaches to drawing a 'scientific' poverty threshold is 'the question of *who* decides what necessities are' (1987: 188, emphasis in original). Three main answers to the question 'who decides?' are represented by what can be labelled as the 'professional expert', 'democratic' and 'participatory' approaches. In practice, though, they overlap, particularly as all approaches involve experts' judgements to some extent. Each approach also raises questions about possible variations in perspective, such as those associated with ethnicity, gender, class, disability and age, which are difficult to take adequately into account (Gordon et al., 2000a; Van den Bosch, 2001; Platt, 2002).

Professional expert   The main example of the 'professional expert' approach is the use of 'budget standards' through which a specified basket of goods and services is costed for different kinds of household to establish a poverty threshold.

This involves expert judgements about the items to be included, together with their quantity, quality and price. Veit-Wilson (1998) identifies two versions. In the original, more 'prescriptive', mode 'experts lay down what are to be the minimum standards of food, clothing, housing, income and so on' based on their own views of how people on low incomes should be able to live (Veit-Wilson, 1987: 188). This was the approach adopted by Rowntree. It underlies the US poverty line, which has been widely criticized for not reflecting changing consumption patterns since the 1960s, when it was established.

More recently, a 'social science' version has been developed, most notably by Jonathan Bradshaw in the UK and by the National Research Council in the US. Rather than prescribing how people on low incomes *should* live, it draws on empirical social scientific evidence as to how the general population actually *does* live. Although budget standards are often associated with a subsistence approach, Bradshaw, among others, has demonstrated how they can incorporate social needs and how they 'have the capacity to bring the analysis of living standards alive' (1997: 51).

Bradshaw is also involved in the development of another social scientific expert approach to fixing poverty thresholds, based on a measure of 'constrained expenditure'. This utilizes 'data on the *absence of expenditure* on durable goods and luxury items' in order to identify 'the income level at which all income is being spent, but none of it is devoted to purchasing any of the major durable or luxury items'. This is then equated with the 'level at which all resources are being used to meet immediate needs with nothing left over to replace the household's capital stock, nor to consume luxury items' (Saunders et al., 2002: 227, emphasis in original). The difficulty with such an approach is that it cannot accommodate those who choose to spend on major durable or luxury items, even when their immediate needs have not been met. (This reflects Rowntree's warning, quoted in the previous chapter, that people cannot live on a 'fodder basis'.) Conversely, as the authors acknowledge, it cannot distinguish where lack of spending on such items reflects choice rather than constraint nor, as a snapshot measure, can it take into account past expenditures, which affect current consumption needs.

Democratic A number of 'democratic' approaches can be identified (Van den Bosch, 2001). These draw on the views of the general population rather than simply those of professional experts. They are often called 'consensual' in the literature. However, studies that are genuinely consensual, in the sense of reaching a consensus through deliberation, are rare. One of the few examples is a democratic version of the budget studies approach: 'lay people negotiated, refined and agreed a poverty line based on their own views as to the essentials of modern day life' for people in similar household circumstances to themselves (Walker and Middleton, 1995: 20). The emphasis is on '*informed* consensus' (Middleton, 2000: 74, emphasis in original).

The approach more commonly dubbed 'consensual' originates with Mack and Lansley's 1985 Breadline Britain Survey and has been widely adopted. Its most recent application in Britain is the 2000 PSE Survey. The essence of the consensual approach lies in its aim: 'to identify a minimum acceptable way of life not by reference to the views of "experts", nor by reference to observed patterns of expenditure or observed living standards, but by reference to *the views of society as a whole*' (Mack and Lansley, 1985: 42, emphasis in original). However, these views are expressed within a framework established by professional experts (Levitas, 2000). Three steps are involved, all using social surveys. The first identifies the items (goods and activities) a majority considers necessities – that is, a majority view rather than a negotiated consensus as such; the second identifies those who are forced to do without these necessities for lack of resources; and the third attempts to establish the income levels at which people risk not being able to afford them.

The reference to observed expenditure patterns and living standards distinguishes their approach from that adopted in Townsend's survey (1979). The latter deploys a range of social indicators of material and social deprivation chosen by the researcher to identify first those without the items chosen and second a band of income beneath which the risk of deprivation intensifies. One of the criticisms it drew, addressed by Mack and Lansley, is that it does not distinguish between choice and constraint as the reason why people lack a particular item on a list that reflected the researcher's own cultural perceptions. Thus, for instance, lack of fresh meat and a Sunday roast may be a function of vegetarianism rather than low income.

The democratic approaches discussed so far all aim at establishing a poverty threshold through the identification of a list of perceived necessities and the income then needed to meet them. An alternative democratic method – variously labelled the 'subjective poverty line', the 'income proxy or evaluation', the 'attitudinal' or, after its birthplace, the 'Leyden' method – in effect asks a sample of the whole population directly what they think the poverty line should be for their own household. In its original form, the word 'poverty' is not used; instead respondents are usually asked about the level of income at which the household 'can just make ends meet'. Qualitative research has, though, identified as problems the complexities of the task facing respondents and the effect of different understandings of the question on the outcome (Institute for Research on Poverty, 1998; Middleton, 1998). There are also potential gender differences, reflecting women's and men's roles in the management and control of household resources (see chapter 3). Nevertheless, the approach is widely used, sometimes in conjunction with the perceived necessities approach.

Where respondents are asked directly to judge their income in relation to the level required to keep them out of poverty, as in the PSE Survey, there is a degree of overlap with attempts to gauge subjective feelings of deprivation and poverty, which are not used to establish a poverty threshold (Atkinson et al., 2002). This was one element of Townsend's survey. While he found that in the majority of cases there was a clear relationship between objective indicators and subjective feelings of deprivation, a minority 'with extremely low resources [denied] feelings of deprivation' (1979: 426). This raises questions about people's willingness to identify with the stigmatized label of poverty, discussed in chapter 5. More generally, it raises an issue for all democratic and subjective approaches: the phenomenon of 'preference-deformation' or 'adaptation' (Sen, 1985a; Nussbaum, 2000). In other words, people who do not have very much may reduce their expectations and aspirations as a way of adapting to their situation. (In the PSE Survey, though, 'poorer groups were sometimes more likely than the better-off groups to consider certain items to be necessities' – carpets and a TV for instance (Gordon et al., 2000a: 17).) These issues have implications also for the final – participatory – approach.

Participatory Participatory research represents less a method than a philosophy – committed to principles of democracy and empowerment. Unlike the other approaches discussed, it is not typically geared to establishing a poverty line. Nevertheless, its proponents claim that 'engaging with the poor leads to better technical diagnosis of problems and better design and implementation of solutions' (Robb, 2002: 104). It is premised on the belief that people in poverty are themselves experts in poverty and that therefore, ideally, their views should be taken on board at all stages of the research process – as subjects and not just objects from whom information is to be extracted. From the perspective of mainstream poverty research in the North, the participatory approach is conspicuous for its rarity rather than its influence. Nevertheless, the case is beginning to be made, influenced by participatory research in the South, the work of organizations such as ATD Fourth World, growing user-involvement in welfare services, and the challenge from the disabled people's movement to traditional research paradigms (Bennett with Roberts, 2004).

As indicated in the Introduction, participatory research is particularly valuable in the development of the conceptualization of poverty. Baulch suggests that most development 'practitioners would recommend a "walking on two legs" strategy in measuring poverty', whereby the kind of methods discussed so far are complemented by participatory methods which better identify the 'more subjective dimensions of poverty' (1996b: 41). There is no reason why the same should not apply to poverty research in the North. Indeed, the choice of indicators for measuring progress in tackling poverty could itself usefully be informed by the views of those experiencing that poverty, as illustrated by UK Government consultations on measuring child poverty and the European Project on Poverty Indicators starting from the Experience of People Living in Poverty (DWP, 2003b; Hacourt, 2003). Evidence suggests that, in the UK, debt levels would emerge as important, although they have hitherto been ignored in the official set of indicators (Galloway, 2002; DWP, 2003b).

Unit of analysis

A further 'who?' question concerns the unit of analysis. Although poverty estimates generally refer to individuals, they are usually based on measures of *household/family* income rather than of that of each *individual* within a household/family. This raises difficult measurement issues, which have gendered implications both for the analysis of poverty and for policies to combat it (see chapter 3). The unit adopted will partly reflect the purposes of the measurement and partly feasibility.

The case for taking the household as the unit is that people living in households pool their resources and share living standards, at least to some extent. If this is ignored, it can give a misleading picture of individual income and living standards. On the other hand, if resources are not shared fairly within households (as research indicates can be the case) this can result in an underestimate of the numbers living in poverty, particularly of women and children, and can give a biased account of the gendered patterns of poverty. Moreover, ultimately poverty is experienced by individuals and it is the well-being of individuals for which we are striving (Nussbaum, 2000). The individual is also clearly the appropriate unit, if poverty is understood in terms of a right to a minimum level of resources (A. B. Atkinson, 1989, 1990; Atkinson et al., 2002).

A related issue is how to compare households of different compositions. The technical device used is called an 'equivalence scale'. This, among other things, is a means of taking account of economies of scale and of the different needs of adults and children so that like can be compared with like. Standard equivalence scales typically do not take account of the additional costs associated with disability, the significance of which is highlighted by Sen's capabilities approach (see chapter 1). The result is that income poverty among disabled people is underestimated (Heady and Room, 2002; Bradshaw et al., 2003). The choice of equivalence scales, although a technical matter, thus involves normative judgements with considerable consequences for the numbers and composition of those counted as poor. It is, therefore, the source of considerable disagreement.

Subjects of comparison

The final 'who?' question concerns the appropriate subjects of comparison in any measure of relative poverty. This question has emerged in two forms. The first concerns the appropriate geographical basis for comparison. Traditionally, poverty has been measured in relation to national comparators. Rainwater et al. (2001) have, however, asked whether the comparison should not be made within a more local unit, such as, in the US, individual states (or in the UK individual nations). The justification would be that people's reference groups for comparing living standards are more likely to be local than national. Using state rather than federal averages in the US produces some very different results for child poverty rates, with a big increase in the richer states and decrease in the poorer. One problem with this argument is that it neatly removes from the policy equation regional economic inequalities, which might be contributing to differential poverty rates. Moreover, mass culture makes it unlikely that people compare themselves only with those in the same state or community. Indeed, in this globalized world, 'there is as strong a case for enlarging the basic unit of comparison as for shrinking it' (UNICEF, 2000: 22).

The second issue has been raised in relation to children: should child poverty be measured against the living standards of other children only rather than of the whole population? The argument put is that 'if children are excluded from social participation by low living standards, the most important form of this may be exclusion from the lifestyle typically enjoyed by other children' (Bradbury et al., 2001: 43; Micklewright, 2002). The problem with this, otherwise plausible, argument is that in those countries where children are at greater risk of poverty than adults, it would camouflage this disparity and serve to depress the estimates of child poverty (see chapter 3).

Conclusion

The general conclusion reached in the literature is that no single method of measurement is sufficient, let alone perfect. Measures inevitably represent proxies for definitions of poverty. The consensus, therefore, is that 'in attempting to understand the changing nature and extent of poverty it is unwise to rely on any single measure' (Layte et al., 2000: 571). Nevertheless, in the UK there appears to be majority support for the view I would endorse that low income should remain central to any official measure (DWP, 2003b, 2003e). More generally, 'triangulation' – the combination of a range of methods – is needed to improve the accuracy of the operationalization of definitions of poverty aimed at measuring its extent, depth and composition (Bradshaw and Finch, 2003). Moreover, further triangulation with qualitative, including participatory, methods will help to achieve a deeper, multidimensional and multi-perspective picture, which goes beyond measurement and which is consistent with the conceptualization of poverty developed here.

3
Inequality, Social Divisions and the Differential Experience of Poverty

The inequalities and social divisions that shape and interact with poverty and that mediate how people experience it are the main focus of this chapter. It thus reflects a structuralist perspective. As argued in chapter 1, poverty is best understood as a function of social, economic and political structures and processes which create and perpetuate an unequal distribution of resources both within and, in a global context, between societies. A structuralist perspective does not necessarily write human agency out of the script, as we shall see in chapter 6. Individuals and groups who experience poverty do so as active agents who will react in different ways and forge their own lives within the structural constraints facing them. This needs to be borne in mind when reading this chapter in which the emphasis is on structure rather than agency.

The chapter begins by placing poverty briefly but firmly in the context of socio-economic inequality and social class. It then paints an impressionistic picture of the material impact of poverty in wealthy societies before turning to look at the ways in which the social divisions of gender, 'race' and disability shape and mediate how it is experienced. In addition to structural inequalities, it considers how poverty is experienced at the two ends of the life-course (a notion that captures the complexity of individuals' passage through a lifetime): childhood and old age. In practice, individual social divisions interact with each other and with phases of the life-course either to reinforce or to mitigate their individual impact, but for ease of analysis they will be discussed separately here.

The final dimension considered is spatial. This also raises an issue about the levels at which poverty is lived simultaneously: most basically as an individual of a particular gender, 'race', ethnicity, religion, social class, age, sexual orientation and with or without disabilities; plus, in many cases, within a family or multi-person household, which can affect the degree and nature of poverty; and finally within the wider neighbourhood and the physical and social environment created by it (Burchardt et al., 2002a). Moreover, power is exercised at these levels and beyond – from the micro-household to the macro-national/global – to exclude individuals and groups from access to adequate resources (Jordan, 1996).

Inequality, Social Class and Polarization

John Scott has analysed this process of exclusion through the representation of deprivation and privilege as 'polarised departures from the normal range of lifestyles that are enjoyed by the citizens of a society' (1994: 173). Differential power and opportunity at each end of the hierarchy of inequality mean that 'the deprived are excluded from public life; the privileged are able to exclude the public from their special advantages' (1994: 151). He concludes that the causes of poverty are inseparable from the causes of wealth. This echoes R. H. Tawney's famous dictum that 'what thoughtful rich people call the problem of poverty thoughtful poor people call with equal justice the problem of riches' (1913). Scott emphasizes that deprivation and privilege are distinct 'conditions and social statuses' and not simply rankings at the bottom and top of a statistical hierarchy (1994: 173).

Poverty, relatively understood, and inequality are not synonymous, as underlined in chapter 1. Nevertheless, poverty is closely associated with inequality. Cross-national analysis demonstrates that the countries with the lowest levels of poverty tend to be more equal overall than countries with higher levels (UNICEF, 2000; Esping-Andersen, 2002). The greater the inequality the less likely it is that those at the top will identify with those at the bottom and be sympathetic to redistributive policies to improve their position (Phillips, 1999). Social class still 'underpins the distribution of poverty and economic inequality' (Mooney, 2000: 156; Savage, 2000). Despite their identification of a 'new poverty' to which the middle classes are also vulnerable, Leisering and Leibfried acknowledge that 'the risk of poverty is obviously higher for families in the lower economic classes' (1999: 240). In unequal societies like the UK, social class continues to affect profoundly life-expectancy, health, education and employment opportunities.

Inequality of both income and wealth intensified in many countries in the late twentieth century (Esping-Andersen, 2002; Townsend and Gordon, 2002). This is best described as a process of socio-economic polarization. The process has been operating at the global level also. Although the subject of some dispute, many argue that an intensification of poverty is associated with growing global inequality, the level of which has been described as 'grotesque' (UNDP, 2003: 39). Townsend is foremost among those who have linked developments in the world economy with the growth in poverty and inequality in many wealthy countries, most notably the US and the UK (1993; Townsend and Gordon, 2002). The conclusion reached by many poverty analysts is that poverty cannot be effectively tackled unless inequality is reduced at both national and international levels. 'Rising inequality is not inevitable' (T. Atkinson, 2002: 45).

The Experience of Poverty

What distinguishes poverty from inequality is the experience of deprivation in both its material and social forms (see chapter 1). The depth and nature of this deprivation will depend, in part, on the length of any spell of poverty and whether it is a one-off or recurrent phenomenon. Of significance also – both psychologically and in terms of how poverty is managed – is whether there is any certainty as to when it will end.

In the UK there has been a series of quantitative and qualitative studies of the material impact of poverty. The major PSE Survey used a deprivation index derived from what a representative sample of the British population considered necessities. It found that of a population of 58 million:

- some 9.5 million cannot afford to keep their homes adequately heated, free from damp and decently decorated;
- around 8 million cannot afford one or more essential household items or to replace electrical goods or furniture when needed;
- nearly 7.5 million do not have the money to participate in common social activities;
- a third of children go without at least one necessity such as adequate clothing and three meals a day, and nearly a fifth go without two or more;
- roughly 6.5 million adults cannot afford essential clothing;
- some 4 million do not have enough money for an adequate diet (Gordon et al., 2000a).

Qualitative studies give more of a feel of what such deprivation means for those experiencing it. A synthesis of thirty such studies by Elaine Kempson (1996) reveals that 'life on a low income . . . is a stressful and debilitating experience' especially for those on social assistance who 'face a struggle against encroaching debt and social isolation where even the most resilient and resourceful are hard pressed to survive' (Barclay, 1996: ix). Generally, the picture painted by qualitative studies is one of: constant restrictions; doing without; running out of money at the end of the week; limited choice; no room for spontaneity; damaged family relationships (Cohen et al., 1992; Kempson et al., 1994). 'Existing not living' is a recurrent phrase used by people in poverty to describe its material impact.

How that impact is subjectively experienced may vary according to the items individuals themselves consider as essential to 'living not existing'. As hinted at in chapter 2, perceptions of necessities may to some extent be patterned according to factors such as gender, ethnicity, disability, social class and age. Thus, for example, disabled and non-disabled people may vary in their views as to what constitute essential items (Knight et al., 2002). Research in both Britain and Sweden suggests that 'ideas about what constitutes poverty and deprivation may be different for men and women' (Payne and Pantazis, 1997: 113). This underlines the main argument of this chapter: intersecting social divisions and position in the life-course, to which we now turn, structure the impact and experience of poverty.

Gender

Gender constitutes the most profound differentiating division. A gendered analysis of poverty reveals not simply its unequal incidence but also that both cause and effect are deeply gendered. The conceptual and methodological implications go well beyond simply 'adding women in'. 'The reverberations are fundamental', as Townsend acknowledges (1993: 106). Moreover, a gendered analysis can illuminate men's as well as women's relationship to poverty (Buhaenko et al., 2003; Ruxton, 2003).

The 'feminization of poverty'

In both North and South poverty all too often wears a female face (UNDP, 1995, 1997). The evidence from the EU and the US shows that, to varying degrees and with the clearest exception of Sweden, women face a greater risk of poverty than men (Bradshaw et al., 2003; Daly and Rake, 2003). The gender disparity is most visible among female-headed households, notably lone mothers and single pensioners (Barnes et al., 2002; Proctor and Dalaker, 2003). Women are also more likely to have experienced poverty at some time in their lives (Payne and Pantazis,1997) and to suffer recurrent and longer poverty spells (Ruspini, 1998, 2001; DWP, 2003a). Moreover, longitudinal analysis, which tracks people over time, has produced 'fairly compelling evidence that the effects of childhood disadvantage are more powerful for women than for men' (Hobcraft, 2003: iii).

The 'feminization of poverty' is the term now widely used to capture these patterns. Although powerful rhetorically, it is in some ways misleading. It implies a new phenomenon, yet 'women have always experienced more poverty than men', as Diana Pearce, who coined the term, observes (1990: 266). What has changed is that the growing number of at-risk female-headed households has dispelled the fog that previously shrouded female poverty. Awareness has increased too of the poverty experienced by female-dominated groups such as carers.

Most statistics deployed in support of the 'feminization of poverty' thesis are based on household heads rather than individuals in households. Alternatively, in the absence of data on the latter, they are rough 'guesstimates' (Marcoux, 1998: 132). The prime example is the widely cited UN claim that 70 per cent of the world's poor are female (UNDP, 1995). A preoccupation with the risk of poverty among female-headed households masks both the heterogeneity within this group and female poverty within male-headed households (Daly, 1992; Razavi, 2000). Poverty head-counts that purport to count individuals but in fact do so on the basis of household income, on the heroic assumption that it is shared fairly, are likely to underestimate female poverty.

Hidden poverty

This 'hidden poverty' results from the unequal distribution of both income and consumption within families. It can mean either that women are poor when their male partners are not or that women experience poverty more intensely than their partners. UK studies of money management show that income is not always shared fairly within the family and that women have less 'personal spending money' than men (Pahl, 1989; Goode et al., 1998) – although this was not the finding of a recent Irish study (Daly and Leonard, 2002). Most of this research has been small-scale and qualitative; nevertheless support for its conclusions comes also from a larger, quantitative survey. This found that 'the orthodox model of households as egalitarian decision-making units, within which resources are shared equally, applied to only a fifth (20 per cent) of the households' surveyed (Vogler, 1994: 241). 'Wives generally experienced greater financial deprivation than husbands', although this varied with systems of household financial allocation, as did women's access to personal spending money (1994: 234).

With regard to consumption, qualitative research again indicates that men tend to be 'privileged consumers' in terms of both everyday commodities such as food and consumer durables such as a car. Moreover, as Millar and Glendinning point out, ' "his" car and "her" washing machine are hardly equivalent in terms of the benefits and freedoms which each confers' (1989: 367). Similar findings on food and basic consumption goods have emerged in the South (World Bank, 2001). The small amount of relevant quantitative research available in Europe points weakly in the same direction but does not 'reveal a substantial reservoir of hidden poverty' (Cantillon and Nolan, 1998: 169). This may, though, be in part due to methodologies that were not designed to measure intra-household inequalities (Bradshaw et al., 2003).

Economic dependence

Hidden female poverty reflects, on the one hand, structural factors associated with women's economic dependence and male power and, on the other, the agency of women who sacrifice their own needs on behalf of other family members, especially children. Women's economic dependence (full or partial) is the price they pay for caring within a gendered division of labour, in which men do the greater share of paid work and women of unpaid, domestic work. This continues both to inhibit the access of many women to an adequate independent income and to facilitate male economic independence and power (Daly and Rake, 2003; EOC, 2003). Complete economic dependence on male partners is now less common and women's earnings play an increasingly important role in keeping families out of poverty (Rake, 2000). The extent and degree of female economic dependence varies over the life-course and between groups and countries. In both the

UK and the US, for instance, Black women are less likely to be economically dependent than White and the phenomenon is generally less marked in the Nordic countries.

Nevertheless, in most countries, women's earnings, particularly where they are part-time, are frequently insufficient to provide genuine economic independence in terms of the balance of economic power within households or the ability to maintain an independent poverty-free household (when, increasingly in practice, families rely on two earners) (Stier and Mandel, 2003). This in part reflects the continued, albeit weakening, hold of the ideology of women's economic dependence, under which women are deemed to have a male provider. It serves to legitimate their inferior economic position in both the public sphere of the labour market and the private sphere of the home. Thus, it is only the more privileged women who are immune to the ideology's material impact.

The implications of female economic dependence extend beyond hidden poverty resulting from the unequal distribution of income and resources within the family. Even where resources are shared fairly, a woman who has insufficient income in her own right to meet her own and her children's needs is vulnerable to poverty because she is reliant on the discretion of her partner and is ill-prepared should the partnership break down. Half of the married women in a UK study were found to be 'at risk of poverty' in that sense (Ward et al., 1996). Other UK research indicates how the unequal power relationship, typical of full or partial economic dependence, is experienced by many women as a lack of control over resources, a lack of rights and a sense of obligation and deference (Burgoyne, 1990; Goode et al., 1998). Some women thus prefer the poverty of lone motherhood because of the financial autonomy that it gives them (Graham, 1993).

Self-sacrifice

The second aspect of hidden poverty results from female self-sacrifice; it has a long history (Vincent, 1991). Contemporary studies of how low income families manage find mothers frequently going without food, clothing and warmth in order to protect other family members, especially children, from the full impact of an inadequate income (Middleton et al., 1994; Farrell and O'Connor, 2003). This 'compulsory altruism' is all too often taken for granted (Land and Rose, 1985). It is one facet of how women tend to act as the shock-absorbers of poverty as they manage poverty and debt as part of their general responsibility for money management in low-income families (Daly and Leonard, 2002; Yeandle et al., 2003). The stress involved can have a damaging effect on physical and mental health, although some women simultaneously report a sense of pride (Bradshaw and Holmes, 1989; Goode et al., 1998).

Time

Managing poverty can be very time-consuming. Yet 'poor people's time is regarded as valueless' (Toynbee, 2003: 34). Where better-off people often substitute money for time through purchase of labour-saving goods or the services of others, those in poverty often do the opposite – expending time in order to save money (Payne, 1991). And it is largely women's time: 'by increasing their work day and intensifying their time use, women internalize the costs of poverty' with implications for their personal well-being (Floro, 1995: 18). Women's time spent on work in the home converts income into the living standards enjoyed by other family members: meals, clean clothes and so forth.

This has implications for the conceptualization and mea-surement of poverty (Millar and Glendinning, 1992; Daly, 1992; Ruspini, 2001). Time is a resource that interacts with financial resources. To understand fully the gendered nature of poverty, we need to know how much of that resource women and men expend on converting income into living standards or, following Sen, into capabilities and function-ings. Thus within a household a woman might be poorer than a man not just in terms of income, capabilities and con-sumption but also in terms of the time and energy left over after the process of conversion. Of course, time poverty can exist in the absence of material poverty but where the two coexist it represents an additional dimension of poverty and in some cases it may be that material poverty is avoided only at the expense of time poverty (Douthitt, 1994). A further dimension, interacting with both material and time poverty, is mobility. Women rely particularly heavily on public transport in the process of managing poverty (Hamilton and Jenkins, 2000). Poor public transport exacerbates their time poverty (Turner and Grieco, 2000; Kenyon et al., 2003). Attempts to incorporate time into the measurement of poverty are rare (but see Vickery, 1977), and the complexities of doing so have been underlined (S. P. Jenkins, 1991). However, the recent development of 'household satellite accounts' that measure and value unpaid domestic work, as required following the 1995 UN Beijing World Conference on Women, might at least facilitate the development of measures of poverty that include 'a monetary valuation of non-market time' (S. P. Jenkins, 1994: 9).

Individuals or households?

The other main implication of a gendered perspective for the conceptualization and measurement of poverty (touched on in chapters 1 and 2) lies in its emphasis on poverty as experienced by individuals rather than households. Irrespective of the material living standards a woman may enjoy at any one time, she is vulnerable to poverty if she lacks control over resources and the independent means to support herself (Millar and Glendinning, 1992; Bradshaw et al., 2003). The individualized nature of Sen's capabilities approach and of the notion of well-being means that together they provide a helpful framework for thinking about women's poverty (Jackson, 1998; Razavi, 1997, 2000). However, given my earlier argument that low income is a key element of the definition of poverty, we still face the methodological challenge raised in chapter 2: that is, how to measure the incomes of individuals within households, including in relation to the expenditure for which they are responsible (S. P. Jenkins, 1991, 1994; Ruspini, 2001).

There is a tension between this individualistic focus, necessary to the exposure of different aspects of female hidden poverty, and an understanding of this poverty as rooted in women's relationships to other family members (Jackson,

1998; Millar, 2003). If an undifferentiated household analysis is the thesis and an individualized analysis the antithesis, we need to achieve a synthesis in which the individualized experience of poverty is understood within its relational context. As commentators on individualization point out, the desire for control over one's own resources and personhood implied by the idea should not be mistaken for selfishness and atomization (Lewis, 2001; Beck and Beck-Gernsheim, 2002).[1]

Family, labour market and state

Women's hidden poverty reflects their inferior position of power in the gendered division of labour, continued sex discrimination and gender stereotyping and the realities and ideology of female economic dependence. Together these underpin women's position in the labour market, family and welfare state and it is the interaction between the three that determines women's economic status over their lifetimes and that distinguishes the causes of female from male poverty. The exact constellation of the three resource systems, however, varies between welfare regimes, reflecting different labour market and welfare policies (Christopher, 2002; Daly and Rake, 2003).

Effective policies to tackle women's poverty need to ensure access to an adequate independent income from the labour market and/or the state, through a combination of labour market, welfare services and income maintenance measures, together with action to tackle the gendered division of labour. Access to an independent income strengthens women's economic position within couples as well as providing them with the capacity to establish autonomous households. This is of particular importance where there is domestic violence and abuse.

'Race'

We have seen how poverty is gendered in terms not just of its incidence but also of cause and effect. The gendered experience of poverty is, in turn, mediated by other social divisions, most notably that of 'race'. Poverty is a racialized phenomenon in three main senses relating to its incidence, the role of racial discrimination and racism, and racialized stereotyping.

Incidence

Poverty in both North and South is racially and ethnically patterned: non-White groups are disproportionately likely to be poor in White-dominated societies, and immigrants, asylum-seekers, Roma and indigenous peoples are particularly vulnerable to poverty (World Bank, 2001; Revenga et al., 2002). In the North, poverty's racial patterning is most visible in the US, where poverty rates for Blacks and Hispanics are roughly three times higher than for non-Hispanic Whites (who nevertheless constitute the largest group in poverty) (Proctor and Dalaker, 2003).

The links between poverty and 'race' are less well documented in Europe, as poverty research has tended to downplay their significance (with a few exceptions such as Craig, 2002). In the UK the inclusion of an ethnic breakdown in the official low-income statistics is relatively recent. It shows that, despite the diversity of experience between minority ethnic groups, overall their members' incomes are 'skewed towards the bottom of the income distribution. This pattern [is] particularly marked for the Pakistani and Bangladeshi group, with approximately three out of five individuals in these families having incomes in the bottom quintile [fifth] of the income distribution' (DWP, 2003a: 19). Not surprisingly, there is also greater deprivation among minority ethnic children than among the White majority, with 'an extraordinary level of concentration among Pakistani and Bangladeshi children' (Platt, 2002: 59; Marsh and Perry, 2003).

Racial discrimination and racism

What accounts for these racial patterns of poverty? Most analysts identify racism and discrimination as key factors. The World Bank, for instance, acknowledges that 'the cumulative effects' and psychological impact of 'discrimination in education, employment opportunities and information' under-mine the economic position of Blacks in White-dominated societies (2001: 124). Spatial concentration in deprived areas reinforces this economic disadvantage (Kushnick and Jennings, 1999; SEU, 2000). Despite a growing divergence between the labour market experiences of different minority ethnic groups, there is ample evidence in the UK of their general disadvantaged position in terms of unemployment, pay and quality of jobs (Platt, 2002; Pilkington, 2003). An official report points to continuing racial discrimination, which 'can often take subtle yet powerful forms' (PIU, 2002: iii). The available evidence suggests the same is true for Europe more widely (Craig, 2002).

Minority ethnic groups also tend to be disadvantaged within the welfare state. A number of factors are involved. They include: rules that discriminate against first-generation immigrants; universal services that fail to accommodate cultural differences; racist attitudes amongst officials; and low take-up among minority ethnic communities (Platt, 2002; Ahmad and Craig, 2003). Moreover, there has been a wide-spread trend to reduce access to welfare among immigrants and asylum-seekers (www.clasp.org). Humiliating treatment of Black welfare users, especially women who are more likely to mediate with welfare institutions, is one example of how everyday racism can exacerbate the experience of poverty. More generally, 'racial harassment and racist crime are wide-spread'; they 'can create a climate of fear' and contribute to the social exclusion of minority ethnic group members (SEU, 2000: 32–3).

Racialized stereotyping

Closely linked to such racism is a process of racialization. On the one hand this serves to stereotype and stigmatize Black people through association with poverty and 'welfare dependency' within an individualistic rather than structural analysis of poverty. On the other, it can stigmatize welfare recipients through the racist coding of welfare (Gilens, 1999). This dual process is most clearly marked in the US where 'the racialization of poverty has been a central feature of the political delegitimation and pacification of poor people' and has served to camouflage underlying wealth inequalities (Jennings and Kushnick, 1999: 6). The parallel process of the (gendered) 'racialization of welfare' facilitated the successful dismantling of welfare rights in the 1990s (Orloff, 2002). The media have played an important role in this process (Gilens, 1999; Jennings and Kushnick, 1999) – not least in the propagation of (in the US context) the deeply racialized construct of the 'underclass' (see chapter 5). This construct is widely deployed by commentators 'as little more than a crude synonym for inner-city blacks over whom they cast the old mantle of the undeserving poor', at the same time ignoring the numerically larger group of poor Whites (Katz, 1989: 234). 'The black underclass ideology not only helped legitimise existing racial inequalities, but it also de-humanised inner-city blacks and pointed to them as the cause of many social evils' (Raup, 1996: 164). In other words, the racialization of poverty and 'welfare dependency', together with the deployment of the 'underclass' label, has performed the classic function of 'blaming the victim'.

Disability

The relationship between poverty and disability in some ways parallels that between poverty and 'race', involving: incidence; specific causal factors, which in part reflect discrimination; and the treatment of disabled people by the wider society. It overlaps in particular with gendered poverty, as the majority of disabled people are female.

Incidence

Although poverty is not an automatic outcome of disability, it is closely associated with it in North and South in differing ways, as both a causal factor and a consequence (Beresford, 1996). It has been estimated that disabled people 'may account for as many as one in five of the world's poorest' and that 'as many as 50 per cent of disabilities are preventable and directly linked to poverty' (DfID, 2000a: 1,

3). UK data show that, on the one hand, the economically and educationally disadvantaged face a significantly above average risk of disability and that, on the other, disability carries a high risk of poverty (Burchardt, 2003). The latter is evident from the official statistics (DWP, 2003a). However, arguably these underestimate the true level of poverty for they do not make adjustment for the additional costs of disability (Burchardt, 2000a, 2003). Moreover, it is often not just the disabled person affected but also family members, especially those (generally women) who restrict their labour market activity to provide care (Barnes and Baldwin, 1999).

Causal factors

The impact on carers is sometimes described as an indirect cost of disability. More fundamentally, the additional needs associated with many forms of disability create expenses not faced by others on a low income. The main examples are: special diet; equipment or adaptations; additional heating because of immobility; and transport costs (Barnes and Baldwin, 1999). Moreover, disabled people are much more likely than the general population to consider access to information technology to be essential (Knight et al., 2002). Sen (1992, 1999) uses the example of the costs associated with disability to illustrate how the translation of incomes into capabilities varies between groups. All other things being equal, an income of 'x' may be adequate for a non-disabled person but may mean lack of capabilities and poverty for a disabled person because of the additional costs they face. This means that disabled people tend to experience greater material deprivation than others living in poverty (Barnes et al., 2002).

Not only do disabled people tend to have higher costs, they also have lower incomes because of their disadvantaged labour market position. Disabled people are disproportionately likely to be out of work, and if they do find work are more likely than non-disabled people to lose it again. Average hourly earnings are below those of their non-disabled peers (Burchardt, 2000a). Barnes and Baldwin sum up: 'the overwhelming majority of disabled people are thus either not employed or are employed in jobs which are poorly paid, undemanding and unrewarding' but this is not inevitable (1999: 161). Disabled people's disadvantaged labour market position is a function both of factors shared with others, most notably social class and lack of educational qualifications, and of factors specific to disability.

Exclusion and discrimination

The disability-specific factors are best understood within the framework of the social model of disability. This represents a rejection of an understanding of disability in individualistic, medicalized terms in favour of locating its source in societal reaction or inaction, leading to the exclusion of those with physical and mental impairments from full participation in mainstream social, economic and political activities. It is institutional and environmental discrimination, through for instance the failure to adapt workplaces and public transport, rather than individual lack of ability that accounts for disabled people's inferior labour market position. Poverty, therefore, 'should be seen as one expression of the institutional discrimination disabled people face' (Beresford, 1996: 557).

Disabled people are also subjected to inter-personal discrimination as a result of negative and hostile attitudes and behaviour: world-wide, 'negative stereotypes are commonly attached to disability. People with disabilities are often assigned to a low social status and in some cases are considered worthless' (DfID, 2000a: 5). Social attitudes contribute to the exclusion and marginalization of disabled people (Knight et al., 2002). Small-scale qualitative research in the UK reveals feelings of '[being] patronised, avoided, ignored, abandoned, mocked by strangers, assumed to be stupid, treated as an inconvenience and regarded as unfit for public view' (Knight and Brent, 1998: 6). A larger-scale study points to 'overwhelming evidence . . . that people who are disabled experience discrimination and prejudice' (Grewal et al., 2002: 91). The underlying attitude, according to Jenny Morris, is one of 'lack of respect' (2001: 177). As in the case of racism, such attitudes exacerbate the experience of poverty, which itself is also experienced as a denial of respect (see chapter 5).

Age

For many, disability is experienced in later life. This brings us to the question of how poverty affects people at different points in their lives. Rowntree identified a 'life-cycle of poverty' in which childhood, parenthood and old age represented troughs. The pattern still holds true, albeit in more complex and dynamic forms, captured in the notion of the 'life-course' (Barnes et al., 2002; Dewilde, 2003). Moreover, poverty is experienced in particular ways at the beginning and end of the life-course. Although this represents a shift of focus from inequality and structured social divisions, these shape individuals' passage through the life-course.

Older age

'Poverty is the main threat facing older people worldwide' (Heslop, 2000: 1). This is particularly true of the South. In the North, the relative position of older people varies between countries according to the effectiveness of their pension arrangements (Barnes et al., 2002). In the UK, the overall relative risk of poverty among older people is not as great as it was. The same is true in the US, although there the poverty line is set at a lower level for older people than the rest of the population, despite the additional needs often associated with ageing (ILC, 2001). A distinguishing feature of poverty in old age is that escape is more difficult, especially for the oldest and most frail, as paid work is rarely an option in societies that construct older age as incompatible with continued involvement in the labour market. The risk of long-term poverty thus remains relatively high. In the UK, next to lone parents, pensioners are the demographic group most likely to have a persistently low income (DWP, 2003a). This makes them very vulnerable to deprivation (Scharf et al., 2002). European research indicates that retired people on low incomes suffer higher levels of material deprivation than other low-income groups (Barnes et al., 2002).

Even in countries where the overall poverty rate among older people has declined, there tend to be considerable differences within the older population. Not surprisingly, the most notable reflect the underlying class, gender and ethnic divisions that frame the experience of poverty more generally. These differential poverty rates in older age are due to both the inequalities during working life discussed earlier and inequitable pension arrangements that fail to mitigate their impact after retirement (Ginn et al., 2001).

Childhood

Childhood is also a time of vulnerability to poverty. Children bring additional costs to households at a time when in many countries parental earnings are lower because of mothers' reduced labour market activity. However, trends in and rates of child poverty and their level relative to overall poverty rates vary considerably between societies (Vleminckx and Smeeding, 2001; Bradshaw, 2002). The US, UK, Canada and Italy stand out as having child poverty rates well above their overall poverty rates, whereas the opposite is true for the Nordic countries (Bradshaw, 2000b). In the EU as a whole, the risk of poverty, including persistent poverty, among children is higher than among adults (Ruxton and Bennett, 2002). Class and 'race' are important determinants.

Concern about high levels of persistent childhood poverty in some countries tends to focus on the effects it has on children's future life chances (Bradbury et al., 2001). A large body of research demonstrates poverty's damaging impact on a child's development and subsequent educational outcomes, job prospects, health and behaviour (Ermisch et al., 2001; Vleminckx and Smeeding, 2001). The UK New Labour Government, for instance, places great emphasis on the long-term effects of child poverty as justification for prioritizing expenditure on this group as an investment in the country's future.

The importance of such a longer-term perspective is not in dispute. However, there have been a growing number of voices calling also for a child-centred perspective on poverty that places due emphasis on what poverty means for childhood itself and that treats children as agents in their own lives. Seeing poverty 'through children's eyes would', it is argued, 'provide a more rounded and informative picture' (Ruxton and Bennett, 2002: 35; Adelman et al., 2003). Tess Ridge's child-centred study of poverty found a particular concern about stigma; being 'different'; and difficulties in 'fitting in' and 'joining in', which can lead to bullying (Ridge, 2002: ch. 4). While, as we shall see in chapter 5, stigma is an issue for adults also, the impact can be particularly devastating for a child or young person who is developing a sense of her own identity.

Geography

Having seen how social divisions and the life-course shape individuals' experience of poverty, we turn now to its geographical dimension, expressed through notions of 'place' and 'space'. 'Poverty has a geography' in three senses: the spatial distribution of, first, 'people poverty' and, second, 'place poverty' (which do not necessarily coincide) and, third, its lived experience within the physical and social space of the neighbourhood (Philo et al., 1995: 177; Powell et al., 2001). In these ways, geography both contributes to and mediates poverty.

The spatial distribution of 'people poverty' has generally been associated to some extent with its urban concentration and segregation from more affluent neighbourhoods, though the patterns may vary between countries. Urban segregation has been particularly marked in the US where the, deeply racialized, process intensified in the late twentieth century (Massey, 1996). Poverty has also become more geographically concentrated in the UK in recent years (Glennerster et al., 1999; Lupton and Power, 2002). Minority ethnic groups overall are more likely to be concentrated in deprived neighbourhoods (SEU, 2000). Although the patterns are more complex and less stark than in the US, 'the disadvantages faced by many people from minority ethnic groups are among the key drivers of neighbourhood poverty' (Lupton, 2003a: 218). The growing concentration of poverty is also part of a wider process of spatial polarization, as affluence too becomes more concentrated (Massey, 1996; Byrne, 1999). This is symbolized by the spread of 'gated communities' in which a growing number of the affluent protect themselves from 'the poor'. Such processes reduce the visibility and political salience of people in poverty and insulate the better-off from engagement with them and their circumstances (Philo et al., 1995; Ehrenreich, 2001). Even where rich and poor live side by side in cities, as in gentrified areas of London, the latter can be invisible to the former as the two inhabit 'parallel space' (Toynbee, 2003: 19). Distance is social as well as spatial (Silver, 1996).

The notion of 'place poverty' and the label of poor or deprived neighbourhood are used to describe more than just the concentration of individuals in poverty (Powell et al., 2001; Spicker, 2001). A neighbourhood is where people interact within and with a particular physical space and environment, the boundaries of which are not fixed (Lupton, 2003b). A neighbourhood's social and physical aspects, together with the infrastructure of public and private services and facilities, shape the experience of poverty (Forrest and Kearns, 1999; Richardson and Mumford, 2002). An EU survey found a clear relationship between low income and perceptions of run-down local surroundings, although there was considerable variation between countries (Gallie and Paugam, 2002). The typical characteristics associated with disadvantaged urban neighbourhoods are: poor housing; a run-down physical environment; neglected public space; inadequate services and facilities; lack of job opportunities; and high levels of crime and anti-social behaviour (Lupton and Power, 2002; Lupton, 2003a). Such an environment is damaging for physical and mental health and general well-being, especially at vulnerable points in the life-course (Ghate and Hazel, 2002; Scharf et al., 2002). It can erode morale and engender feelings of lack of control and powerlessness (Wacquant, 1996; Lupton and Power, 2002; Mumford and Power, 2003). In sum, a disadvantaged physical and social environment can aggravate the effects of individual poverty and 'compound the misery of living on a low income' (SEU, 2001: 17).

Views differ, however, as to the independent effect of neighbourhood on life-chances (*Urban Studies*, 2001). On the one hand, the damaging impact on educational and labour market opportunities associated with residence in such neighbourhoods has been analysed as part of the wider process of social exclusion discussed in chapter 4 (Madanipour, 1998; Byrne, 1999; Lupton and Power, 2002). On the other, there have been warnings against exaggerating the specific impact of neighbourhood, especially outside the US (Friedrichs, 1998; Kleinman, 1999). Analysis of the British Household Panel Study suggests a middle position: 'area is an important influence but there are other equally and more important influences at the individual and household levels' (Buck, 2001: 2272). According to Ruth Lupton (2003b), the disagreements are in part a function of limitations of methodology and data.

Some further words of caution are also in order. First, while deprived neighbourhoods share many problems, there is at the same time considerable diversity amongst and within them and a concentration of low-income residents does not inevitably mean inadequate services or a poor physical and social environment (Powell et al., 2001). Lupton and Power (2002) suggest that a number of 'protective factors' can help prevent or reverse neighbourhood decline. As well as good mainstream services and neighbourhood management, they include collective action and strong social networks (Richardson and Mumford, 2002). The stereotypical image of hopeless deprived neighbourhoods frequently conceals the extent and vigour of community participation and action, often spearheaded by women (Forrest and Kearns, 1999; Mumford and Power, 2003). Second, not all people in poverty live in the poorest areas. Indeed, in both the UK and the US the majority does not (although in the US this is not true of African Americans) (Glennerster et al., 1999; Tunstall and Lupton, 2003).

Nor is poverty a purely urban phenomenon. From a global perspective, the majority of the world's poor live in rural areas, and that is the main concern of the international development literature (Gordon and Spicker, 1999). In the North, rural poverty exists but in more dispersed and even less visible form than its urban counterpart. Isolation and immobility because of lack of transport are key spatial markers of rural poverty (Shucksmith, 2000). Also, the invisibility of the rural poor may take a different form from that typical of the urban: they are more likely to live 'cheek by jowl' with the affluent but, whereas they see that affluence all too clearly, the affluent do not see them (Cloke and Little, 1997). This makes for a different 'geography of stigma' than that typically associated with urban deprived areas (McCormick and Philo, 1995: 16). It is the stigma and shame of being different 'in a small or scattered community [which] can be very hard to carry' (Simmons, 1997: 25). In parts of the rural US, however, the geography of rural poverty can be more akin to that of urban, 'the have-nots live worlds apart from the haves, socially isolated and outside the mainstream', segregated along lines of class and/or race (Duncan, 1999: xiii).

In urban deprived areas, neighbourhoods themselves can become stigmatized, often by the media, and their residents looked down on and discriminated against as a result (Forrest and Kearns, 1999; Bourdieu, 1999; Lupton, 2003a). Distorted media images of 'crime, dysfunction and disaster' turn such areas into 'the badlands of national imagination' (Toynbee, 2003: 149). Area stigma can be tenacious, even in the face of large-scale regeneration (Hastings and Dean, 2003). Studies of deprived estates reveal how the stigma attached to them 'impoverishes all areas of residents' lives' (Dean and Hastings, 2000: 1), including job opportunities (Atkinson and Kintrea, 2001; MacDonald and Marsh, 2001). Such a stigma is felt keenly by many and is often bitterly resented (Corden, 1996; Wood and Vamplew, 1999; see also chapter 5). Nevertheless, despite the problems, in some deprived neighbourhoods pride in and identification with the locality, as well as a strong community spirit, can exist alongside the shame associated with its stigmatization and dissatisfaction with its shortcomings (Ghate and Hazel, 2002; Mumford and Power, 2003). Both sets of responses reflect the importance of place to well-being and identity, particularly where mobility, in the sense both of narrow everyday geographical horizons and of ability to move out, is constrained by lack of money (Gilroy and Speak, 1998; Charlesworth, 2000).

Conclusion

An understanding of how poverty is framed by geography, inequality, social divisions and the life-course throws light on both underlying structural causal factors and the differential experience of poverty. One implication is that policies to combat poverty need to address underlying inequalities and be embedded within broader gender, 'race' and disability equality and anti-discrimination strategies. Given the salience of place to the experience of poverty, there is a case for area-based policies (Tunstall and Lupton, 2003; Lupton 2003b). But they must be sensitive to the dangers of reinforcing the stigmatization of the areas targeted and not be deployed as a substitute for macro-policies that address the wider structural causes of poverty (Lupton, 2003a). A focus on place has been described as 'bridging the gap between the concepts of poverty and social exclusion' (Powell et al., 2001: 254). The same is true of a focus on cross-cutting social divisions. Social exclusion is the subject of the following chapter, marking the beginning of the shift to more relational/symbolic conceptualizations of poverty.

4
Poverty and Social Exclusion

The concept of social exclusion has partially eclipsed that of poverty in European political and academic debate. Despite its popularity, there is only limited consensus as to either its meaning or its relationship to poverty. While some write of it as a novel empirical phenomenon describing a particular group of people, a state or a process, others argue that it is better understood purely at the level of concept or political discourse. The flexibility and ambiguity of the concept have tended to favour political expediency over analytical clarity. Nevertheless, in this chapter I will pull out some common threads running through much of the burgeoning literature on the topic.[1] The chapter first traces its emergence before reviewing the range of discourses and paradigms (shared frameworks of understanding) in which the concept is embedded. It then focuses on the relationship – empirical and conceptual – between poverty and social exclusion. I will argue that, provided it is not used politically to camouflage poverty and inequality, social exclusion can usefully be understood and used as a lens that illuminates aspects of poverty discussed in subsequent chapters (see also de Haan, 1999). In other words, it is a way of looking at the concept of poverty rather than an alternative to it. It is moreover a multi-focal lens that can encompass the social divisions that were the subject of the previous chapter, thereby encouraging the analytic and policy integration argued for there.

The Concept of Social Exclusion

A travelling concept

Social exclusion's theoretical roots lie in classical sociology. In the work of Max Weber the idea referred to the ways in which groups can, through a process of 'social closure', secure and maintain privilege at the expense of those different from their own members (Berting and Villain-Gandossi, 2001). The underlying concern with social integration and cohesion has been identified with the theoretical stance of Emile Durkheim and Robert K. Merton (Levitas, 1998; Born and Jensen, 2002). In contrast, the emphasis in some formulations on a denial of civil, political and social rights stands in the tradition of T. H. Marshall.

Social exclusion's modern usage is, however, more political than sociological in origin (Daly and Saraceno, 2002). It is usually traced to France, where it was deployed in the 1970s and early 1980s to refer to a range of marginalized groups who had fallen through the net of the French social insurance system (Evans, 1998). With rising unemployment and the spread of poverty to new groups, the concept was applied more broadly (though not universally) to analyse processes of social disintegration and conditions of precariousness (Martin, 1996; Choffé, 2001). For some commentators, these trends, together with the failure of social protection systems, mean that social exclusion represents 'a qualitatively new phenomenon' (Raveaud and Salais, 2001: 48). The term was adopted by the European Commission in the late 1980s, partly to accommodate the reluctance of some member governments to use the word 'poverty' (Berghman, 1997; Veit-Wilson, 1998). It is now firmly embedded in EU discourse, with 'the combating of exclusion' one of the social policy objectives of the 1997 Amsterdam Treaty. This was followed by agreement on an 'open method of co-ordination' of action on social *inclusion* at the 2000 Lisbon Summit (Mayes et al., 2001).

The concept has been adopted, with varying degrees of enthusiasm, in individual member states (R. Atkinson and Davoudi, 2000). Most notable has been its embrace by the

UK New Labour Government on coming to power in 1997, when it quickly established the Social Exclusion Unit at the heart of government. This is a rare example in recent years of adoption by a UK Government of a European rather than North American policy discourse, for the concept of social exclusion has hitherto had little purchase in the US. Although not yet deployed widely in the South, attempts have been made 'to fashion a notion of social exclusion which is not Eurocentric but relevant globally, in a wide variety of country-settings', on the grounds that 'social exclusion occurs within all societies, but has different meanings and manifests itself in different forms' (Gore and Figueiredo, 1997: 3, 8).[2]

Paradigms and discourses

Even within a purely European context, the meanings attached to social exclusion vary between and within countries, reflecting different cultural, economic and institutional contexts, political and sociological traditions and both dominant and critical political and intellectual stances (SOSTRIS, 1997). These different inflections are in turn mirrored in the shifting discourses of social exclusion deployed at EU level (R. Atkinson and Davoudi, 2000). Typologies developed by Hilary Silver and Ruth Levitas help to make sense of its multiple meanings.

Silver identifies three social scientific and political paradigms within which the various interpretations and applications of social exclusion 'are embedded' (1994: 536). She labels them 'solidarity', 'specialization' and 'monopoly' paradigms. Each 'attributes exclusion to a different cause and is grounded in a different political philosophy: Republicanism, liberalism and social democracy' (1994: 539). The 'solidarity' paradigm originates in France and is concerned with the breakdown in the bonds of solidarity between individual and society. In the Republican citizenship tradition the emphasis is on the *state*'s responsibility to reintegrate the excluded (Spicker, 1997; Rosanvallon, 2000). The 'specialization' paradigm is located in Anglo-American liberalism. In contrast to the 'solidarity' paradigm it is individualist in outlook. Exclusion is understood as a consequence of specialization: 'of social differentiation, the economic division of labour, and the separation of spheres' (Silver, 1994: 542). Typically it results from market failure, discrimination or unenforced rights. Greater emphasis is placed on *individual* responsibility within a construction of citizenship as a contractual exchange of rights and obligations. The 'monopoly' paradigm reflects Weber's formulation of 'social closure'. 'Exclusion arises from the interplay of class, status, and political power and serves the interests of the included', who thereby maintain their monopoly of power and resources within a structure of inequality (Silver, 1994: 543). It is combated through the extension of full citizenship. Its influence, Silver suggests, can be found in much of continental Europe, especially on the Left (for instance, Jordan, 1996).[3]

Comparing France and the UK, Martin Evans (1998) underlines the importance of institutional context, in particular the ways in which understandings of social exclusion reflect different national social protection systems. Silver nevertheless stresses that her ideal-types should not be confused with institutional classifications of welfare states, despite some overlap between them, since welfare states reflect the historical interplay of different paradigms. Moreover, there exist divergent interpretations of social exclusion *within* individual welfare states. This is illustrated by Levitas's analysis of the UK, in which she emphasizes that social exclusion is a *concept* used to describe and explain reality rather than the reality itself.

Levitas (1998, 2000) analyses how the concept has been deployed in the UK in terms of a set of competing discourses or matrices of meaning which both help us make sense of our social world and shape our perceptions of what actions are possible and desirable within it. She dubs these discourses RED, MUD and SID. RED refers to a redistributive, egalitarian discourse that embraces notions of citizenship, social rights and social justice. Its deployment by critical thinkers and activists predates the mainstream absorption of a discourse of social exclusion in the UK (see Golding 1986; Lister, 1990). In contrast, MUD is a moralistic discourse, frequently articulated through the divisive and stigmatizing North American language of the 'underclass' and 'dependency culture' to portray those excluded as culturally distinct from mainstream society (see chapter 5). It emphasizes individual values and behaviour. Some are therefore critical of the idea of social exclusion because of its perceived affinity with 'underclass' discourses and an individualistic account of poverty (Novak, 2001; Procacci, 2001). SID, a 'social integrationist discourse', increasingly dominant in the UK and at EC level, is preoccupied with social cohesion and, in relation to policy, is focused primarily, and sometimes exclusively, on exclusion from paid work. Hartley Dean (2004) identifies two versions of SID: a 'liberal' version exemplified by New Labour's approach and a 'conservative' version associated with the French solidarity paradigm. Levitas sums up the differences between the three discourses according to 'what the excluded are seen as lacking', namely money (and we might add power) in RED, morals in MUD and work in SID (especially the liberal version).

The Labour Government's approach to tackling social exclusion reflects a shifting amalgam of the three. Although it initially deployed a definition of social exclusion in the RED tradition, there is a definite spattering of MUD, particularly in the recourse to the language of 'welfare dependency'. More centrally, both its general concern to build social cohesion and its policies are firmly rooted in SID, most notably in the identification of paid work, supported by education and training, as the key route to social inclusion. At EC level also, a number of paradigms and discourses intermingle, resulting in a lack of definitional clarity (Shoukens and Carmichael, 2001). Although the original and most dominant influence has been the French solidarity paradigm, Levitas suggests that its translation into official European policy papers is more redolent of the narrower (liberal) discourse of SID. At the same time some EC documents reflect (to a lesser extent) the analysis of the official European Observatory on Social Exclusion. With shades of RED, this defined social exclusion in relation to social rights in the British Marshallian citizenship tradition.

The politics and social geometry of inclusion/exclusion

Implicit in the idea of social exclusion is its opposite: social inclusion. The latter discourse is increasingly being deployed by the EC. The same is true in Scotland, where an official consultation exercise elicited rejection of the terminology of social exclusion, as divisive, in favour of the more aspirational politics of social inclusion. Yet, the concept of social inclusion is as contested as that of social exclusion and is even less clearly articulated. Critical, yet not always explicit, are 'the *terms* of inclusion' (Gore and Figueiredo, 1997: 41, emphasis added; Witcher, 2003). Social inclusion policies are typically aimed at social integration, primarily through paid work. In some countries, notably France, the aim is broader: 'insertion' into social structures as well as the labour market through a range of activities which embrace not just job search and training but also, for instance, parental education and help with literacy and social skills (Martin, 1996; Saraceno, 2002). Levitas has described it as a 'performative' construction of inclusion (2000: 362). In an increasingly contractual model of citizenship, in which rights are contingent on obligations, individuals are charged with the responsibility to pursue and equip themselves for inclusion in exchange for the opportunities opened up by government. Thus, for example, the French Revenu Minimum d'Insertion (a form of conditional social assistance introduced in 1988) is presented as a 'contract of inclusion' (Rosanvallon, 2000). The UK New Labour Government labelled its employment-centred welfare reform strategy a 'new contract for welfare'.

Criticisms of the dominant SID approach to social inclusion focus on its 'normalizing' logic, which leaves 'unquestioned the efficacy of capitalist social relations from which people are axiomatically excluded if they cannot or do not sustain themselves through paid employment' (Dean with Melrose, 1999; 48). The equation of social inclusion with paid work is challenged on two main grounds. First, inclusion in the labour market through marginal, low paid, insecure jobs under poor working conditions does not constitute genuine poverty-free social inclusion (A. B. Atkinson, 1998; Gallie and Paugam, 2002). Instead, it has been characterized as 'unfavourable inclusion' (Sen, 2000: 28–9) or 'a disempowering form of inclusion' (Anthias, 2001: 839). Second, both the (gendered) unpaid work of reproduction and care and community and voluntary activities are thereby discounted and effectively devalued and marginalized.

Faced with this narrow, normalizing interpretation of social inclusion, some have proposed participatory citizenship as a preferable antonym of social exclusion (Anthias, 2001). In the words of Martin Longoria from the 'Cry of the Excluded' (a decentralized movement of over 12 million urban dwellers, peasants and indigenous peoples in the Americas, originating in Brazil): 'You know what is the opposite of exclusion for us? It is not inclusion, but participation. Active participation is what makes you a full citizen' (Cabannes, 2000: 19). Others paint a RED-hued picture of the inclusive society, which incorporates not just the ideal of participatory citizenship but also an egalitarian understanding of social justice and recognition of diversity (Askonas and Stewart, 2000; Witcher, 2003). As part of its concern with inequalities, a social justice perspective problematizes the self-exclusion from the bonds of common citizenship of the wealthy (Barry, 2002). An expansive construction of the inclusive society, moreover, needs to be internationalist in spirit, embracing progressive asylum, immigration, trade and overseas aid policies (Lister, 2000).

The RED-style construction of social inclusion/exclusion locates it within the wider relations of inequality, polarization and differentiation described in chapter 3. The underlying social geometry is that of a vertical, hierarchical relationship of 'top' to 'bottom', cross-cut with horizontal social divisions that structure distance from centres of power (Daly and Saraceno, 2002). The social geometry of SID and MUD is, in contrast, a simple flat, horizontal, dichotomous relationship of 'in' or 'out' (Jackson, 1999). Criticisms of this dichotomous insider/outsider model reflect both empirical and political concerns.

From an empirical perspective, it is argued that the model represents an oversimplification of more complex social structures and dynamics (Rosanvallon, 2000; Born and Jensen, 2002). Empirical analysis in the UK by the Centre for Analysis of Social Exclusion (CASE), for instance, indicates 'a more fluid picture of people along a continuum of exclusion, rather than a clear division between those who are "in" and "out"' (Richardson and Le Grand, 2002: 499; Burchardt et al., 2002a). It is, though, the political implications of the in/out model that have been the subject of particular criticism, for the model aggravates an all-too-common 'us' and 'them' relationship between 'non-poor' and 'poor'. In this way, groups defined as 'excluded' are constructed as problems outside mainstream society. It obscures the dynamics of inequality and polarization at the heart of society, affecting the 'included' majority also (Levitas, 1998, 2000). A preoccupation with the boundary between 'included' and 'excluded' encourages a minimalist policy response of 'treating marginal people marginally', in which the goal is merely to move them across the boundary, leaving underlying structural divisions largely undisturbed (Goodin, 1996: 357).

The Relationship between Social Exclusion and Poverty

From an overview of the debates around social exclusion as an academic and political concept, we turn now to consider its relationship to poverty. Given the concept's contested nature, it is hardly surprising that no single clear picture of this relationship emerges from the literature. The relationship is expounded both in terms of different descriptions of empirical reality and at the conceptual level. We will look at each in turn.

The empirical relationship

Formulations of an empirical link Any empirical link between the phenomena described respectively as 'social exclusion' and 'poverty' can be presented in causal/sequential and/or descriptive terms. Walker and Park, for instance, posit a *sequential* trajectory of 'moving from income poverty to social exclusion', which is akin to 'slipping from a point of keeping their heads above water, through "sinking", to "drowning"', possibly involving a simultaneous process of detachment from social institutions (1998: 40). The Council of Europe advances both a *sequential* and a *causal* relationship: 'Poverty may lead to social exclusion, in the sense that people are cut off from the labour market, do not take part in dominant behavioural and cultural patterns, lose social contacts, live in certain stigmatised neighbourhoods, and are not reached by welfare agencies' (2001: 17).

In the first formulation, the trajectory from poverty to social exclusion is articulated more as a matter of degree or depth; in the latter it is painted more as a qualitative difference. Graham Room is among those adopting the second position. He argues that social exclusion, understood in its 'core' sense, is associated with intense 'multi-dimensional disadvantage'; carries with it 'the connotation of separation and permanence'; and represents 'a rupture' or 'catastrophic discontinuity in relationships with the rest of society', which is 'to some considerable degree irreversible' (1999: 171; 2000).

The causal/sequential arrow can also point in the opposite direction. Sen, for instance, stresses 'the diverse ways in which social exclusion can cause deprivation and poverty' (2000: 40). By social exclusion he is, however, referring not to the extreme condition evoked by metaphors of 'drowning' and 'rupture' but to a more variegated phenomenon embracing a variety of specific exclusions such as those pertaining to the labour market and gender relations (see below). Thus social exclusion is sometimes identified as an effect of poverty and sometimes as a cause.

Similar differences of understanding can be discerned in the varying ways in which a *descriptive* empirical link is presented in the literature. Typically this link is expressed in terms either of a 'nested' pattern or of degree of overlap (Gore and Figueiredo, 1997). In some articulations of the former, social exclusion is *'nested'* within poverty, typically as an extreme form, involving linked multiple disadvantages and sometimes also the kind of rupture described by Room (Leisering and Leibfried, 1999). In other formulations poverty is, conversely, nested within social exclusion as a particular form of the latter, or as one of a number of dimensions of disadvantage that, together, constitute a broader condition of social exclusion (Berghman, 1997). New Labour frequently portrays social exclusion as more than just poverty. The notion of an *overlapping* relationship conveys the idea that some people experience material poverty and social exclusion simultaneously while others can be in poverty without being socially excluded or can be socially

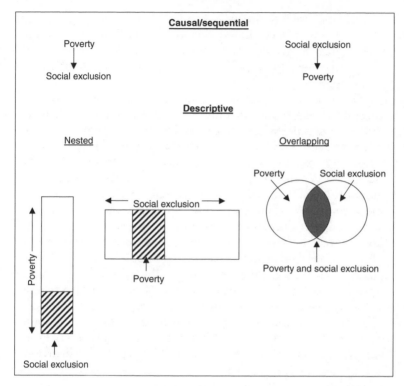

Figure 4.1　Empirical relationships between poverty and social exclusion

excluded without being poor. This is a common formulation; the relative size of the three groups is then a matter for empirical measurement, the results of which, in turn, are likely to be sensitive to the definition and choice of indicators of social exclusion.

Evidence of an empirical link　In the small, but growing, body of empirical research these indicators measure social exclusion along a number of separate dimensions. Typically, in addition to the dimension of material poverty and deprivation, they include different permutations of: exclusion from the labour market (and, in some instances, from other economically or socially valued activities); social isolation; political exclusion; exclusion from public and private services. This research throws some light on the extent to which financial and other indicators of social exclusion coincide and the degree to which individuals are excluded on a range of dimensions, as implied by most formulations of social exclusion.

The European empirical evidence points to a (varying) degree of overlap between material poverty and other dimensions of social exclusion. Burchardt et al.'s analysis of the British Household Panel Survey (BHPS) found a clear association between income level and exclusion from productive activities (including family care) and to a lesser extent political engagement and social interaction (2002b). While this suggests that 'low income is a frequent concomitant of exclusion on other dimensions', in no instance was a majority of the poorest fifth of the population excluded on any one of those other dimensions (Burchardt, 2000b: 395). Initial analysis of the PSE Survey (which unlike the BHPS includes specially devised indicators of social exclusion) suggests a 'strong association' between poverty and other dimensions of social exclusion, with the exception of social isolation and support (Bradshaw, 2000c). Further analysis also points to a strong association between severity of poverty and degree of children's exclusion from social activities and services (Adelman et al., 2003).

The lack of a strong association between poverty and *social isolation* is of particular significance because, as an indicator of lack of integration into solidaristic social networks, social isolation represents the essence of social exclusion within the 'solidarity paradigm' (Martin, 1996; Spicker, 1997). It has also, in some formulations, become associated more widely with the meaning of social exclusion (Gallie, 1999). Indeed, there is some indication from cross-EU surveys that the public 'are attuned to physical and social isolation when talking about social exclusion' (Golding, 1995: 230), although we need more research into popular understandings of the term. Social integration figures in a slightly different form in Anglo-Saxon 'network' models of social exclusion (which focus on 'links to more advantaged, mainstream groups' and potential networks of support) and in the associated preoccupation with strengthening 'social capital' (Buck, 2001: 2255; 6, 1997).[4] The importance of social relationships to a child-centred understanding of social exclusion, in the context of the 'complex social world' of childhood, has also been emphasized by Tess Ridge (2002: 143).

What little evidence there is tends to support the PSE finding of a relatively weak link between poverty and social isolation, although it is stronger in some countries than others and among some groups than others (Paugam, 1996; Barnes et al., 2002; Apospori and Millar, 2003). Most research indicates a weaker association between poverty and isolation among women than men (Russell, 1999). However, this may not be true for young women (EOC, 2003). Social isolation may be greater among those suffering extreme and persistent poverty (ATD Fourth World, 1995). There appears also to be a stronger association with *subjective* feelings of isolation (Gallie and Paugam, 2002). Related research throws light on the relationship between social isolation and another key dimension of social exclusion: labour market exclusion. Again, despite considerable variation between European societies, the general picture is not one of social isolation among those excluded from the labour market (Clasen et al., 1998; Gordon et al., 2000a). However, a common pattern is of relatively segregated social networks involving other unemployed people, poorly placed to provide material support or to act as a link to the formal labour market (Gallie and Paugam, 2000; Gallie et al., 2003).

The author of a British study of social exclusion in three deprived housing estates suggests that his finding of a group 'whose members are mostly well integrated with their local community, even if they are less well connected to mainstream society' 'poses a challenge to the concept of "social exclusion"' (Page, 2000: 46). He therefore posits that it is 'lack of "connectedness" to people and places off the estate' that is 'one of the defining features of social exclusion' (2000: 83). This reading is consistent with the argument that jobless people need wide networks 'rich in weak ties' (6, 1997: 6) with people unlike themselves to connect them to job opportunities (although arguably lone mothers need 'strong tie' local networks to help with child-care). This line of argument does not, however, reflect the meaning of social isolation in the solidarity paradigm, which attaches a less instrumental significance to social networks.

What this discussion suggests is that we need to differentiate between different kinds of social isolation: it is disconnection from the wider society (other than through authority figures such as social workers, who are frequently feared) rather than loss of personal networks (which are often strong in deprived areas) that appears to be more characteristic of joblessness and poverty. This would also help account for why some people defined as 'socially excluded' do not necessarily feel so (Johnston et al., 2000; Page, 2000; MacDonald and Marsh, 2001) or can feel integrated within their community but excluded from the wider society (Wood and Vamplew, 1999). The possibility that some people are simultaneously excluded and included raises the issue of what it is they are excluded from (see also below). The question then also arises as to whether one has to *feel* socially excluded to *be* socially excluded (Richardson and Le Grand, 2002). Both aspects matter and neither is irreducible to the other.

The discussion so far has cast doubt on the strength of the empirical link between material poverty and the pivotal social isolation dimension of social exclusion. Another key question raised by the existing empirical evidence in the UK is whether it is even possible to identify a significant group of people who can be categorized as socially excluded. Burchardt et al.'s study found that under half a per cent of the population were excluded on all the dimensions measured and none were so over the full five years of the panel. The conclusion reached, and endorsed by John Hills (2002) in a major book on social exclusion, was that:

> given the complexity of the associations between the different dimensions of exclusion, and the relatively high proportions of those excluded on one dimension who are not excluded on others, no clear-cut multidimensional category of socially excluded people can be identified using these indicators. The results suggest that the dimensions of exclusion are best treated separately rather than amalgamated into a single category of the 'socially excluded'. (Burchardt et al., 1999: 241)

A study of London comes to a similar conclusion and warns against over-dramatizing social exclusion at the expense of overlooking 'a very great deal of old-fashioned poverty' (Buck et al., 2002: 371). The evidence is not yet conclusive – for instance, a different set of indicators might produce variant results and it is possible that the 'truly excluded' are under-represented in the kind of surveys undertaken. The authors of a more in-depth study of young people in a 'severely excluded' locale in north-east England, for example, suggest that, insofar as the phenomenon of social exclusion exists, it can be found in its 'most entrenched forms' among the small number whose lives revolve around the 'poverty drug' of heroin (MacDonald and Marsh, 2002: 27, 38).

Room argues that the idea of social exclusion as 'catastrophic rupture' can still serve as a benchmark (2000: 413). Nevertheless, with the possible exception of the few people subject to such 'catastrophic rupture', the empirical evidence suggests that it is not necessarily helpful to treat different forms of exclusion as an undifferentiated phenomenon (Gore and Figueiredo, 1997: 45). Inclusion and exclusion may coexist in different spheres – the economic, social, political and cultural – and in sub-spheres of each (Witcher, 2003). This, in turn, reinforces Levitas's argument that social exclusion, in its wider usage, is better understood as a concept than as an empirical reality (see also de Haan, 1999; Born and Jensen, 2002).

The conceptual relationship: what is the 'value-added'?

Having explored the empirical relationship between poverty and social exclusion, we turn now to the conceptual level. Here, the debate largely centres on the issue of the 'value-added' that social exclusion brings to the analysis of poverty (Micklewright, 2002: 28). Very broadly, three main positions can be identified. The first is represented by a relatively small number who are, at best, unconvinced of the value of the concept of social exclusion and, at worst, dismiss it as unhelpful or even dangerous. Øyen is particularly critical of what she considers to be a political rather than analytical concept, with 'limited theoretical underpinning'. Its usage, she contends, means that 'poverty, the real and nasty poverty, becomes invisible because it is being hidden under the umbrella of social exclusion which embraces several other phenomena' (1997: 63, 64). Although less hostile, Nolan and Whelan are similarly sceptical of this 'amorphous' concept. While they concede that social exclusion may sensitize researchers and policy-makers to important aspects of poverty, they fear that this is 'at a cost': loss of 'the spark that "poverty" ignites because of its everyday usage and evaluative content' (1996: 190, 195). They also argue that those who favour social exclusion over poverty tend to base their comparisons on a caricature that confuses the conceptualization of poverty with its narrower, often uni-dimensional, measurement. Perceptions of social exclusion's 'value-added' are, in part, a function of how poverty itself is conceptualized (Sen, 2000).

The second and third positions are taken by the proponents of social exclusion: one is that the new insights that it brings to the analysis of poverty constitute a significant conceptual shift; the other is that these insights are not *new* but that the concept nevertheless acts as a catalyst, which has foregrounded important aspects of poverty and encouraged a broad and dynamic analysis. Although exponents of social exclusion frequently differ in the aspects that they identify as quintessential to its 'value-added', there are a number of key recurrent themes that we will look at in turn. Broadly, they fall into two categories: the first three themes (relations and rights, social divisions and multidimensionality) emphasize its breadth and the last theme its dynamic quality.

Relations and rights   One of the most prominent claims is that social exclusion is primarily about *relational* issues (Room, 1995, 1999; Allen et al., 1998). The notion of social exclusion necessarily involves a relationship with the wider society or subsections of society from which an individual or group is excluded. This, A. B. Atkinson (1998) argues, makes it inherently relative. Some, such as Room, contrast social exclusion's relational focus with the distributional core of poverty. In contrast, Bhalla and Lapeyre dismiss this dichotomy as 'rather simplistic', arguing that social exclusion 'pertains to the *interaction* of distributional and relational problems of human relations, and is thus more comprehensive than the concept of poverty' (1999: 34, 33, emphasis added). A different perspective is provided by Sen, who suggests that the value of social exclusion lies not in its novelty or greater comprehensiveness but in its illumination of the 'role of relational features in the deprivation of capability and thus in the experience of poverty' (Sen, 2000: 6). Such a relational focus has been shown to be of particular value when looking at poverty from a child and youth-centred perspective (Morris, 2001; Ridge 2002; Adelman et al., 2003).

Room lists social exclusion's relational features as 'inadequate social participation, lack of social integration and lack of power' (1995: 5; 1999: 169). We consider each in turn. With echoes of Townsend's definition of relative deprivation, *participation* is central to the working definition of social exclusion propounded by researchers at CASE: 'an individual is socially excluded if he or she does not participate in key activities of the society in which he or she lives' (Burchardt et al., 2002b: 30). (In increasingly diverse societies, though, it may not always be that easy to identify what are agreed 'key activities' (Parekh, 2000).) The 'community experts' they consulted understood social exclusion in similar terms and emphasized the importance of communication skills for social, political and economic participation (Richardson and Le Grand, 2002).[5] Lack of *social integration* refers to detachment from different social networks, discussed above. Lack of *power* in many ways goes to the heart of social exclusion, yet it is often more implicit than explicit in the literature, perhaps, in part, because of its nebulous nature (Byrne, 1999).

Room also analyses social exclusion in relational terms as the denial of social rights or 'the extent to which the individual is bound into membership of [the] moral and political community' (1995: 7). This understanding is reflected in the reports of the EU Observatory on Social Exclusion in which Room played a leading role. These reports also underline the significance of political, civil and broader human rights for social exclusion and participation, as do a number of other analysts, particularly when applying the concept to the South (Gore and Figueiredo, 1997; Clert, 1999). For Bhalla and Lapeyre it is the denial of such rights that is the 'distinguishing feature' of social exclusion (1999: 34; but see chapter 7 below). This view is echoed in the South in the claim by the movement of the Cry of the Excluded (originating in Brazil) that the notion of exclusion is more helpful than that of poverty because it refers to access to rights rather than goods (Cabannes, 2000). In the North it is reflected in the views of a group of young disabled people in the UK for whom ' "being shut out of society" is about being denied their human rights' (J. Morris, 2001: 178). At an institutional level, the French law against social exclusion is couched in a discourse of interdependent rights (Choffé, 2001).

Another aspect of the relational meaning of social exclusion, less frequently discussed, is the symbolic dimension (explored in relation to poverty in later chapters). This 'refers to how excluded individuals and groups are defined by themselves and the wider society' (R. Atkinson and Davoudi, 2000: 441; Choffé, 2001). An EU report on non-monetary indicators of poverty and social exclusion includes 'symbolic references' in its discussion of social exclusion. Among the associated indicators are a number that attempt to measure self-image and social identity (CEC, 1998).

Social divisions　Social exclusion's relational perspective also facilitates a broad framework of analysis, which embraces the social divisions discussed in the previous chapter. It thus 'allows us to look at issues to do with social and cultural injustices generated by inequalities of gender, race, ethnicity, sexuality, age and disability and the ways these may intersect and be compounded by issues of distribution' (F. Williams, 1998: 15). Discrimination and prejudice, as well as poverty, can exclude people from full participation in society and from full effective rights of citizenship (which is not to say that all members of affected groups are necessarily excluded) (Witcher, 2003). This dimension of social exclusion has received particular emphasis in some of the *disability* literature, which demonstrates that the exclusion of disabled people 'is not solely material. It has a lot to do with society's attitude to disabled people' (Knight and Brent, 1998: 4). Barriers to physical access, together with prejudicial attitudes, serve to exclude disabled people from public and private services and general social and political participation (Knight et al., 2002).

Likewise, '*race*' and *ethnicity* have been identified as 'an important dimension of social cleavage along which processes of social exclusion run throughout Europe' (Cars et al., 1998: 284). The broad framework of social exclusion has been used to analyse both exclusion at nation-state borders and processes of economic, political and cultural exclusion faced by established minority ethnic groups to varying degrees (Roche and van Berkel, 1997). Some, though, warn that this could dilute and marginalize the particularity of *racial* exclusion.

Gender has, hitherto, not figured prominently in social exclusion analysis. The few feminist commentators who have discussed it point to both the potential and difficulties of its application to gender relations and the position of women. Its potential lies, in part, in its relational, multidimensional and dynamic nature (Ulshoefer, 1998). Daly and Saraceno highlight two advantages in particular. First, in their view, the concept's horizontal social geometry (criticized above) is a useful supplement to more traditional 'vertical thinking' because it can illuminate distance from centres of power (2002: 97). Second is its potential to give due recognition to the importance of the family 'as one of the most important solidaristic social networks' (2002: 96).

However, this recognition stands in tension with the centrality commonly ascribed to labour market participation in social inclusion policies: the possibility that 'social inclusion can take place in conditions of exclusion' is rarely recognized (2002: 98). Thus, a lone mother's care responsibilities, for example, could simultaneously be a source of exclusion from the labour market and of integration into local social networks.[6] Conversely, social exclusion can take place in conditions of inclusion when long or unsocial working hours impede social and political participation outside the workplace (Gordon et al., 2004). A gendered analysis of social exclusion illuminates how such tensions affect women and men differently, reflecting their respective positions in relation to family and labour market (Daly and Saraceno, 2002; Bradshaw et al., 2003). It also reinforces and genders the conclusion that social exclusion is better understood as a differentiated rather than monolithic process, as 'gendered subjects experience simultaneous exclusion and inclusion' (Jackson, 1999: 132). In terms of women's position more generally, though, Daly and Saraceno conclude that 'while a critical gender perspective enriches the social exclusion discourse in referring to specific gender-based risks and vulnerabilities' and while 'social exclusion is certainly gendered', it does not follow that women as a category are socially excluded (2002: 101).

Overall, this discussion suggests that, while social exclusion provides a helpful conceptual link to the social divisions that interact in different ways with material poverty, it does not provide a broad 'synthesizing umbrella' under which these divisions can best be understood (Gore and Figueiredo, 1997: 45; Anthias, 2001). Analysis needs to examine the specificities of different forms of exclusion as well as any commonalities.

Multidimensional and multi-level   Social exclusion's ability to embrace social divisions represents one aspect of a broader, central claim: that it offers a more comprehensive, *multidimensional* understanding than traditional formulations of poverty (Berghman, 1997; de Haan, 1998; 1999). In the words of the EC:

> more clearly than the concept of poverty, understood far too often as referring exclusively to income, it also states the multi-dimensional nature of mechanisms whereby individuals and groups are excluded from taking part in the social exchange, from the component practices and rights of social integration and identity. (CEC, 1992: 8)

On the face of it, the multidimensional nature of social exclusion is no more than a restatement of the multidimensional concept of relative deprivation discussed in chapter 1 (Burchardt et al., 2002a). There are, though, ways in which it goes further. One is the focus on the extent to which these dimensions interact and are cumulative (Clert, 1999). Typical metaphors are 'vicious cycle' or 'circle' (SEU, 2001: 10; Gallie et al., 2003: 28), 'spiral' (Page, 2000: 5) and 'web' (Henderson and Salmon, 2001: 15–16). What is not always clear, however, is whether such metaphors indicate cause, consequence or simply description of the experience of poverty.

Another distinctive feature is the greater breadth of social exclusion's multidimensionality. As well as its potential to illuminate non-material aspects of social divisions, in some formulations it places greater emphasis more generally on *political* and *cultural* forms and arenas of exclusion alongside the economic and the social (Madanipour et al., 1998). Such breadth was endorsed by the 'community experts' consulted by Richardson and Le Grand (2002). The *political* dimension of social exclusion includes both political and civic participation and lack of a voice in and influence on decision-making (Bhalla and Lapeyre, 1999; Percy-Smith, 2000). At one level, the *cultural* refers to culture in a relatively narrow, albeit important, sense: exclusion from opportunities to enjoy art, music, theatre and poetry and denial of 'all outlets of creative self-expression' (ATD Fourth World, 2000b: 1). The French law against social exclusion thus 'affirms the right to equal opportunities through access for all to culture' (Choffé, 2001). More broadly, the cultural embraces also effective access to new information and communication technology (Warschauer, 2003). At another level, culture acts as 'a marker of difference' (Clarke, 1999: 72). This involves a more fundamental process by which people's identities are devalued by the 'norms and symbols of mainstream society' and they are unable to live up to 'cultural expectations' (Cars et al., 1998: 280; Kronauer, 1998: 64).

Separating out the cultural from the social for analytical purposes also makes more explicit the cultural dimension of Townsend's original formulation of relative deprivation, discussed in chapter 1. Consumption is understood not just as a potential site of relative deprivation but also as a signifier of identity. Zygmunt Bauman writes that 'the poor of a consumer society are socially defined, and self-defined, first and foremost as blemished, defective, faulty and deficient – in other words, inadequate – consumers' (1998: 38). It is not just a question of what items people are able to buy but also their quality (for example, new or secondhand, branded or own brand) and their source (for instance, mainstream retailer or alternative informal channels such as car boot sales). The 'resentment' at the 'stigma attached . . . to *having* to buy cheap "own brand" goods', revealed by a UK study of low-income families, prompted the observation that 'social identities are increasingly being defined by expenditure . . . families can experience social exclusion in simple and painful ways' (Stephenson, 2001: 51, emphasis added). Likewise, a study of consumption patterns in rural England found that it is not enough to possess items included in a list of poverty indicators: where such items were obtained by necessity from informal (inferior) retail channels, people 'still view themselves as excluded from mainstream consumption practices'. For them, such channels 'produce meanings and constitute identities' (C. C. Williams, 2002: 210). The criticism that such a reading of social exclusion fails to challenge 'the cultural foundations of capitalism' (Bowring, 2000: 307) may be valid, but is of little comfort to those who face a 'large No Entry sign to the consumer society where the rest of us live' (Toynbee, 2003: 239).

Consumption practices also involve a *spatial dimension* in terms of 'a complex geography of exclusion and inclusion' in terms of where people shop (P. Williams and Hubbard, 2001: 284). Room identifies 'a shift of emphasis from the individual or household to the local community in its spatial dimension' as a key aspect of the 'broadening of perspective' produced by the concept of social exclusion (1995: 238, 233; 1999). Such a shift of emphasis was supported by Richardson and Le Grand's 'community experts' who objected to the researchers' use of the individual as the sole unit of analysis, for they 'felt strongly that social exclusion affected both individuals and areas' (2002: 512). Spatial issues do not distinguish the study of social exclusion from that of poverty, as we saw in chapter 3. Nevertheless, it is probably true to say that the former accords a more central, constitutive, role to 'spatiality' (Madanipour, 1998: 86). This is reflected in the analysis and policies of the Social Exclusion Unit, alongside an emphasis on specific groups vulnerable to social exclusion.

Dynamics   In addition to the multidimensional and spatial aspects of social exclusion, Room identifies a further key shift of emphasis: 'from a static to a dynamic analysis' (1995: 236; 1999). This dynamic analysis variously involves a concern with *process*, in terms of both individual trajectories and wider societal forces, and with *agency*, again at the level both of the individual and of societal agents of exclusion.

Many accounts emphasize that social exclusion should be understood as a *process* rather than as a condition or category (see, for example, Castells, 2000; Rosanvallon, 2000); others suggest that it constitutes both a state and a process (for example, Silver, 1994; Gore and Figueiredo, 1997). Either way, there is a broad agreement that the emphasis on process is one, or even the most, useful distinguishing feature of the concept of social exclusion (even if UK politicians and officials tend to conceive it as a condition or outcome). However, the nature of its distinctiveness depends on how process is understood and this is not always made explicit. Broadly, we can identify two approaches and, although they are not necessarily mutually exclusive, most analyses tend to deploy one or the other. The first focuses on individual trajectories (sometimes described as a series of stages such as precariousness), as well as the factors or events that can trigger entry into or exit from a situation of exclusion (Room, 1995, 1999, 2000). A. B. Atkinson goes further with his argument that studying social exclusion is not just a question of tracing *past* trajectories but also of developing 'forward-looking indicators' that can measure people's expectations of the future: 'people are excluded not just because they are currently without a job or income but because they have little prospects [*sic*] for the future' – their own and their children's (1998: 8). This lone mother expresses the point graphically: 'Every day is the same to me. I get up. I get the kids ready. The furthest I go is the shops and I don't see anything else for me. In five years time, I'd say I'll still be doing that' (Daly and Leonard, 2002: 117).

A focus on past trajectories is not unique to social exclusion, as increasingly poverty research itself has taken a dynamic approach, with the development of the methodological tools needed to trace people's incomes and living standards over time (see chapter 6). Some, therefore, conclude that a focus on process is nothing new (Spicker, 1997). However, the second understanding of process does arguably constitute a distinguishing feature of social exclusion. Here the focus is on process as *causal mechanism* – at the societal and institutional level (de Haan, 1998, 1999; Madanipour et al., 1998). Behind the noun 'exclusion' stands an active verb 'to exclude', which implies the question 'who or what is excluding?'. This draws attention from outcomes and individual trajectories to 'social actors and institutions' (Rodgers, 1997: 73). A distinction then needs to be made, Sen (2000) argues, between 'active' and 'passive' exclusion. The former constitutes deliberate policy or action such as the denial of social rights to or xenophobic attacks on asylum-seekers; the latter is where social or economic circumstances, such as unemployment, have an exclusionary effect. However, as Sen points out, the absence of direct intent in the latter case does not absolve governments from responsibility. Indeed, policies and practices can themselves unwittingly exacerbate social exclusion. An example is those housing allocation processes that 'segregate the poorest into the worst areas' and confirm 'the stigmatised and residualised role of social housing' (Pawson and Kintrea, 2002: 663).

Implicit in this understanding of process is acknowledgement of the role of both structure and *agency*: the operation of social, economic and political structures and institutions and the agency of the *more powerful* (Rodgers et al., 1995). However, if the analysis stops there, there is a danger of casting 'the excluded' themselves merely as passive victims of structural processes and of more powerful actors' agency, without any authorship of their own biographies (Chamberlayne and Rustin, 1999; Jackson, 1999). Charles Gore, therefore, argues that social exclusion is 'a practice of the more powerful which structures the possible field of action of the *less powerful*' without blocking all 'possibility of agency on the part of excluded groups' (1995: 113, emphasis added). One issue for empirical analysis is then the extent to which the latter 'feel themselves able to realize their objectives as a result of their own decisions' (Hills, 2002: 240).

Agency also raises the issue of the status of *voluntary exclusion*: does the process have to be involuntary to be categorized as exclusion (Burchardt, 2000b; Le Grand, 2003)? This is a question that can be applied to those at the top of a socio-economic hierarchy who 'isolate' themselves from the wider society as well as those at the bottom who, for instance, may refuse job opportunities (Barry, 2002: 15). The 'community experts', consulted by Richardson and Le

Grand (2002: 509), considered both forms of voluntary exclusion to be damaging, but were particularly critical of the former process, which they described as 'withdrawal'. While they agreed that, for those at the bottom, there was an important distinction between exclusion 'from choice' and exclusion because of factors beyond the individual's control, they pointed out that, in practice, it is not always easy to distinguish the two.

The 'value-added': framework and focus   We have seen the ways in which the concept of social exclusion can stimulate insights into social relations and rights, social divisions, multidimensionality and dynamic processes. As indicated in a number of places, each of these insights can be, and in some expositions has been, applied to the concept of poverty. Indeed, even Room, who has analysed poverty and social exclusion in terms of two different intellectual traditions (the Anglo-Saxon and continental European) and who has described social exclusion as representing a 'conceptual shift', concedes that none of its elements 'is so novel as to render irrelevant previous research into poverty' (1999: 169, 171). Many therefore take the view that the value of social exclusion as a concept lies not in any specific *new* insight it affords but in its function as a broad and dynamic integrating framework and focus that 'stimulates fresh thinking in the area' (Chamberlayne and Rustin, 1999: 42; de Haan, 1998, 1999; Burchardt et al., 2002a).

As such it complements rather than replaces the concept of poverty. It thereby informs anti-poverty policies. How it does so depends largely on the dominant paradigm or discourse of social exclusion and inclusion. Typically, it has encouraged a wider policy focus, embracing, for example, transport as well as more traditional social policies (Kenyon et al., 2003; SEU, 2003). As well as greater breadth, this focus also places emphasis on prevention (through, for instance, education and training policies) and the promotion of exit from poverty (most commonly through 'welfare-to-work' schemes) (Hills, 2002). I have suggested elsewhere a more RED-inspired strategy that would tackle exclusion 'at both the material and the symbolic level and across a range of dimensions of inequalities' (Lister, 2000: 51).

Conclusion

This discussion of social exclusion, from both a conceptual and empirical perspective, suggests that, while it is possible to identify processes of exclusion and even states of specific forms or dimensions of exclusion, we currently lack empirical evidence of a clearly distinguishable, more generalized phenomenon of social exclusion. Instead, other than in its most acute form (which appears to be rare), social exclusion is better understood as a potentially illuminating concept and as a set of political discourses with a range of policy implications. Provided social exclusion is not treated as an alternative to poverty, it can serve a useful conceptual function as a lens, which both sharpens the focus on a number of important aspects of poverty and also advances the kind of broad framework of analysis of poverty advocated elsewhere in this volume.

5
Discourses of Poverty: From Othering to Respect

'Tis still my maxim that there is no scandal like rags, nor any crime so shameful as poverty.

George Farquhar, *The Beaux Strategem*, 1707

The worst blow of all is the contempt of your fellow citizens. I and many families live in that contempt.

Moraene Roberts, National Poverty Hearing. Russell, 1996: 4

The location of the Other is primarily in language. It is through language that selves and others are mediated and represented.

Pickering, 2001: 72

We hear how the media, and some politicians, speak about us and it hurts.

Parent living on benefit, participating in meetings of the APPGP, 1999

The worst thing about living in poverty is the way it gives others permission to treat you – as if you don't matter.

Statement by group of low income parents to the APPGP. Galloway, 2002: 13

The above quotations illustrate the key themes of this chapter, as our attention turns to the relational/symbolic rim of the poverty wheel presented in the Introduction. As argued there, poverty cannot be understood purely in material terms. Both as a concept and as a lived reality, it has to be understood also as a social relation – primarily between 'the poor' and 'the non-poor' (Waxman, 1977; Becker, 1997). It is a two-way relationship, but one which is largely defined by the 'non-poor' whose discourses, attitudes and actions can have a profound impact on how poverty is experienced. The subject of this chapter is, therefore, how the more powerful 'non-poor' construct 'the poor' as Other. I will leave to the following two chapters the question of the agency of people in poverty themselves within their relationship with the 'non-poor'. The discussion in chapter 6 of poverty dynamics, together with the earlier reflection on the arbitrariness of any dividing line between 'poor' and 'non-poor', also reminds us that we are not talking about fixed, totally separate groups (Veit-Wilson, 1999). Nevertheless, as we shall see, the division acts as a powerful symbolic marker of those classed as poor at any one time and in particular of those in severe and persistent poverty.

The main focus of the chapter is how 'the poor' are 'Othered' through language and images. It therefore starts with a more general discussion of the process of Othering and of the power of language and images – and the discourses they articulate – to label and stigmatize marginalized social groups, with fundamental implications for how members of those groups are treated. The previous chapter elaborated on the discourse of social exclusion. Here we consider the discourses of the 'underclass', 'welfare dependency' and poverty itself, having first put them in historical context. Finally, the chapter explores the stigma, shame and humiliation associated with poverty. It suggests that, for many, it is the lack of respect and loss of dignity that result from 'living in the contempt of your fellow citizens' that can make poverty so difficult to bear. This points to the importance of political struggles at the relational/symbolic rim of the poverty wheel as well as at its material core.

Othering and the Power of Discourse

The notion of 'the poor' as Other is used here to signify the many ways in which 'the poor' are treated as different from the rest of society. The capital 'O' denotes its symbolic weight. The notion of 'Other*ing*' conveys how this is not an inherent state but an ongoing process animated by the 'non-poor'. It is a dualistic process of differentiation and demarcation, by which the line is drawn between 'us' and 'them' – between the more and the less powerful – and through which social distance is established and maintained (Beresford and Croft, 1995; Riggins, 1997). It is not a neutral line, for it is imbued with negative value judgements that construct 'the poor' variously as a source of moral contamination, a threat, an 'undeserving' economic burden, an object of pity or even as an exotic species. It is a process that takes place at different levels and in different fora: from everyday social relations through interaction with welfare officials and professionals to research, the media, the legal system and policy-making (Schram, 1995). Valerie Polakow, for example, describes how, in the US, schools, teacher training institutions and research institutes are all 'implicated in the framing of poor children as *other*, and in institutionalizing the legitimacy of their *otherness* status' (1993: 150, emphasis in original).

Othering is closely associated with, and reinforced by, a number of related social processes such as stereotyping, stigmatization and the more neutral categorization. Stereotyping is a discriminatory form of labelling, which attains a taken-for-granted quality and serves to portray particular social groups as homogeneous. It is a discursive strategy that magnifies and distorts difference (Riggins, 1997). Michael Pickering writes that 'stereotypes operate as socially exorcistic rituals in maintaining the boundaries of normality and legitimacy' (2001: 45). He suggests that normally 'stereotyping attempts to translate cultural difference into Otherness, in the interests of order, power and control' (2001: 204). In contrast, in the case of 'the poor', stereotyping functions to *create* cultural difference and thereby the Other. At the same time, as we saw in chapter 3, those groups who are more likely to be poor – women, racialized minorities and disabled people – are themselves groups that are frequently Othered.

Processes of classification and categorization effected by governmental and legal institutions, the media and social scientists, although analytically distinct from stereotyping, can draw on stereotypes and thereby reinforce them. These processes can have implications for how 'the poor' are treated by fellow citizens as well as by powerful classificatory institutions (Edelman, 1977). As we shall see, the bifurcation of 'the poor' into 'deserving' and 'undeserving', each with their associated stereotypes, has had a profound impact on their treatment by the welfare state and its antecedents. The label of 'undeserving' poor has been negatively charged by the process of stigmatization, which, historically and today, has had implications for how society sees 'the poor', how they see themselves and how they are treated by welfare institutions. Erving Goffman's classic text referred to stigma as 'an attribute that is deeply discrediting' and to the belief that 'the person with stigma is not quite human' (1968: 13, 15). In this way, stigma contributes to the dehumanization involved in Othering (Oliver, 2001).

Othering and associated processes such as stigmatization have various effects on 'us' and 'them' and the relations between the two. With regard to 'us', Othering helps to define the self and to affirm identity (Sibley, 1995). In contrast, it divests 'them' of 'their social and cultural identities by diminishing them to their stereotyped characteristics' and by casting them as silent objects (Pickering, 2001: 73; Oliver, 2001). In doing so, it denies them their complex humanity and subjectivity. Othering operates as 'a strategy of symbolic exclusion', which makes it easier for people to blame the Other for their own and society's problems (Pickering, 2001: 48). The Othering of 'the poor' also acts as a warning to others; poverty thereby represents a 'spectre – a socially constituted object of wholesome horror' (Dean with Melrose, 1999: 48). As regards the *relationship* between 'us' and 'them', Othering legitimates 'our' privilege – rooted in superiority – and 'their' exploitation and oppression – rooted in inferiority – together with the socio-economic inequalities that underlie poverty (Riggins, 1997; Young, 1999). This underlines the ways in which power relationships are inscribed in the process of Othering. It suggests that Othering may be most marked where inequality is sharpest.

An additional effect of Othering is that it denies the Other the 'right to name and define themselves' (Pickering, 2001: 73). The power 'to name one's Self' has been described as 'a fundamental human right' (Riggins, 1997: 8) and as a key 'political resource' (Silver, 1996: 135). Naming 'the poor' is an exercise in power, for 'we' invariably name 'them', even when sympathetically (Polakow, 1993). Naming or labelling of the Other has symbolic, cultural, psychological and material effects. 'How we name things affects how we behave towards them. The name, or label, carries with it expectations' (Clarke and Cochrane, 1998: 26). Likewise 'we' create images of 'them – the poor', which have a similarly powerful effect on attitudes and actions. 'The politics of representation' is therefore a crucial element in the politics of poverty (hooks, 1994: 169). As we shall see, it has taken on greater salience today as some groups of people in poverty, following the disabled people's movement, are resisting the ways they are represented by the wider society, in recognition of the power of language and images.

It is through language and images that the discourses that frame how we perceive and act in the social world are articulated. Othering can thus be understood as a discursive practice, which shapes how the 'non-poor' think and talk about and act towards 'the poor' at both an interpersonal and an institutional level. Although it does not represent the only available poverty discourse, its impact on policy and the practice of officials and professionals has been profound in some countries, notably the UK and US.[1] Moreover, welfare policy and administration can themselves be understood as a discursive and symbolic practice, which constructs 'the poor' and the nature of the problem of poverty in various ways (Schram, 1995; Saraceno, 2002). A focus on discourse thus helps to illuminate the relationship between the material and relational/symbolic dimensions of poverty and the ways in which the fibres of power are interwoven through them.

Rooted in History

Contemporary discourses of poverty are rooted in history. While the precise language and labels have changed with time, they are, in the UK, imbued with deeply sedimented 'punitive and negative images of the poor' (Jones and Novak,

1999: 5). These images were transplanted and adapted to the 'New World' of North America where they continue to shape attitudes and policies towards 'the poor' (Waxman, 1977; Handler and Hasenfeld, 1997). They reinforce a belief in self-help and the American Dream, which constitutes poverty as failure. Attempts by Progressive era social investigators at the turn of the twentieth-century to 'de-pauperize thinking about poverty' and the short-lived ascendancy of more structural accounts in the mid-twentieth-century represented mere 'brief detours' from the more deeply entrenched 'societal line drawing and moral censure' (O'Connor, 2001: 8; Ross, 1991: 1506). The nineteenth-century is pivotal to understanding modern Anglo-American discourses of poverty, including in particular that of the 'underclass', although the roots run deeper in earlier vagrancy laws and the Elizabethan Poor Law (Waxman, 1977).

At each stage, processes of categorization and classification have been critical to the Othering of 'the poor' and in particular those deemed 'undeserving'. Golding and Middleton detail how, from the sixteenth century, 'classification of the poor into the necessarily and voluntarily indigent became the central purpose of poverty relief'. The consequent 'growing physical and psychological separation of the poor from other classes left free rein for the creation of a rich and only minimally informed mythology about the monstrous underworld of the wretched poor' (1982: 10). This underworld loomed large in the psyche of Victorian Britain. On both sides of the Atlantic, classification of 'the poor' by charities, the state and social researchers was elevated to new heights of precision and refinement, as demarcation lines were drawn more firmly in order to 'Separate! Separate! Separate!' (Himmelfarb, 1984: 398).

The lines of demarcation were drawn with a moral divider (Himmelfarb, 1984). They were designed to protect the respectable from the morally undesirable and to facilitate 'a vast machinery of disciplinary social intervention' aimed at remoralization (Squires, 1990: 55). The effect was, perhaps paradoxically, to 'tarnish all the poor' as more or less morally defective, as pauperism became established as 'a moral category' (Katz, 1989: 14). Pauperism denoted both the people who were subjected to the Poor Law and their condition. It was not an extreme form of poverty but, in its association with character, behaviour and moral degradation, was constructed as qualitatively different (Golding and Middleton, 1982; Squires, 1990). The essence of this difference lay in economic dependency, which was opposed to the 'self-provision of subsistence' achieved by 'the independent labourer' (M. Dean, 1992: 237–8). Dependency spelt degradation and infirmity of character and was characterized as primarily moral and psychological rather than economic (Himmelfarb, 1984; Fraser and Gordon, 1994).

Although they were constructed as qualitatively different, the dividing line between pauperism and poverty was, in practice, a thin and permeable one, as individuals slipped between the two. Welfare policy therefore attempted to 'prevent the poor from lapsing into pauperism by making that prospect repugnant. This was the rationale of less-eligibility and of the stigma of pauperism' (Himmelfarb, 1995: 142). Less-eligibility was the principle underlying the workhouse's treatment of the able-bodied pauper: that conditions in the workhouse should be 'less eligible' or desirable than those of the poorest independent labourer. A further distinction was involved here: between the ('undeserving') 'able-bodied' and the ('deserving') 'impotent' or incapable pauper. The bifurcation of 'undeserving' and 'deserving' has, under various labels, subsequently been deployed to categorize 'the poor' more generally, most notably in the US as well as the UK (Handler and Hasenfeld, 1997).

Another axis of classification of the nineteenth-century poor was aimed at charting and containing 'the dangerous and criminal classes' (Squires, 1990: 54). The notion of the 'dangerous classes'– or 'residuum' as they were also known – invoked fears of criminality, vice, sexual immorality, pollution and a threat to the social order. Women, as failed moral guardians on the one hand and sexualized beings and unmarried mothers on the other, were the object of particular disgust and blame (Mooney, 1998; Carabine, 2000). Impoverished children, although everywhere, were largely invisible (Ridge, 2002). Dirty, diseased and depraved, the dangerous classes were feared as a source of both physical and moral filth and contamination, to be kept at a distance (Sibley, 1995). Henry Mayhew, an influential nineteenth-century chronicler of the London poor, was typical in his conflation of the physical and the moral in his recurrent imagery of 'pestilence' and his description of vagrants as a 'stream of vice and disease' (Himmelfarb, 1984: 340).[2] More fundamentally, the dangerous classes were constructed as a 'species' or 'race apart' (Himmelfarb, 1984: 399; Mann, 1994: 48). As such they were the object of a form of 'domestic colonialism', as middle-class 'explorers' and 'missionaries' entered 'alien and unknown' territory in order to investigate and contain the threat they represented (Mooney, 1998: 57).

The intervention of social workers and other professionals to support and control 'problem families' (a label dating from the 1940s) can be seen as a twentieth-century equivalent (Macnicol, 1987; Welshman, 2002). Nineteenth-century echoes also reverberate in the pathological discourses of poverty deployed by twentieth-century social reformers such as Daniel Moynihan in his important and highly controversial 1965 official US report, *The Negro Family* (O'Connor, 2001; Deacon, 2002). Similar controversy surrounded the influential notion of a 'culture of poverty', coined by the American anthropologist Oscar Lewis. Lewis defined the culture of poverty as 'a subculture with its own structure and rationale, as a way of life which is passed down from generation to generation along family lines' (1967: xxxix). This subculture was driven by a set of values, attitudes and beliefs, different from those held by the majority. Its existence was, however, challenged by critics, including a fellow anthropologist, Charles Valentine (1968).

Lewis emphasized that the culture's 'considerable pathology' should not obscure its function as 'an adaptation and a reaction of the poor to their marginal position' in unequal, capitalist societies. He wrote of poor families' 'fortitude, vitality, resilience and ability to cope with problems which would paralyze many middle-class individuals' (1967: xxvii, xli; Harvey and Reed, 1996). At the same time, in *The Other America*, a pivotal intervention, Michael Harrington married the culture of poverty to a structural analysis (O'Connor, 2001). Nevertheless, the concept lends itself to 'a stigma theory of the tribal type' (Waxman, 1977: 90). It therefore proved useful to those who, unlike Lewis and Harrington themselves, blamed 'the poor' for their poverty, as both supporters and critics of Lewis have observed (Harvey and Reed, 1996; O'Connor, 2001).

The idea of a culture of poverty was more influential politically in the US than the UK. In the latter a parallel notion of the 'cycle of deprivation' emerged in the 1970s, popularized by a senior Conservative politician, the late Sir Keith Joseph. It was concerned with the intergenerational transmission of deprivation, primarily through parental attitudes and values, and how to prevent it through behavioural solutions such as better parenting and education. There are echoes here of an 1838 Poor Law Commissioners Report, which emphasized the importance of education as 'a means of eradicating the germs of pauperism from the rising generation' (cited in Ridge, 2002: 15). The original cycle of deprivation thesis was not confirmed by an ambitious Government-sponsored research programme. New evidence on intergenerational continuities in disadvantage has, though, led to renewed Government interest in 'the cycle of disadvantage', although with some attention to structural as well as behavioural factors (Deacon, 2003: 123; *Benefits*, 2002).

The 'Underclass' and 'Welfare Dependency'

The cycle of deprivation has been described as 'a chronological stepping stone' between the earlier discourses described above and that of the 'underclass', which gained ascendancy in the US and UK (but not elsewhere) in the 1980s and early 1990s (Welshman, 2002). The 'underclass' is the most contested of contemporary poverty discourses in both the academic and the political arenas. It has operated simultaneously as a tool of social scientific analysis and as a popular media and political construct, but with the frequent blurring of the dividing line between the two. The controversy centres on the very existence of an 'underclass' as well as causal mechanisms and language.

Although the term had been used previously by social scientists, the 'underclass' surfaced in the US in the late 1970s and early 1980s as a creature of journalism. It described an alien ghetto group, stuck at the bottom of society, whose values and behaviour set them apart from mainstream America and the American dream of opportunity (Katz, 1989; Gans, 1995). Later in the 1980s an alternative, more sophisticated, perspective on the same phenomenon was provided by the sociologist William Julius Wilson (1987). He too has been criticized for subscribing to a pathological reading of behaviour in the ghetto (O'Connor, 2001). Nevertheless, Wilson did also emphasize the structural labour market position of the 'underclass', together with the way in which 'race' and class divisions have created 'the truly disadvantaged' among inner-city Blacks. Significantly, in his 1990 presidential address to the American Sociological Association, Wilson then distanced himself from the term, as having become 'hopelessly polluted in meaning'.

Foremost among the polluters has been the much publicized and hugely influential Charles Murray. He was also instrumental in popularizing the idea of the 'underclass' in the UK in a series of newspaper articles and pamphlets, starting in 1989. The label has subsequently been deployed, often thoughtlessly, by the media and politicians across the political divide. Tony Blair, for instance, soon after coming to power, set out the case for tackling 'what we all know exists – an underclass of people cut off from society's mainstream, without any sense of shared purpose' (1997). New Labour has, though, since become more circumspect in its use of the term, favouring instead social exclusion, which is generally seen as less pejorative in tone, even if in some formulations it shares certain assumptions with the notion of the 'underclass' (see chapter 4).

Popularization of the idea of an 'underclass' preceded attempts to define it. There is still no single agreed definition. Different definitions tend to reflect whether the underlying explanation is structural or behavioural/cultural in origin, although attempts have been made to straddle the two (for instance, MacDonald, 1997). Murray makes clear that 'the underclass does not refer to degree of poverty, but to a type of poverty', defined by behaviour (1996: 23). The main indicators he uses are illegitimacy (to which he has attached increasing significance), violent crime and drop-out from the labour force among young males. He emphasizes that 'by underclass, I do not mean people who are merely poor, but people who are at the margins of society, unsocialised and often violent' (2001: 2). It is the elasticity of behavioural definitions, which lump together disparate marginalized groups under one stigmatizing and fear-inducing 'umbrella label', that is the source of much criticism of the 'underclass' as an analytical and a political concept (Gans, 1995: 18; Bauman, 1998). As Dean and Taylor-Gooby (1992) observe, it serves to marginalize symbolically those it defines rather than to define the marginalized.

An alternative approach towards definition can be found among British sociologists. They attempt to locate the 'underclass' within – or rather beneath – the class structure, with varying emphases on its members' economic position in relation to the labour market and/or the state and on the existence, or not, of a shared cultural outlook and values (Runciman, 1990; Morris, 1994). What the various definitions do have in common is the distinction drawn between the 'underclass' and the wider group of 'poor'. The media, on the other hand, frequently treat the two as synonymous, as they deploy the label in an undefined way. As with pauperism in the nineteenth-century, the effect is to tarnish 'the poor' more generally with the label's stigmatizing brush. An example is the right-wing commentator Bruce Anderson's assertion:

> Almost all the poverty in contemporary Britain is to be found among the members of a demoralised and indeed dangerously detached underclass. But they do not lack for subsistence. They merely lack stability . . . Above all, these underclass households lack fathers. (*The Independent*, 23 June 2003).[3]

The lack of agreement as to what constitutes the 'underclass' renders problematic attempts at empirical quantification. Indeed, Murray avoided such attempts with the admission that it is a waste of time trying to count the 'underclass', as 'it all depends on how one defines its membership' (1996: 41). Moreover, the balance of empirical evidence does not support claims of a culturally distinct group displaying 'underclass' characteristics in either the US or UK.[4]

The lack of empirical evidence has not, however, diminished the popular potency of the concept of the 'underclass'. This potency lies in part in its success in tapping into and providing a repository for anxieties about the consequences of growing social – and in the US racial – polarization and very real social and economic change. Two elements stand out: 'dangerous youth' (MacDonald, 1997; MacDonald and Marsh, 2001) and the instability of gender relations in the labour market and family (Mann, 1999; Morris, 1994, 1996). Lone mothers, the most vilified members of the 'underclass', have been made the scapegoat for many of these troubling changes and, at times, cast as a social threat. It is the traditional family and men's position in it which, the argument goes, are under particular threat. In the US the threat has been explicitly racialized as part of a wider racially coded welfare politics forged by the White middle class (Franklin 1991; see also chapter 3); in the UK any racial connotations of the 'underclass' and lone motherhood have tended to be more subterranean.

Lydia Morris has described the notion of the 'underclass' as 'an exercise in conceptual containment' (1996: 161). It provides a seemingly simple explanation and set of policy prescriptions for these anxiety-provoking social changes. It does so in a way that locates the problem in the behaviour of marginalized individuals and outside the mainstream of society. This deflects attention from underlying unequal class, gender and 'race' relations and structural causes (Katz, 1989; Novak, 2001). The discourse of the 'underclass' re-frames the problem of poverty as the twin behavioural threats of dependency and delinquency (Dean and Taylor-Gooby, 1992).

'Welfare dependency' is a particularly salient theme. There are differing understandings of its nature – most notably a rational response to 'generous' welfare payments or a passive moral/psychological state induced by reliance on welfare (Fraser and Gordon, 1994). They are, though, articulated through a common discourse, which pathologizes welfare and those who rely on it – especially, in the US, lone mothers and African-Americans (Misra et al., 2003). Its ideological power is underlined by analysts of late twentieth-century US welfare reform.[5] In the face of widening inequality, 'the new consensus' on welfare recast the problem of poverty as a moral problem of 'behavioural dependency' among the 'underclass' (Novak 1987: 88). It helped to change the terms of the welfare debate, thereby paving the way for what President Clinton heralded as 'the end of welfare as we know it'. Its influence has spread to infect debates about welfare reform more generally in advanced Western welfare states. The clearest example is the UK where the discourse was appropriated by both Conservative and Labour politicians and has now become embedded in common-sense assumptions about welfare (Dean, 2003b). Yet, as with the 'underclass' itself, research has not supported the thesis (Dean and Taylor-Gooby, 1992; Leisering and Walker, 1998; Johnston et al., 2000).

Welfare dependency is often popularly associated with (far from passive) illicit work in the informal economy (see chapter 6). Although less virulent than during the British 'scroungerphobia' of the mid-1970s (analysed by Golding and Middleton, 1982), in the UK a recurrent discourse of 'fraud and abuse' continues to delegitimize social security recipients (Cook, 1997; Hills, 2001). More generally, the demonization of the 'underclass' is heightened by its association with crime, violence and anti-social behaviour. Mickey Kaus, for example, blames the 'threat' that the 'underclass' constitutes and the 'fear' it instils for the demise of the public civic sphere in American cities (1992).

The historical echoes in the association of the 'underclass' with both delinquency and dependency are unmistakable, as is the very language of the 'underclass'. It is a similar language to that used in the nineteenth-century to describe that group of 'the poor' perceived as undeserving and threatening (Macnicol, 1987; Katz, 1989). Indeed American proponents of the term, such as Murray (1996) and the journalist Ken Auletta, explicitly draw parallels with the undesirable Victorian substratum depicted by Mayhew. The contemporary 'underclass' discourse is thus steeped in negative historical sediment.

Together with the imagery conveyed by the language of the 'underclass', these resonances render it the most pejorative of contemporary poverty labels, as its indelible stamp separates 'them' from 'us'. It is, as Murray himself acknowledges, a deliberately 'ugly word' (1996: 23). So too is the language of many who write about it. It is frequently a language of disease and contamination. Murray (1996) uses the metaphor of 'plague'; others, such as Ralf Dahrendorf (1987), of 'cancer'.

Animal imagery is also sometimes deployed to convey a sub-human quality. For instance, the British media have created a new object of fear: 'the feral child' running wild in the no-go areas inhabited by the 'underclass' (see *The Observer*, 25 April and *Daily Mail*, 26 April 2002). 'Brood mares', 'breeding mules', 'monkeys' and the more generic 'animals in the Government barn' are among the animal epithets applied by US legislators to mothers on welfare (Kushnick, 1999: 160; Kingfisher, 2002: 22). Such dehumanization legitimates the vilification and exclusion of the Other (Sibley, 1995; Oliver, 2001). Not surprisingly, therefore, people in poverty (though rarely asked) perceive the 'underclass' label as stigmatizing (Beresford et al., 1999). A British politician who used the term in a meeting was met by 'a storm of protest from people [in poverty] objecting to the term as demeaning' (ATD Fourth World, 2000a: 39).

Critics of the 'underclass' concept are divided about use of the term. Some maintain that it should be dropped altogether, on the grounds that it is sociologically unhelpful and politically damaging; others suggest that, used carefully, it can perform a useful function in drawing attention to the problem of poverty in a way that the word 'poverty' itself is no longer able to do. My own view is that use of the term for benevolent purposes is playing with fire. Labelling a group in such a pathologizing and explicitly Othering way makes it easier for the rest of society to write them off as beyond the bonds of common citizenship. The outcome is more likely to be defensive tougher law and order policies than an inclusive anti-poverty strategy. Stigmatizing labels can produce stigmatizing policies, which, as Alan Deacon (2002) observes, is exactly what some 'underclass' proponents seek in the name of promoting responsible behaviour.

The 'p' Words

I have argued against the use of the language of the 'underclass' and 'welfare dependency' in the context of the historical categorization of the 'undeserving poor' that they echo.

This should not be taken to imply that less value-laden discourses of poverty are necessarily unproblematic. Herbert J. Gans draws a distinction between stigmatizing 'labels' and descriptive terms (1995: 12). Although the 'p' words of 'poor' and 'poverty' fall into the latter category, their historical and contemporary connotations mean that they are not neutral terms (Novak, 2001). They form part of 'a vocabulary of invidious distinction', which constructs 'the poor' as different or deviant (Katz, 1989: 5). The 'p' words are used by 'us' about 'them' and rarely by people in poverty themselves (Polakow, 1993; Corden, 1996). Typically, the latter are not asked how they want to be described (Silver, 1996). The terms 'poverty' and 'poor', therefore, are frequently experienced as stigmatizing labels by their 'unasked, unwilling targets' (Gans, 1995: 21).

Research with people with experience of poverty in the UK elicited negative responses to the 'p' words from a number of them: 'horrid' or 'horrible' words; 'stigma'; 'socially worse'; 'puts you down' were among their reactions (Beresford et al., 1999: 64–5). The adjective 'poor' is also tainted by its double meaning of inferior, as in 'poor quality' or 'deficient'. Its use as an adjective can be experienced as insulting and demeaning (CoPPP, 2000). Moreover, it carries a definitional implication for identity that is inappropriate given that poverty is a circumstance that a person experiences rather than a personal quality (Warah, 2000; see also chapter 6).

Drawing partly on another UK study (of social security claimants), Hartley Dean identifies a range of images or discourses used to make sense of the 'p' words. Broadly these either serve to distance the speaker from the phenomenon or they convey a negative image of 'something blameworthy, threatening or unspeakable' (Dean with Melrose, 1999: 29; Dean, 1992). Certainly, poverty is 'not something that many people will readily admit to' (Dean with Melrose, 1999: 29). As many as two-thirds of the social security claimants in the study did not admit to poverty, with men less likely to do so than women. Even those who did call themselves 'poor' often did so reluctantly. The same refusal to wear the stigmatizing label of poverty emerges in other qualitative studies (Cohen, 1997; Yeandle et al., 2003). Quantitative surveys also frequently identify a minority who are classified as poor under the criteria used but who do not consider themselves poor (Townsend, 1979; Gordon et al., 2000a). There may be various reasons for this. One interpretation is that, in line with W. G. Runciman's theory of relative deprivation, people may be using a narrow range of 'reference groups' to assess their own economic situation (Runciman, 1966; Dean with Melrose, 1999). Frequently these reference groups may be people worse off than themselves (Stephenson, 2001). Here, there is sometimes a sense that people believe that to call themselves 'poor' would be to belittle the plight of those in worse circumstances, either in the same or poorer countries (Beresford et al., 1999). Nevertheless, it remains likely that 'fear of shame-based humiliation is a primary factor' in people not wanting 'to identify themselves as poor' (hooks, 1994: 169).[6]

This aversion to the stigmatization associated with poverty comes through very strongly in Anne Corden's description of a study in a deprived area in the UK. Her account also illustrates the dilemmas this raises for researchers and campaigners. Participants in the study had made clear that they did not want themselves or their community to be associated with the term 'poverty'. When the study was published, a local paper presented it in just the kind of stigmatizing way that residents had resisted, leaving them feeling 'angry . . . powerless and frustrated'. Corden writes of the dilemma this creates for her:

> If I look for ways of avoiding the use of the word 'poverty' in my written and spoken language then it is hard for me to join the poverty debate. What might be a powerful contribution on behalf of the poor people I met may be suppressed. Unless I use the term 'poverty' when I write I effectively collude with a government view that poverty has disappeared. (1996: 18)

Participatory research in the South often uses terms such as 'ill-being' in order to avoid the 'p' word (Bennett with Roberts, 2004). However, it is then difficult to know whether participants necessarily equate 'ill-being' with poverty (see chapter 1). There is also the political issue Corden raises in her reference to the previous Conservative Government which deleted the 'p' word from the official lexicon. This was not because of the word's stigmatizing connotations (although this argument was used opportunistically) but represented an attempt to deny the phenomenon's existence. In Germany too the word (Armut) has been 'virtually taboo' (Leisering and Leibfried, 1999: 196).[7] Despite the reluctance to identify with the term, some people with experience of poverty nevertheless argue that it is still needed as the basis for political action (Beresford et al., 1999). Likewise, the general consensus among anti-poverty campaigners and researchers is that to replace 'poverty' with a sanitized language such as 'less well off' is to blunt the moral and political sword that the word can represent in sympathetic hands (H. Dean, 1992). 'Avoiding the word' makes 'avoiding the problem' easier (Dundee Anti-Poverty Forum, 2003: 11). It also neutralizes the problem by eliding the painful experience of poverty behind colourless terms like 'low income'.

This discussion of the 'p' words and of the 'underclass' label raises a number of issues. One is the responsibility of those who research and write about poverty to use language that is respectful and 'less distancing' (O'Connor, 2001: 293). Another is the paradoxical way in which the 'p' words can simultaneously represent both a stigmatizing classification and a moral and political challenge (see Introduction). The relative weight of the two shifts according to the political and economic climate. Yet, whether 'victims or villains' (Becker, 1997), 'the poor' tend to be constructed as Other, either responsible for their own fate or passive objects of concern, without agency. They are targets of, at best, 'the non-poor's' pity or indifference and, at worst, their fear, contempt or hostility, to be 'helped or punished, ignored or studied' but rarely treated as equal fellow citizens with rights (Katz, 1989: 236).

Representations of Poverty

Such constructions and the problems associated with the 'p' word are reinforced through more general representations of 'the poor'. These representations are an important element in the Othering process. The image created by many commentators is that of 'strangers in our midst' (Katz, 1989: 7). Sometimes this is a deliberate mechanism for 'blaming the victim'. Sometimes it is deployed by more sympathetic observers to shock society into action. An example is Harrington's *The Other America,* in which he deployed imagery such as 'internal alien' and 'underworld' (1962: 17, 2, cited in Rimstead, 1997). In the UK, the radical journalist Nick Davies wrote a widely publicized book called *Dark Heart: The Shocking Truth about Hidden Britain.* The book is an example of what we might call 'sympathetic Othering'. Davies presents himself as a 'Victorian explorer penetrating a distant jungle': it is 'another', 'undiscovered country' inhabited by 'the poor'. He frequently uses the adjective 'different' to reinforce the message. While Davies emphasizes the damage wrought on people by poverty, the use of such images arguably does more to distance them from his readers and to engender fear than to inspire the 'crusade against poverty' he seeks (1998: 305).

Journalists are an important source of images of 'Others', informing attitudes and frequently confirming negative stereotypes and creating distance between 'us' and 'them' (Sibley 1995; Lens, 2002). Research in the UK and US has underlined the contribution of such images to the development of punitive attitudes and policies towards recipients of welfare (de Goede, 1996; Golding, 1999). A particular theme of US research is the racialized nature of such images (Gilens, 1999; Misra et al., 2003).

Alongside 'undeserving' welfare recipients are also images of the 'deserving poor'. At their most positive these may be portrayals of 'heroic survivors', which set impossible standards for more everyday survivors; more often they 'serve up people in poverty as pathetic, hopeless and crushed, passively accepting their plight' (Beresford et al., 1999: 16). Such images, particularly visual images, are sometimes used by charities and campaigning groups. They are, though, increasingly being challenged in relation to poverty in the South, images of which have 'stripped . . . dignity away' (Nyoni, 1988/9: 9). The disabled people's movement has also shown the way in challenging the demeaning and victimizing imagery traditionally used by charities.

The passive representation of poverty's victims is reinforced by the way in which people in poverty are typically the objects rather than subjects of media representations (Illouz, 1994). For much of the time, 'the poor' live below the media radar screen – unseen and unheard (Toynbee, 2003). To the extent that poverty is covered by the media, it tends to be mediated by 'experts' (Devereux, 1998). When 'the poor' themselves do appear and are allowed to speak, it is usually to illustrate the journalist's agenda rather than to provide their own analysis of their situation (Lens, 2002). This restricted voice and conditional visibility accorded people in poverty, in turn, reinforces the media's individualization of the problems they face at the expense of an exploration of the wider structural context (Devereux, 1998; Bullock et al., 2001). This can affect how the wider society understands the causes of poverty (Iyengar, 1991).

Stigma, Shame and Humiliation

People in poverty are, of course, themselves consumers of the media. They see and hear the stigmatizing images and language (Goffman, 1968; Soss, 1999). As observed already, residents of deprived areas may bitterly resent the stigmatization of their neighbourhoods. Stigma can also operate at the personal and institutional levels (Waxman, 1977). It can attach in particular to receipt of means-tested welfare (more predominant in liberal welfare states such as the US and UK). It can be reinforced by the manner in which welfare is sometimes administered so as to degrade its recipients and act as a warning to others (Handler and Hasenfeld, 1997; Jones and Novak, 1999; Gilliom, 2001). The degree and nature of the stigma attached to poverty and welfare receipt varies between societies, reflecting factors such as the historical treatment of 'the poor' and the nature of the social security system. Relevant too are popular explanations of poverty, which vary markedly between countries but which can also shift over time (van Oorschot and Halman, 2000; Gallie and Paugam, 2002).

   In their discussions with people with experience of poverty, Beresford et al. deliberately did not use the word 'stigma'. Nevertheless 'it was an issue to which they repeatedly turned. Almost every group discussed stigma as a key consequence of being poor. Stigma shaped, overshadowed and was the context for their relationships with other people, particularly their relationships with the non-poor and official agencies' (1999: 96). Of particular concern were the media and the stigma many felt when claiming benefits (see also Dundee Anti-Poverty Forum, 2003; Farrell and O'Connor, 2003). Treatment by social services professionals can also be experienced as stigmatizing (Buhaenko et al., 2003).

The impact of stigma can be profound, although not all will react in the same way and its effects can depend on the situation (Rogers-Dillon, 1995; *Journal of Social Issues*, 2001). Internalization, with all its damaging implications for identity and self-esteem, and for resistance, are two polarized reactions (Rimstead, 1997). Both were found in a Scottish study of rough sleepers, people who begged and *Big Issue* vendors.[8] Most were keenly aware of the negative perceptions of them held by the wider public and this impacted upon their self-image (Kennedy and Fitzpatrick, 1999; see also Dean, 1999).

Where the stigma of poverty is internalized, shame is a likely consequence (Goffman, 1968). As noted in the Introduction, participatory research in the South has underscored the centrality of shame and humiliation to the experience of poverty. Narayan et al. note that, because of the stigma associated with poverty in eastern Europe as well as the South, 'poor people often try to conceal their poverty to avoid humiliation and shame' (2000: 38). So too in some more affluent countries feelings of shame and experiences of humiliation are recurrent themes when people in poverty are asked what poverty and claiming welfare mean to them (Polakow, 1993; Kempson, 1996). Indeed, in a report of a visit to the UK, two community workers from south India, Stan and Mari Thekaekara, comment that 'the stigma attached to being poor is far greater here in the UK' and observe a strong 'sense of shame' (1994: 21).

As Adam Smith recognized over two centuries ago, clothing, as a key signifier of relative poverty (see chapter 1), represents a visible badge of shame and humiliation (Gilroy and Speak, 1998; C. C. Williams, 2002). This is particularly so for children. Ridge's study of childhood poverty found that wearing the (unaffordable) appropriate, fashionable clothing is crucial to 'fitting in', friendships and avoidance of both bullying and social exclusion. One child explained that 'if you don't wear trendy stuff . . . not so many people will be your friend 'cos of what you wear'; another that 'you've got to keep going with the trend otherwise you kind of get picked on' (Ridge, 2002: 68). This study and earlier research by Middleton et al. (1994) underline the importance to children and young people of clothing as an expression of their emergent identities. More generally, the shame and humiliation associated with poverty can be particularly difficult to bear for this age group. Willow observes that discussions about poverty with children living in deprived areas were all 'woven with the threads of stigma and shame' (2001: 12). This is likely to be a contributory factor in the lower self-esteem of many children who have grown up in poverty (Ermisch et al., 2001; Ruxton and Bennett, 2002).

The significance of shame and humiliation is not to be underestimated. They play an important role in maintaining inequality and social hierarchy. They are painfully injurious to identity, self-respect and self-esteem, in other words to how we feel about ourselves (Rawls, 1973; Honneth, 1995). A participant in a UK Coalition against Poverty workshop describes what the loss of self-esteem feels like: 'You're like an onion and gradually every skin is peeled off of you and there's nothing left. All your self-esteem and how you feel about yourself is gone – you're left feeling like nothing and then your family feels like that' (UKCAP, 1997: 12). Shame and humiliation peel away self-esteem and negate the identity of many people who experience poverty. In his study of social identity, Richard Jenkins suggests that Goffman's analysis of stigma demonstrates how 'others don't just perceive our identity, they actively constitute it. And they do so not only in terms of naming or categorising, but in terms of how they respond to or treat us' (1996: 74). While labelling does not determine identity in a fixed way, Jenkins argues that 'public image may become self-image. Our own sense of humanity is a hostage to categorising judgements of others' (1996: 57).

Questions of identity have implications for the political agency of people in poverty; these will be explored in chapter 6. Here, I simply want to make a related link between identity and the desire of people in poverty to be treated with dignity and respect. This desire represents the foundation stone of what political and social theorists have dubbed a 'politics of recognition' (discussed in the Conclusion). Recognition, argues Charles Taylor, is 'not just a courtesy we owe people. It is a vital human need' (1992: 26).

Dignity and Respect

> Lack of respect, though less aggressive than an outright insult, can take an equally wounding form. No insult is offered another person, but neither is recognition extended; he or she is not *seen* – as a full human being whose presence matters. (Sennett, 2003: 3, emphasis in original)

In the South, participatory research attests to the struggles of the powerless 'to find a place of dignity and respect in society' as they attempt to resist the shame and humiliation they face (Narayan et al., 2000: 260). Similar reactions can be identified in the North. One mother in Beresford et al.'s study explained that 'poverty strips your dignity. You can't have any dignity with poverty' (1999: 90). Millicent Simms, a young unemployed woman, told a UK National Poverty Hearing that 'You shouldn't have to be made to feel as though you are useless. I just feel very angry sometimes that people are ignorant to the fact that we are humans as well and we do need to be respected' (Russell, 1996: 10). Her anger was reflected in much of the evidence received by the UK Commission on Poverty, Participation and Power. Its Report took as its starting point the observation that:

> too often, people experiencing poverty are not treated with respect, either in general or by the people they come into contact with most . . . The lack of respect for people living in poverty was one of the clearest and most heartfelt messages which came across to us as a Commission. (CoPPP, 2000: 3; see also Galloway, 2002)

When people in poverty are treated with respect, it can increase their self-confidence and sense of agency. Carol, a resident of Easterhouse in Glasgow, writes of how she was elected chairperson of a food co-op and of how other volunteers 'respected me and it gave me more confidence' (Holman, 1998: 45; see also Wood and Vamplew, 1999).

According to John Rawls, self-respect is 'perhaps the most important primary good' (1973: 440). Sen (1999) identifies self-respect as a key functioning (see chapter 1) and its significance is explored in greater depth in the work of Nussbaum. She includes in her list of central human functional capabilities: 'having the social bases of self-respect and non-humiliation; being able to be treated as a dignified being whose worth is equal to that of others' (2000: 79). The achievement of this principle with regard to people living in poverty has implications not just for how they are treated in everyday social relations but also for the organization of society. This is acknowledged, in principle at least, in the 1998 French Law against Social Exclusion. Article 1 states that 'the struggle against exclusion is a national necessity based on respect for the equal worth of all human beings'. At European level, the EC has recommended that Member States should recognize the right to a level of social assistance sufficient to enable members 'to live in a manner compatible with human dignity' (cited in Veit-Wilson, 1998: 86).

Yet, by and large, society tends to pay only lip-service to the principle of equal worth and human dignity. In reality, where socio-economic inequalities are wide, it is a fiction. As Anne Phillips observes, 'a society that condones excesses of poverty in the midst of wealth, or arbitrarily rewards one skill with one hundred times the wages of another, is not recognizing its citizens as of equal human worth' (1999: 131). The better-off are too far removed socially, and sometimes geographically, from those in poverty to feel that the latter are 'dignified beings' who are their equals. Respect does not easily transcend 'the boundaries of inequality' (Sennett, 2003: 23). The denial of dignity contributes to 'the injury of class' (Sennett and Cobb, 1972: 118). Meritocratic societies, such as the US and increasingly the UK, make 'no room for failure in [their] schemes of respect' (1972: 183). Poverty denotes failure. The equation of receipt of welfare with stigmatized 'dependency' strips away another skin of the onion of self-esteem.

Indeed, this is the intention of some 'underclass' theorists. Despite acknowledgement of unpaid contributions to society, including those made by 'conscientious mothers', Murray maintains that the long-term welfare recipient *'cannot* feel self-respect no matter what is done on behalf of her dignity', for she is not a 'net contributor' to society (1988: 123, 130–1, emphasis in original). Less pejoratively, Kaus promises *'respect'* to members of the 'underclass' in return for assimilation into low paid work (1992: 139, emphasis in original). In contrast, the American writer Barbara Ehrenreich comments that what most 'surprised and offended her', when she tried to live as a low-paid worker, was the 'routine indignities' and 'the extent to which one is required to surrender one's basic civil rights and . . . self respect' (2001: 208–9). The more fundamental point being made implicitly by many people in poverty is that recognition of their dignity and their right to self-respect should not be conditional on 'success' or, *contra* Murray, on undertaking paid work.

Conclusion

This chapter has underlined the importance of the 'politics of representation' to the achievement of this ideal. bell hooks has argued that the affirmation of the 'dignity and integrity' of people living in poverty requires 'constructively changing ways [they] are represented in every aspect of life' (1994: 170–2). This raises wider issues of cultural citizenship, one element of which is 'the right to dignifying representation' (Pakulski, 1997: 80). According to Jan Pakulski, 'cultural citizenship involves the right to be "different", to re-value stigmatised identities' (1997: 83). In the case of 'the poor', however, it is about the right to be 'the same'. The fear of appearing different comes across particularly strongly in children's accounts of poverty (Ridge, 2002; DWP 2003b).

A central theme of the chapter has been the power of discourse – as articulated through language and images – in constructing 'the poor' as 'different' or Other. This Other may be irresponsible, criminal or inadequate – to be censured, feared or pitied. At the same time, the discussion has hinted at another, underlying, form of power: the power of more dominant groups to define 'the poor' as Other. Behind the language stand cultural attitudes, economic divisions and power relationships that will not be dissolved by a 'politics of renaming' alone (Schram, 1995: 22). This means that, as hooks (1994) recognizes and as is developed in the Conclusion, a politics of representation and recognition has to be linked to a politics of redistribution. Moreover, as I shall argue in chapter 7, such a politics has to involve people in poverty themselves as social actors. This, in turn, requires acknowledgement of their agency, which is the principal message of the next chapter.

6
Poverty and Agency: From Getting By to Getting Organized

A central message of the previous chapter was that Othering reduces 'the poor' to passive objects – in either the benign form of the helpless victim or the malign spectre of the lazy, work-shy, welfare dependant. This passive characterization contributes to the social distancing of 'them' from 'us'. Until recently, there has been only limited recognition of the agency – or capacity to act – of people living in poverty. To the extent that agency *has* been acknowledged it has tended to be in terms of attribution of responsibility for the individual's poverty rather than recognition of the complex subjectivity of fellow human beings trying to negotiate their lives in adverse circumstances.

After a general discussion of the notion of agency and of how it figures in different explanations of poverty, this chapter explores four aspects of the agency of people in poverty: 'getting by' or everyday coping; 'getting (back) at' through 'everyday resistance'; 'getting out' of poverty; and 'getting organized' to effect change. 'Getting organized' to effect change depends in part on a sense of identification as 'poor' or as a member of a group in poverty. This, final, section will therefore begin with a more general exploration of the question of how people in poverty see themselves and their position, which links back to the previous chapter.

This chapter exemplifies in particularly sharp form how writing a book of this nature involves walking some difficult tightropes. Most fundamentally, the very act of writing *about* people in poverty – even as subjects and actors – from a position of affluence, is, at one level, an act of objectification of a group that already suffers excessive objectification and scrutiny. There is also a fine line between acknowledgement of the agency of people in poverty, including their capacity to make mistakes and 'wrong' decisions like the rest of us, and blaming them for that poverty. One commentator, for instance, has used evidence of how some people manage to cope on low incomes to argue that those who do not do so demonstrate 'domestic incompetence' and lack of 'moral commitment', and need 'rebuking with public disapproval' (Anderson, n.d.: 5, 27).

Alternatively, an emphasis on agency runs the risk of romanticization and idealization. Not all agency is necessarily constructive either for the individual or others (Hoggett, 2001; Hunter, 2003). Agency can, for instance, be expressed through acts of violence. Moreover, the flip-side of idealizing agency can be that those who do not manage to 'get out' or 'get organized', or who are too ground down or depressed even to 'get by' or to 'get (back) at' those in authority over them, can be the object of even greater contempt, thereby aggravating feelings of failure and shame (Greener, 2002). Depression has been described as 'equivalent to a collapse of agency' (Hoggett, 2001: 47). Depression and psychological distress are all too common among those in poverty, especially women (Payne, 1991; Davis and Hill, 2001; Gallie and Paugam, 2002). Yet pilot studies in the US suggest that, when treated for depression, people in poverty had been 'introduced to agency and had begun to exercise it; even when they were up against nearly insurmountable obstacles, they progressed – often fast, and sometimes far' (Solomon, 2001: 340).

Agency

The idea of agency is typically used to characterize individuals as autonomous, purposive and creative actors, capable of a degree of choice. A conscious sense of agency is important to an individual's self-identity and sense of self-esteem. Survival in the face of oppression and deprivation is helped by a belief in the ability to exercise some measure of control over one's own life, however limited. Three, interrelated, aspects of sociological debates about agency are of particular relevance to understanding the situation of people in poverty: the relationship between agency and structure; models of agency; and types of agency.

Agency and structure

How far what happens in society can be understood as the product of individual actions (agency) or of wider social, economic and political institutions and processes (structure) has long been a central problem in sociological theory. The theoretical pendulum has swung at different times between an emphasis on agency and on structure but has, more recently, been preoccupied with the relationship between the two. Of particular significance for the study of poverty is the extent to which, on the one hand, structure enables or constrains the agency of different groups and, on the other, the agency of different groups is able to impact on structure. Re-phrased in line with contemporary theories of individualization, which emphasize individual choice and action (Beck and Beck-Gernsheim, 2002), the question is posed in terms of how far people in poverty are able to be authors of their own biographies (Chamberlayne and Rustin, 1999; Leisering and Leibfried, 1999). The answer lies in the extent to which they are able to exercise 'generative' power to control their own lives despite their subordinate position in wider 'hierarchical' political, economic and social power relationships (Giddens, 1991; Kabeer, 2000a).

Post-war British social policy has been characterized as, until recently, denying the agency of individuals in poverty in its preoccupation with structural causes and aversion to 'blaming the victim'. In fact, not all structuralist explanations denied any room for individual agency and responsibility (see, for instance, Holman, 1978; George and Howards, 1991). Nevertheless, it has been argued that the general downplaying of agency left a vacuum, which exponents of the 'underclass' such as Charles Murray were able to fill (Deacon and Mann, 1999; Deacon, 2002). In the US too, the second half of the twentieth century saw an increasingly polarized debate between those who attribute the causes of poverty to social and economic structures and those who hold culture and individual behaviour responsible, with the latter group's views increasingly dominant (O'Connor, 2001).

The treatment of agency in this chapter reflects a recent development in welfare theorizing, which aims to transcend the dichotomy between individualist and structuralist approaches. Central to this 'new paradigm of welfare' is an emphasis on 'the capacity of people to be creative, reflexive human beings, that is, to be active agents in shaping their lives, experiencing, acting upon and reconstituting the outcomes of welfare policies in various ways' (F. Williams et al., 1999b: 2). The analytical framework locates agency in the context of the individual's social position 'in relation to wider forms of stratification and social relations of power' (1999b: 179). In this way, the framework offers a means of focusing on the agency of individuals in poverty without losing sight of the ways in which their agency is constrained by lack of material resources and power. An example of the application of such an approach can be found in a cross-national study of social exclusion. The researchers used the notion of 'individual life-trajectories' as shaped by aspirations, resources (material and human) and external opportunities (to which I would add constraints). They viewed the research subjects 'as they viewed themselves, as agents in their own lives, as they attempted to realise aspirations and goals in the [often difficult] circumstances in which they found themselves' (Chamberlayne and Rustin, 1999: 43).

Models of agency

The model of agency embedded in this new welfare research paradigm is very different from that driving 'underclass' theories in which agency is equated with individual responsibility for poverty. In the latter, the model is generally that of 'economic rational man' instrumentally pursuing his (or her) self-interest and responsive to economic incentives. From a very different political position, Bill Jordan has also deployed an economic model of agency to portray 'the poor as rational actors' rather than victims (1996: 78).

From a sociological perspective such models have been criticized for their 'narrow conceptualization of human action' which, 'in atomizing human agency, largely ignores culture and social structures in which human agents are embedded' (Burns, 1994: 198, 227). Agency is exercised within a social and cultural context and research indicates that 'cultural values play an important role in influencing economic choices' (Taylor-Gooby, 1998: 222). Two studies of lone mothers – one American, one British – illustrate the point. The American study points to competing 'cultural models', which underlie 'women's tacit [and sometimes explicit] conceptions of what constitutes "proper" approaches to finding work, raising one's child, and negotiating high-quality preschooling' (Holloway et al., 1997: 12). The British study counters the model of 'economic rational man' with the notion of contextualized 'gendered moral rationalities', defined as 'collective and social understandings about what is the proper relationship between motherhood and paid work' (Duncan and Edwards, 1999: 3). Thus the exercise of agency in relation to economic choices is motivated by 'socially negotiated, non-economic understandings about what is morally right and socially acceptable' as well as by financial calculations (1999: 118).

Another model of agency to be found in the poverty literature derives from the work of Sen (Leisering and Leibfried, 1999; Korpi, 2000). The very notion of capabilities (see chapter 1) implies agency. Moreover, 'understanding the agency role is,' in Sen's view, 'central to recognizing people as responsible persons: not only are we well or ill, but also we act or refuse to act, and can choose to act one way rather than another . . . It makes a difference' (1999: 190). Indeed, what makes a difference is not only how those in poverty choose to act but also how those with more power choose to act in relation to them. In other words, structures are perpetuated (and modified) by agency – individual and collective actions or non-actions.

Types of agency

The complex, delicate juggling act of making ends meet on an inadequate budget; refusal to comply with the demands of welfare agencies; deciding whether to combine caring for children with paid work; and involvement in collective action to improve neighbourhood conditions or to defend welfare benefits are all examples of agency. However, they each represent a different kind of agency. The literature offers a number of classifications (see, for instance, Hoggett, 2001).

An important dimension for our purposes concerns the consequential, strategic significance for people's lives of the choices involved (Kabeer, 2000a). A decision about whether to take paid work, for instance, involves *strategic* agency, which then has consequences for the more *everyday* agency involved in making ends meet. The latter, though less consequential for the course of individuals' lives, nevertheless shapes how they experience poverty (Leisering and Leibfried, 1999). We can also distinguish between, on the one hand, *personal* and, on the other, *political* and *citizenship* agency. As used here, the former focuses on the individual's livelihood broadly understood ('getting by' or 'getting out') whereas the latter involves, respectively, acts of defiance or trying to effect wider change ('getting (back) at' or 'getting organized'). Personal and political/citizenship agency are to some extent interrelated: to act politically or as a citizen requires a sense of agency, the belief that one can act; acting politically or as a citizen, especially collectively, in turn fosters that sense of agency (Lister, 2003).

The dimensions of 'everyday–strategic' and 'personal–political/citizenship', which form the basis of the taxonomy in figure 6.1, should be understood as continua rather than dichotomies. The taxonomy categorizes actions not actors and therefore any one individual may be exercising all four forms of agency identified in the quadrants. Moreover, as we shall see, not all expressions of agency can be neatly classified. Figure 6.1 will now be used to structure the discussion of poverty and agency, as we consider each of the quadrants in turn.

Figure 6.1   Forms of agency exercised by people in poverty

Getting By

'Getting by' in poverty stands in the *everyday–personal* quadrant of the taxonomy. The cloak of invisibility surrounding getting by tends to be lifted only when it breaks down and the situation becomes classified as a 'problem'. Getting by can all too easily be taken for granted and not recognized as an expression of agency. The 'fight to keep going' in the face of adversity 'is not given any weight or significance' (ATD Fourth World, 1991: 43). Yet the broader notion of 'coping', of which 'getting by' is one example, represents a key building block in the new paradigm of welfare, mentioned earlier (F. Williams et al., 1999b; Williams and Popay, 1999). One of its architects, Michael Titterton, emphasizes 'the role of creative human agency' in coping with threats to personal welfare. He contends that the 'new paradigm should, above all, generate respect for informal modes of coping and helpseeking, and should create a new sensitivity towards the creative and diverse ways in which people respond to their own problems and the ways in which they help other people to respond' (1992: 1, 19).

Titterton uses the notion of unequally distributed coping 'resources' – personal, social and material – as one factor in people's differential ability to cope with stressful circumstances (see also Erikson, 1993). Cultural resources, which enable people to make sense of their situation and access necessary information especially to escape poverty, also play a part (Duncan, 1999; Wessels and Miedema, 2003). Time too is a resource and one that is highly gendered, as we saw in chapter 3. The notion of resources links back to Veit-Wilson's definition of needs quoted in chapter 1. The idea of people drawing on a range of resources to manage their lives can be found in both the psychological and sociological literature. In the latter, it serves to mediate between agency and structure (F. Williams and Popay, 1999).

In the context of poverty, the development literature has placed particular emphasis on this idea as part of the increasingly influential 'livelihoods approach'. A livelihood is defined as 'the capabilities, assets (stores, resources, claims and access) and activities required for a means of living' (Chambers and Conway, 1992: 7). The approach is seen as having opened up the space, including within households, for 'addressing in interdisciplinary and policy relevant terms, the multiple, fluid and often convoluted ways that people manage their lives' (Beall, 2002: 83). People in poverty are characterized as 'managers of complex asset portfolios', constantly making decisions about their deployment (Moser, 1998: 1; Narayan, 2000: 49, 64). These portfolios comprise: financial assets; personal assets (including skills, knowledge and health); social assets (including social networks); natural assets (derived from the natural environment); and both collective and individual physical assets (including the infrastructure and household goods). They are frequently represented as different forms of 'capital'.[1]

More critical exponents of the livelihoods approach are wary of reducing social relations to the economistic language of 'assets' and 'capital'. An alternative formulation proposes 'a wide conception of the *resources* that people need to *access* in the process of *composing* a livelihood' (Bebbington, 1999: cited in Beall, 2002: 72, Beall's emphasis). This returns us to the more neutral idea of 'resources', inserts the idea of 'composition' in place of 'management' and places emphasis on the issue of access. Access, in turn, opens up questions of economic, political and social structural context and the wider distribution of resources of various kinds (Rakodi with Lloyd-Jones, 2002). Attention to how people in poverty exercise agency to deploy the resources available to them must not obscure the ways in which, over the life-course, the more privileged are able to draw on their considerably greater resources to perpetuate their privilege (Skeggs, 1997; Savage, 2000).

Although primarily a development tool, a number of practitioners and analysts are exploring the relevance of the livelihoods approach in a European context (*Community Development Journal*, 2003; C. C. Williams and Windebank, 2003). An exploratory Oxfam study in urban Scotland found that the livelihoods framework resonated with poverty 'professionals', who believed that it offered a more 'holistic' approach to anti-poverty work (Long et al., 2002: 61; Hocking, 2003). However, as the authors observe, in the global North the scope for 'asset building' is more constrained by government policy than in the South (Long et al., 2002: 57). Such constraints vary according to the particular institutional arrangements of different welfare states – for example, the constraints are generally greater in the more developed social assistance systems of many northern European countries than in southern Europe (Saraceno, 2002; Steinert and Pilgram, 2003).

The notions of coping and of resource or asset-management can be understood as a mediating link between a person's capabilities and her achieved functionings, within the context of the overall distribution of resources (see chapter 1). They help to illuminate the ways in which getting by when in poverty involves the exercise of agency. In the complex interplay of agency and structure, many researchers, rightly, emphasize the constraints and lack of choice faced by people in poverty and their sense of having no control over their lives.

Yet, despite the constricted nature of the agency that people in poverty can exercise, 'even the material conditions and life experiences of most of the poor are not so constrained in every sense that they are not capable of making decisions about how to cope with their situation' (Leisering and Leibfried, 1999: 40).

Coping strategies

At a very minimum, coping or getting by is an active process of juggling, piecing together and going without (Kempson et al., 1994; Daly and Leonard, 2002). Children frequently play a part, for instance through part-time work or self-denial and moderation of their demands (Loumidis and Middleton, 2000; Ridge, 2002). Stephen Gilliat observes that 'coping enables those who face deprivation to survive, "get by" or "make out" in a world structured by powerful economic forces and their agents' (2001: 1). It involves 'making space or creating room for manoeuvre within constraints' (2001: 139). In his study of 'how the poor adapt to poverty in capitalism' he identifies three main forms of coping: 'resource augmentation, expenditure minimisation and stress management' (2001: 65). Our main focus here is the agency involved in, first, managing existing resources and, second, augmenting those resources. Both can increase the stress that then has to be managed. Gilliat notes that

> many of the poor are very good managers of their poverty. They are resourceful and use their money and time with great expediency. They are precise about planning household accounts and ruthless about expenditure, savagely cutting back to keep out of debt. They set priorities and cut out luxuries . . . Despite this achievement they understandably describe such work as sacrifice and relentless struggle. (2001: 99)

A similar conclusion is reached by an overview of British research into how people manage on low incomes: 'in general, poor people manage their finances with care, skill and resourcefulness. There is no evidence to suggest that there are two types of poor families – those who can cope and those who can't' (Vaitilingam, 2002: 4). David McCrone does, though, argue that a distinction can be made between 'non-planners' who 'get by' on a day-to-day basis and 'planners' who 'make out' through the deployment of longer-term strategies. He emphasizes that the distinction represents 'a very fine line' and is not a matter of competence, for ' "getting by" involves some intricate and highly competent routines' (1994: 80, 70). Moreover, the very strain of getting by can make it difficult to think or act strategically (Chamberlayne and Rustin, 1999).

Despite this distinction, much of the poverty literature in both North and South describes everyday coping in terms of 'strategies' – both general 'survival' or 'livelihood strategies' and, in the North, more specific 'budgeting strategies'. This use of the term strategy to acknowledge agency represents a 'shorthand for a series of choices constrained to a greater or lesser extent by macroeconomic circumstances, social context, cultural and ideological expectations and access to resources' (Rakodi, 2002: 8). Strategies can be more implicit than articulated and are not necessarily effective (Jordan et al., 1992; Dewilde, 2003). Typical adjectives attached are: 'complex', 'innovative', 'sophisticated' (Middleton and Walker, 1994: 149; Chambers, 1997, 164–5; UNDP, 1997: 61). Vincent's observation of early twentieth-century poverty as representing 'a practice' is still apposite:

> Even the most hopeless pursued intricate strategies of survival which embodied complex normative and material aspirations and involved elaborate negotiations with a wide range of individuals and agencies. At all times, the fewer the resources, the more thought and energy that had to be expended in their use. (1991: vii)

Contemporary British research reveals the diversity of these strategies, as people adapt to particular circumstances and structural constraints (Middleton, 2002; McKendrick et al., 2003b). However, neither of the two main strategies – 'bill juggling and debt' or 'tight money control and cutting back' – produces a 'desirable outcome' in the face of 'a Hobson's choice' between anxiety and debt and 'lives that few of us would find acceptable' (Kempson et al., 1994: 280, 282, 286, 293).

The coping strategies adopted to survive poverty are not limited to managing inadequate material resources. They may include dealing with the kind of Othering attitudes and treatment described in chapter 5. They may also involve coping with and surviving personal traumas (Holman, 1998). Moreover, people in poverty 'experience the same biographical problems which face everyone, such as bringing up children' (Leisering and Leibfried, 1999: 124). Poverty makes it that much more difficult to cope with the problems associated with parenting (ATD Fourth World, 1991, 1996; Ghate and Hazel, 2002). The stress associated with poverty can undermine parental capacity so that the very survival strategies adopted by parents can 'override attention to individual needs of their children' (Wilson and Herbert, 1978: 186). Nevertheless, most struggle to look after their children as well as they can. An American study of lone mothers details the 'daily battle to be good parents' and 'to create a safe zone where their children could be protected from danger, where educational opportunities were provided, where loving family was available, and where material needs were met' (Holloway et al., 1997: 94). At the same time they juggled their paid work and family responsibilities (see also Kemmer et al., 2001). Another study of low-income African-American mothers describes the 'buffering' and 'enhancing' 'maternal management strategies' they deployed to 'protect children from danger and promote positive, social, cultural and academic development' (Jarrett and Jefferson, 2003: 21).

Personal and social resources

As observed in chapter 3, it is women who carry the main strain of eking out inadequate material resources. In doing so they draw on their personal and, frequently also, social resources. Two words are used over and over again in the poverty literature – in both South and North – to describe the *personal* resources that are drawn on in the struggle to survive: resilience and resourcefulness (see, for instance, Forrest and Kearns, 1999; Narayan, 2000; Hill, 2001). British studies show that getting by on inadequate incomes also requires considerable skill in budgeting, shopping and meal-planning (Christie et al., 2002). This can be time-consuming and tiring: 'You're more tired. I mean . . . that being poor is so much work, your whole life' (woman quoted in Beresford et al., 1999: 94).

For some, the very fact of survival and of managing a low income can be a source of satisfaction and pride (Holloway et al., 1997; Stephenson, 2001). Nevertheless, countless studies also point to the 'danger of painting too rosy a picture of women's resourcefulness that ignores the strain that it places on many of them', particularly in the face of debt (Kempson, 1996: 24). It is often difficult to tap into (often depleted) personal resources when exhausted by the very struggle to get by and when overwhelmed by the feelings of demoralization, hopelessness, powerlessness and lack of control that poverty can engender (Holman, 1998; Ghate and Hazel, 2002). This is particularly the case when poverty is associated with ill health, as it frequently is (Marsh and Rowlingson, 2002; Vegeris and Perry, 2003). Personal coping mechanisms, such as smoking, can themselves undermine health (Graham, 1993; Dundee Anti-Poverty Forum, 2003).

Personal resources may be buttressed by the *social* resources that derive from strong social networks (Ghate and Hazel, 2002). An American anthropologist points to 'ongoing ethnographic work in marginalized communities [which] continues to demonstrate that "social capital" and civic engagement among the poor remain at an all-time high, *if* they are measured in terms of community residents' participation in the open-ended social networks that have long been a critical component of self-help strategies among the poor' (Hyatt, 2001: 207, emphasis in original). The continued importance of such networks is also underlined by cross-European and British studies (Chanan, 1992; Lupton, 2003a; Mumford and Power, 2003). Their strength and nature vary between societies and locales, reflecting factors such as the nature of welfare state institutions and the stability of the local population (Paugam, 1996; Steinert and Pilgram, 2003). They also fluctuate over time in response to economic and social change and individual life courses, and they vary between ethnic groups (Ghate and Hazel, 2002; Gallie and Paugam, 2002; Pettigrew, 2003). In some areas, they may be very weak and/or largely confined to kin (Dean and Shah, 2002). Again, it is mainly women who sustain social networks among kin and more widely in deprived communities (Forrest and Kearns, 1999; Daly and Leonard, 2002). The ability to draw on social resources may depend in part on 'fitting in' with local norms and expectations, which can use up resources (time, energy and money) as well as generate them.[2] This illustrates how agency is exercised in the context of personal and social relations, which can be both enabling and constraining.

Social networks – relatives, friends and neighbours – can provide emotional and material support (Ghate and Hazel, 2002; McKendrick et al., 2003b). *Emotional* support can help people to cope psychologically with the strains of poverty (Scott et al., 1999). *Material* support – in cash or kind – can be crucial to getting by (Bourdieu, 1999; Farrell and O'Connor, 2003). Kempson et al. found that 'help in kind was more acceptable than cash, and exchange was better than a loan which, in turn, was better than a gift'. This reflected 'the need both to save face and to maintain independence' (1994: 151). A pattern of reciprocity is revealed here and in other studies (Jordan et al., 1992; Holloway et al., 1997). In other words, drawing on social resources is an *active* process of giving as well as receiving. Reciprocal help can also be in the form of mutual aid – the exchange of practical help between members of social networks. According to C. C. Williams and Windebank the exchange of *unpaid* work is not as common in poorer areas as is sometimes assumed (2000). Instead, they found a preference for *paid* informal work as a means of giving and receiving help. Work for cash in this context, they suggest, represents 'monetized mutual aid', which lubricates social networks (2002: 245).

Child-care is one form of unpaid work that *is* quite commonly exchanged between women (Holloway et al., 1997; Dean and Shah, 2002). In some cases, it represents an example of how people can draw on social resources to help them get out of poverty. In this instance, social resources provide 'social leverage' rather than 'social support' (Buck et al., 2002: 61). Networks, as a source of cultural resources, can also, in certain circumstances, be helpful in finding work, particularly informal work (MacDonald, 1994; C. C. Williams and Windebank, 1998a, 1998b). However, as we saw in chapter 4, this is not necessarily the case where such networks are cut off from the world of work. Indeed, it has been suggested that such networks can hold people back from getting out of poverty, either because of 'downward-levelling' peer pressure (Forrest and Kearns,1999: 9) or because of a reluctance to move to find work for fear of losing the very social networks that help them get by (Walker and Shaw, 1998; Johnston et al., 2000). As we shall see, networks can also help people move into the 'getting organized' agency quadrant.

Augmenting resources through the informal economy

Although drawing on social networks can represent a means of 'resource augmentation' (Gilliat, 2001), the reciprocal nature of many such transactions means that any augmentation of material resources is largely temporary – albeit still important. Kempson et al.'s study identifies a hierarchy of acceptability among the available options for maximizing disposable income. At the top came finding a full-time (or better-paid) job, which we will discuss under 'getting out'. 'At the other extreme, turning to crime was generally acknowledged to be a last resort, while begging was so unacceptable that it did not appear on the list at all' (1994: 275).[3] Casual work in the informal economy came somewhere in the middle. Because of the rules governing social assistance, in welfare states such work often involves fraud. As we shall see, some analysts interpret this as an expression of 'everyday resistance'. However, it is more commonly understood as a form of getting by – part of a, frequently complex, process of 'income packaging'.

Edin and Lein distinguish between three kinds of work done by welfare recipients: that which is 'reported' to the welfare agency; 'unreported' work, either in the formal sector or, more typically, for cash in the informal sector; and illegal 'underground' work, such as drugs-dealing (1996: 258). The welfare literature tends to focus on unreported work. Not surprisingly, it is difficult to gauge the extent to which welfare recipients engage in it to augment their benefits.

Some UK analysts follow Ray Pahl in arguing that a combination of a depletion of work-related social networks, a lack of necessary skills and resources and fear of being reported means that informal work is not typically used as a 'coping strategy' by welfare recipients (Pahl, 1984: 251). C. C. Williams and Windebank, in particular, take this position. Moreover, some of the unreported work that is done in deprived areas is, they suggest, motivated less by financial reward than by a desire to cement social networks and help others (2002). However, they also note that the extent to which across Europe

> the unemployed are using the paid informal sector to 'get by' economically in particular cities and regions is dependent upon the supply of informal labour, the demand for goods and services and the 'institutional' structure of the locality, in terms of both the structure of networks which can organise informal work and the extent of sanctions against informal work. (1998b: 152; see also Saraceno, 2002)

Thus research conducted in particular locations can reveal high levels of unreported work, even if this is not universal (Jordan et al., 1992; Lupton, 2003a). The combination of inadequate benefit levels and labour market deregulation has, it is argued, encouraged resort to unreported work to get by (Jordan and Redley, 1994; Dean, 1998). In this context, unreported work, within the limits set by need rather than greed, can take on a certain legitimacy and is often condoned in deprived areas and sometimes among the wider population also (Elam and Thomas, 1997; Rowlingson et al., 1997). Although illegal, augmenting inadequate benefit payments through unreported work, within the context of limited economic choices, does represent the exercise of agency and a degree of resourcefulness and enterprise (Jencks, 1992). In some cases it can represent a step towards 'getting out' through legitimate self-employment (MacDonald, 1994).

Those who undertake unreported work often justify it with reference to family responsibilities (MacDonald, 1994; Gilliom, 2001). In most cases, it is seen as the only way to get by and meet basic needs when benefits are inadequate and the rules discourage reporting (Dean and Melrose, 1996, 1997; Rowlingson et al., 1997; C. C. Williams and Windebank, 1998b). This is particularly the case for women (C. C. Williams and Windebank, 1998a). Doing unreported work thus represents another, albeit illegal, element of the survival strategies deployed in getting by (Edin and Lein, 1996).

Not surprisingly, even less is known about the extent to which people in poverty turn to 'underground' work in order to get by. Kempson et al.'s (1994) study of seventy-four low-income families found three mothers had shoplifted for food and one was contemplating prostitution – described elsewhere as a 'crime of poverty' (Cook, 1997: 36). A review of qualitative studies of African-American youth growing up in deprived neighbourhoods identifies 'hustling' (stealing) as a 'vital' survival strategy on the streets (Jarrett, 2003: 164). Depending on the target, some underground work, like unrecorded work, is condoned as 'part and parcel of survival' in deprived areas (Wood and Vamplew, 1999: 47). More anti-social forms of underground work such as drug-dealing are less tolerated and are often a source of 'huge worry' among parents, but they offer a tempting alternative to a breadline existence for some young men in particular (Mumford and Power, 2003: 212; Davies, 1998; Bourdieu 1999).

Getting (Back) at

In some cases, such underground work is represented as a form of *resistance,* labelled 'getting (back) at' in the *every-day–political* quadrant of figure 6.1. One study in a deprived inner-city ward found that some young men moved into 'anti-employment careers', fuelled by 'an ethos which involved not merely the rejection of conformist values, such as work commitment, but an inversion of such values, so that the ability to prosper without recourse to waged employment became a virtue in itself' (Craine, 1997: 147). The anger and despair felt by some who feel trapped in poverty can explode into destructive forms of agency against themselves, their families or neighbourhoods or the wider society (ATD Fourth World, 1991; Davies, 1998; Furbey, 1999). (In some instances, dependence on hard drugs represents an attempt to 'blank out' the despair of poverty (MacDonald and Marsh, 2002: 36). While serious misuse is likely to impair *strategic* agency, a study of drug-users in Merseyside underlines the hard work (or *everyday* agency) involved in securing a daily drugs supply in the informal economy (Buchanan and Young, 2000).)

These kinds of activity are not, however, the forms of resistance typically identified in the poverty literature. Instead, the focus tends to be mainly on unrecorded work, dealing with welfare authorities and, to a lesser extent, the rejection of negative labelling, as forms of 'everyday resistance'. The term 'everyday resistance' was coined by James C. Scott, in the context of peasant economies, to refer to 'the ordinary weapons of relatively powerless groups: foot dragging, dissimulation, false compliance, pilfering, feigned ignorance, slander, arson, sabotage, and so forth' (1985: 29). Unlike more institutionalized forms of resistance, it is 'informal, often covert, and concerned largely with immediate, de facto gains' at the expense of the more powerful rather than with 'public and symbolic goals' (1985: 33). The goal is not political change but 'nearly always survival and persistence' (1985: 301). It is animated by 'the fusion of self-interest and resistance': for example, 'when a peasant hides part of his crop to avoid paying taxes, he is both filling his stomach and depriving the state of grain' (1985: 295). Although the action is typically individual rather than collective, it is frequently facilitated by 'networks of understanding and practice' (1985: 300).

Some analysts have used the notion of everyday resistance to interpret the ways in which some social assistance recipients engage with the benefits system, particularly through violation of the regulations. Two examples in the US are studies by Catherine P. Kingfisher (1996) and John Gilliom (2001). Kingfisher's study of women welfare recipients in Michigan identified two 'strategies for dealing with the various inadequacies of public relief' (1996: 38). The more common and more obviously resistant in nature was 'manipulation'. This might involve lying and concealment or 'impression management' – for instance, feigning ignorance or a compliant attitude. A number of the women expressed their resistance in the claim that the welfare system itself encouraged dishonesty. The alternative strategy was 'hyper-truth', which typically 'entailed an exaggerated playing by the rules' (1996: 40). This might also involve fighting to receive one's full entitlements or, less frequently, policing those regarded as 'welfare cheats'.[4]

Gilliom writes of how low-income mothers in Appalachian Ohio pursue 'generations-old' 'survival strategies' (such as cutting hair and selling things), which have been 'illegalized' under the welfare regulations and surveillance regime. He contends that, when they refuse to desist,

> in the face of a massive governmental effort to detect and stop them, they are rejecting and challenging, often by evasion, the political commands of the state. Although the mothers focus their attention on survival, not 'politics', they clearly offer significant symbolic and material opposition to policy mandates . . . It is a pattern of resistance that has clear results: desperately needed material benefits; the maintenance of a zone of autonomy in the face of dependency of life on welfare; the sustenance of a shared identity of mothering [as they support each other as mothers]; and the undermining of the surveillance mission itself. (2001: 100, 112)

In the UK, Bill Jordan has been the main proponent of the 'social security fraud as everyday resistance' thesis. He suggests that such fraud represents more than 'isolated individual action' because through deprived communities' networks 'a culture of resistance develops . . . with its own . . . everyday practices of opposition to the official system of enforcement'. Such resistance, he argues, enables 'the poor to compensate themselves to some extent for their exclusion from the benefits of the mainstream community' (1996: 157). Through unreported work, 'poor people hit back' at the oppressive administrative requirements of the social security system (Jordan and Redley, 1994: 172). They interpret the rules – sometimes ingeniously – 'in such a way as to give themselves room for manoeuvre in managing their resources' (Jordan, 1993: 213; Jordan et al., 1992). Their 'practices of resistance and discourses of dissent' also represent 'attempts to gain autonomy and dignity' (Jordan, 1993: 216).

Hartley Dean, on the other hand, questions the existence of a 'culture of resistance'. His own research with thirty-five fraudulent social security recipients found seven 'for whom fiddling was, in one sense, a self-consciously subversive activity and a reaction to a sense of oppression', but they were not 'especially radical figures' (Dean and Melrose, 1997: 108). In most cases there was still a strong attachment to the work ethic (Dean and Melrose, 1996; Dean, 1998). Mac-Donald found a similar commitment to paid work among those doing 'fiddly jobs', together with a desire 'to maintain their self-identity [and] self-respect' (1994: 526). Dean concludes, from his study, that

> to the extent that respondents were engaged in acts of resistance, it was a very conservative form of resistance: many did feel that their legitimate expectations of the welfare state had been betrayed and believed this justified their dishonesty, but they aspired not to challenge the state, but to get a 'proper' job and achieve a decent but modest living standard. (2002: 216)

Nevertheless, he concedes that, in the minority of 'neighbourhoods or locations in which there are no formal labour market opportunities, engagement with alternative survival strategies may cease to represent isolated acts of resistance and become the norm' (2002: 216). Whether or not this happens, the implication is that 'isolated acts of resistance' in the form of 'alternative survival strategies' do already occur. What is difficult to determine, as J. C. Scott (1985) acknowledges in relation to peasant society, is the extent to which actions, which are primarily about survival, do also reflect more political motives of resistance. Evidence of resentment against a social security system that is perceived to be unfair among many who are willing to 'fiddle' the system suggests that an *element* at least of resistance is not that uncommon, even if survival is the primary motive (Dean and Taylor-Gooby, 1992; Rowlingson et al., 1997). Just occasionally, such resentment leads to more organized and overtly political forms of resistance, such as against the intensification of compulsion in the British benefits system (Rogers, 2002).

As Dean and Melrose (1997) warn, there may be an element of romanticizing or wishful thinking among radicals who interpret social security fraud as everyday resistance. Gilliat (2001), in contrast, argues that such coping strategies represent not resistance but a form of adaptation, which ultimately serves to reproduce the socio-economic order. More generally, some radical socio-legal scholars are sceptical as to the political significance of individual 'very small acts of defiance' and 'near futile incidents of coping and surviving' that rarely effect change (Handler, 1992: 724; McCann and March, 1996: 223). Where unsuccessful, they query whether such actions are, as sometimes claimed, 'likely to enhance dignity and encourage agency' (McCann and March, 1996: 227).

Nevertheless, however insignificant in the broader political scheme of things, acts of everyday resistance do challenge the equation of poverty with passivity and lack of agency. They represent a means whereby people in poverty can assert their rejection of the constraints imposed by the socioeconomic order and 'get (back) at' those with power over them, even if they do not directly challenge that order or power. Broad constructions of 'the political', rooted in feminism and a Foucauldian concern with the micro-processes of power relations, do see significance in everyday 'micropolitics' or 'micro-resistance', even if the actions involved are not motivated by or fail to achieve political goals (Mann, 1997: 234–6; Leonard, 1997: 95). Furthermore, such constructions point to how everyday resistance can also operate more explicitly at the symbolic/cultural level through 'discursive dissent' (Bleiker, 2003: 43). An example is when people in poverty resist the processes of Othering described in chapter 5 and struggle to sustain a sense of self. This is illustrated by a poetry collection based on a creative writing project involving people in poverty. A number of the poems represent moving assertions of human dignity in the face of indifference and disrespect (Prest, 2000). Examples of 'discursive dissent' in the literature also illustrate how resistance is frequently combined with accommodation of dominant values (Broughton, 2003; Dean, 2003a).

Getting Out

A mix of resistance and accommodation can likewise sometimes be found in attitudes towards 'getting out' of poverty

– in the *personal–strategic* quadrant of figure 6.1. Kingfisher describes how female welfare recipients in her study tended to resist the dominant presumption that low-paid work is better than welfare. At the same time, they subscribed to 'mainstream models of achievement and success' in their belief that education 'was crucial to "making it"' (1996: 27). Employment and education are widely seen as the main routes for getting out of poverty. Individuals exercise their strategic agency in negotiating these routes but the routes themselves are forged by structural and cultural factors, which can assist or obstruct the exercise of that agency.

The interplay between agency and structure in shaping individual poverty trajectories is at the heart of contemporary theorization of the dynamics of poverty (Leisering and Walker, 1998; Leisering and Leibfried, 1999). In other words, movements in and out of poverty are a product of both individual actions (taken by poor and non-poor) on the one hand and economic and social processes and Government policies on the other. This theorization represents one of the most important recent developments in the conceptualization of poverty. It has been facilitated in some countries by the establishment of longitudinal data sets that track the same individuals over time. These panel surveys help to identify those for whom poverty is a long-term sentence (and who are therefore particularly vulnerable to the Othering processes described in the previous chapter). At the same time, they reveal high rates of entry into and exit from poverty each year in a range of industrialized countries, with many more people experiencing poverty over a period of time than are identified by snapshot measures.[5] Movement *out of* poverty tends to be associated with changes in employment status or rewards, although improvements in labour market position do not necessarily spell an escape from poverty (Heady, 1997; Jenkins and Rigg, 2001). It is typically short-range and is not always sustained, as people frequently move in and out of poverty – their trajectories constricted by a 'rubber band' model of poverty dynamics (Jenkins, 2000: 115). Women appear to be held particularly tightly by the rubber band (Ruspini, 1998).

This kind of research has been hailed as encouraging a perception of people in poverty as active agents in their own lives

(Vobruba, 2000). However, empirical studies into poverty dynamics tend to be quantitative, providing an overall picture at the impersonal macro level. Important as they are, what such studies cannot do is provide insights into the ways in which these dynamics reflect the agency of the individuals involved or the toll that the struggle to get out of poverty can take on them. From the perspective of understanding agency and its relationship to structure and culture, studies at the micro level are therefore important in complementing longitudinal macro-level poverty surveys.

People in poverty, not surprisingly, differ in the extent to which they deploy strategic agency (through, for example, education or job-search) to try to escape – or help their children escape – poverty. Individuals' exercise of such agency reflects the personal and other resources they can draw on, their social and cultural environment and their perceptions of the (gendered) structural opportunities and constraints they face (Edin and Lein, 1996; Duncan, 1999; Long et al., 2002). The configuration of these factors faced by people in poverty can stifle aspiration among both adults and children and instil fatalism.[6] Politicians talk of the need to tackle 'this poverty of ambition' (DSS, 1999: 45). Nevertheless, research indicates that ambition is not always absent. Often aspirations are centred on children and their education, as parents express a determination and pursue strategies to ensure their children are not condemned to a future of poverty.[7] Yet, the educational odds tend to be stacked against their children, albeit less so in more equal societies such as Sweden.

Education can be important also for *adults* in poverty: both in strengthening a sense of agency and in opening up employment opportunities (Duncan, 1999; John et al., 2001). Research does not support the popular stereotype of passive welfare recipients, content to sink back into a 'culture of dependency'. Instead, most are keen to find paid work, either immediately or, in the case of lone mothers, when their children are older, and some overcome considerable obstacles to do so (Holloway et al., 1997; Mumford and Power, 2003). Job-search can be a demoralizing and costly business. As the journalist Polly Toynbee discovered when she tried living on the minimum wage, 'poor people travel miles they cannot afford, chasing jobs that come and go on the unexplained whim of unseen people they never meet' (2003: 97). The authors of a cross-EU study suggest that 'the resource constraints on job search imposed by lack of income' may explain why they found that poverty itself constitutes an obstacle to unemployed people getting jobs (Gallie et al., 2003: 28). Nevertheless, UK research indicates that 'the vast majority of claimants are engaged in a determined, continuing struggle to find work', even if at times a minority are too discouraged to persevere (Walker and Shaw, 1998: 241). In some instances, people demonstrate their commitment through part-time work or volunteering as possible stepping stones back into full-time employment or by struggling to build up an income from self-employment or through studying (MacDonald 1996a, 1996b; Elam and Thomas, 1997).

Where personal and other resources are limited and the barriers are high, strategic agency is likely to be relatively weak. Sometimes, the daily strain of getting by means that the future is 'framed in terms of hours and days rather than years' (Daly and Leonard, 2002: 117; Wardhaugh and Jones, 1999). Coping can sap the energy needed to seek ways out of poverty. The greater the hardship, the lower morale and self-confidence are likely to be; the lower the morale and self-confidence, the harder it is to escape poverty through paid employment (Marsh and Rowlingson, 2002; Gallie et al., 2003). Morale and motivation to seek ways out of poverty are all too often further undermined by poor health – physical and mental – which acts as an obstacle to paid work for many (Marsh et al., 2001; Kasparova et al., 2003). The 'traumatic' life histories of some workless 'people with multiple problems and needs' can make the most modest work ambitions difficult to achieve (Dean, 2003a: 441). Domestic violence can also check the ability of women in poverty to exercise strategic agency, particularly where male partners sabotage their attempts to get out of poverty (Edin and Lein, 1996; Tolman and Raphael, 2000).

Furthermore, cultural norms and 'gendered moral rationalities', mentioned earlier, can mean that some mothers exercise their agency not to pursue paid employment so long as they feel that their primary responsibility is to care for their children full-time (Duncan and Edwards, 1999; Smith, 2002).

Such norms may particularly influence attitudes towards mothers' employment in minority ethnic communities of Pakistani and Bangladeshi origin (Pettigrew, 2003). In other cases, and more generally, the structural barriers – including lack of suitable employment opportunities, child-care facilities and transport – can be too great. There are also some communities – such as those in rural North America studied by Cynthia Duncan (1999) – where rigid class and race divisions and powerful vested interests can block the exits from poverty almost completely.

Paid work may be the main route out of poverty but it is no panacea. Low pay can continue to spell poverty, especially for women (Dickens and Ellwood, 2001; Bradshaw et al., 2003). The transition from benefits to (often insecure) work can sometimes exacerbate poverty and debt. More complex financial arrangements can make the process of juggling an inadequate income more difficult in low-paid work than on benefit (Farrell and O'Connor, 2003). Income volatility arising from frequent changes in main source of income is associated with severe and persistent poverty among children (Adelman et al., 2003). It is not surprising, therefore, that sometimes taking paid work feels too risky (Walker and Shaw, 1998; Mumford and Power, 2003). Nevertheless, the psychological benefits of paid work encourage some people not to 'give in' even when worse off than on benefit (Farrell and O'Connor, 2003: 61).

Lone mothers who take up paid employment typically face a complex balancing act, which carries its own strains of getting by (Holloway et al., 1997; Kemmer et al., 2001; Mason, 2003). In some instances, this balancing act involves a conflict between paid work and their children's education. Research reveals the strain and time squeeze that conflicting policy pressures – to take paid work and to be more involved in their children's education – can place on lone mothers (Standing, 1999). Moreover, efforts to get out of poverty through paid work can be at the expense of helping to improve their children's educational performance (Newman and Chin, 2003). Thus mothers' exercise of strategic agency to get out of poverty may have perverse longer-term consequences for their children's ability to get out or stay out of poverty. This is one example of how the personal strategic agency exercised by people in poverty has to be understood in the context of the structural, cultural and policy constraints and (more limited) opportunities that they face.

Getting Organized

Structural and cultural context also shapes the opportunities for the exercise of collective strategic agency in the *political/citizenship–strategic* quadrant of figure 6.1. Macro-level surveys suggest that poverty and deprivation tend to be associated with lower levels of political and civic activity and collective action than among the wider population (Verba et al., 1993, 1995; Attwood et al., 2003). This, together with the Othering processes described in chapter 5, can encourage an image of 'the poor' as lacking 'political agency, the capacity for activism' (Goode and Maskovsky, 2001: 14). Yet, micro-level evidence from some deprived communities illuminates the extent to which some residents do 'get organized' and act as citizens, despite the many obstacles they face. Such action may be in the form of collective self-help (often representing more organized forms of 'getting by') or of more directly political activities, with frequent overlap between the two. Less common, though not unknown, is political action beyond local communities. Before reviewing some of the evidence of such collective agency, it is important, first, to be aware of the very real constraints upon it.

The constraints on getting organized

Subjectivities and identities One of the most fundamental constraints concerns subjectivity and identity – 'people's understanding and accounting of their own experiences . . . [and] their sense of being and belonging', which are key elements in the new paradigm of welfare, mentioned earlier (F. Williams and Popay, 1999: 179). Attention to subjectivities and identities allows for greater complexity and fluidity than the kind of rigid, totalizing, ascribed social categories – such as 'the poor' or 'welfare claimants' – referred to in chapter 5 (Taylor, 1998; F. Williams, 1998). Nevertheless, social categories can impinge on subjectivity and identity and, when accepted, can provide the basis for 'categorical identity', namely a sense of *belonging* or sameness with others, which contributes to a sense of collective identity (Taylor, 1998: 340). For instance, a category such as 'disabled' can function, on the one hand, to classify and sometimes stigmatize but can also, on the other, provide the basis for positive collective identification. Categorical identity, in turn, contributes to 'ontological identity' or a person's unique *sense of self* or *being* (Taylor, 1998).

The two, interrelated, elements of identity, together with subjectivity, are pivotal to the development of political agency (Hunter, 2003). How people understand their situation shapes their responses to it (Chamberlayne and Rustin, 1999). The capacity for political agency requires a degree of 'self-esteem – a stable sense of one's own separate identity and a confidence that one is worthy to participate in political life' (James, 1992: 60). Collective political agency and the articulation of collective political claims call also for a sense of shared categorical identity with others in a similar position.

The experience of poverty and of processes of Othering frequently injures identity (ontological and categorical) and subjectivity. The damage to self-esteem, and therefore one's sense of self, was discussed in the previous chapter. With regard to subjectivity, where the problem of poverty is typically individualized and blamed on 'the poor' by politicians and the media, it is likely that those affected will make sense of their situation in individualized, often self-blaming, terms and look for individual rather than collective solutions (Lyon-Callo, 2001; Dean, 2003a). This is particularly likely to be so in English-speaking liberal welfare states where popular 'individual blame explanations' of poverty are widespread (van Oorschot and Halman, 2000: 12). Where there is a sense of hopelessness, powerlessness and fatalism in the face of apparently intractable problems, it can be difficult to believe that real change is possible, so that agency can be limited to 'getting by' (Policy Action Team 9, 1999; Gilliat, 2001; Buhaenko et al., 2003). Not surprisingly, a sense of political efficacy, considered important to political participation, is generally weaker among poorer and less educated groups and in the poorest neighbourhoods (Parry et al., 1992; Cohen and

Dawson, 1993). An American study, however, suggests that this does not necessarily indicate a lack of self-belief in personal political capacities; rather it can reflect negative experiences of welfare institutions, which translate into lack of confidence in the responsiveness of political institutions more generally (Soss, 1999).

In addition, a number of interrelated factors work against the development of a shared categorical identity among people in poverty. First, 'poor' may not even be part of a person's *individual* identity or may be less salient than other identifiers such as gender, ethnicity or age. Poverty represents a socio-economic position rather than a personal defining characteristic (Warah, 2000). The category 'poor', ascribed by more powerful others (politicians, professionals, media, researchers), effaces the subjectivities and identities of individuals so labelled (Beresford and Croft, 1995; Taylor, 1998). As a report on a project developing partnerships between people in poverty and professionals observes, the former 'do not want to be seen only in the context of their poverty' (ATD Fourth World, 1996: 60). Insofar as 'poor' *is* internalized as an element of individual identity, given its negative connotations, a person is unlikely to want to own it publicly. There is little research directly addressing this issue *from the perspective of identity*. One study of a New York soup kitchen did, though, analyse how users spoke about 'the poor' in such as way as to distance themselves from the category in the construction of their own identities (Cohen, 1997).

Second, the ascription of a category such as 'poor' does not necessarily translate into a sense of *collective* categorical identity (Jenkins, 1996). In this case, this is partly because of the increasingly heterogeneous and fragmented nature of the group so categorized, together with the poverty dynamics discussed earlier. To the extent that there is a (semi-)permanent or well-established group in poverty, 'what they share – and what identifies them as a class – is only the economic plight that statistics and everyday life monotonously reproduce' (Coole, 1996: 21). Iris Young suggests that Sartre's notion of 'seriality', a weaker form of collectivity than a group with a shared identity, is helpful in making sense of such a 'structural positioning that conditions the possibility of social agents without constituting their identities' or assuming common qualities (2000: 100; 1994). In other words, seriality implies a common condition but not a shared identity or characteristics. People in poverty may thus constitute a serial collectivity, without necessarily having anything in common other than their poverty and societal reactions to it.

Lack of a collective categorical identity as 'poor' also reflects the frequent reluctance to identify with the label, discussed in chapter 5. In the *Poverty First Hand* study, this was given as one explanation for why many people in poverty had not been involved in anti-poverty campaigning (Beresford et al., 1999). Community workers from India were told in Glasgow that 'no one wanted to stand up and say "I'm poor and I'll fight for my rights with other poor people". There was a sense of shame about being poor'. In contrast 'groups such as Gays and people with physical disabilities . . . were proud to rally together and identify with each other' (Thekaekara and Thekaekara, 1994: 21). Such groups (or at least some of their members) have been able to transform a negatively ascribed category into the positive affirmation of categorical identity as the basis for a politics of recognition of their own difference (Young, 1990).

This type of transformation is not readily open to people in poverty, the vast majority of whom would prefer not to be poor. 'Poor' describes a socially stigmatized *lack* of material resources. A lack of this kind does not constitute a solid basis for a shared identity. 'Proud to be poor' is not a banner under which many are likely to march. It is therefore not surprising that poverty does not typically appear to constitute a salient categorical identity for those affected. Collective action is difficult without common identification.

However, there are other categorical identities that can provide the basis for collective action among people in poverty, such as (lone) mothers, pensioners, local residents (Naples, 1998; Waters, 1999). The saliency of any particular identity will vary according to the situation. However, to the extent that it is poverty that is the focus of their action, there may be a danger that organizing solely around particular identities associated with poverty could reinforce divisions between groups in the competition for resources (Beresford et al., 1999). One way people sometimes try to disassociate themselves from the stigma of poverty is to Other those deemed less 'deserving' than themselves (Broughton, 2003; Dundee Anti-Poverty Forum, 2003).

Barriers to getting organized   I have suggested that a reluctance to identify with poverty's stigmatized condition constitutes the most fundamental constraint on getting organized. In addition, people in poverty face a number of practical barriers. Political scientists emphasize the importance of resources – most notably 'material wealth, education and skills' – to political participation (Parry et al., 1992: 64). Verba et al. identify 'the stratification of resources along lines of socioeconomic and other demographic cleavages [as] a principal explanation for the inequalities in participation' revealed in their major study of participation in the US (1995: 288).

The struggle for day-to-day survival, which, as we have seen, can sap people's energy and health, depletes the personal resources available for collective action (ATD Fourth World, 2000a; CoPPP, 2000). Indeed, 'everything that disadvantages a person, either individually or because they are living in a disadvantaged neighbourhood, also makes it harder for him or her to participate in group activities: poor transport, lack of money, lack of safety, depressing environment, lack of facilities, being stuck at home' (Chanan, 1992: 85). In addition, institutional, political and cultural barriers make collective action difficult for those already lacking political resources (Policy Action Team 9, 1999).

Overcoming the constraints

Nevertheless, what is remarkable is the extent to which a minority of people in poverty does overcome the constraints and barriers and 'get organized' to try to effect change, even if not necessarily under the banner of poverty. The very process of coming together in this way can transform subjectivities and identities so that political agency is developed and strengthened (Buhaenko et al., 2003). We will now look separately at collective self-help activities and more explicitly political action, even though the distinction is not always that clear in practice, and then at the gendered nature of such activities.

Collective self-help We have seen how 'getting by' can involve drawing on the social resources of informal social networks. Such networks can provide the soil out of which more organized forms of collective self-help can grow; these, in turn, strengthen the social resources available to people in poverty (Silburn et al., 1999; Hyatt, 2001). A European study of 'local community action' defines it as 'any collective public or quasi-public effort involving the active unpaid participation of inhabitants which addresses the perceived needs of people living in that locality' (Chanan, 1992: 3). Although only a minority was actively involved, the study underlines the 'vital role [played] in improving conditions in disadvantaged localities', a role that could be enhanced with better resourcing (1992: 140). Community development resources can be particularly valuable (Henderson and Salmon, 2001; SCCD, 2001). Typically, activities focus on the needs of children and young people, lack of local amenities, environmental problems and debt.

Local studies similarly attest to the strength and significance of collective self-help activities in some deprived areas (Buhaenko et al., 2003; Lupton, 2003a; Mumford and Power, 2003). According to the report of a British research programme, 'all the studies emphasise resilience in the face of adversity, widespread commitment to community activities, the importance of mutual aid and neighbourhood support networks, and a belief that if anything is going to be achieved it is up to the residents themselves' (Forrest and Kearns, 1999: 13). Collective self-help activities play an important role in the survival strategies of people in poverty world-wide (Castells, 1997; UNDP, 1997). While their extent and nature vary within and between societies, where they do flourish their importance as an expression of collective agency and active citizenship should not be underestimated (Policy Action Team 9, 1999). Moreover, such activities can provide a 'springboard' for engagement with the economic or political 'mainstream' (Burns and Taylor, 1998).

Political action   Although overall levels of political activity are generally relatively low among people in poverty, a major American survey found that 'once active, they do not do less' and indeed tend to give more of their time to campaigns (Verba et al., 1993: 309). Analysis of a British survey suggests a higher rate of political participation among the unemployed or economically inactive compared with the employed than indicated by the political resources (such as education) available to the two groups (Parry et al., 1992). As noted already, the collective political activities of people in poverty may not necessarily be focused on or carried out under the banner of 'poverty'. Nevertheless, there are examples of collective organization around poverty or welfare rights issues.

Although such action does not always figure on the political radar screen, an example of where it has done is in the US. In the 1960s many people in poverty organized under the banner of the National Welfare Rights Organization (NWRO). Since the 1980s and 1990s, there has been something of a resurgence of welfare rights and anti-poverty and low-wage campaigning (Kingfisher, 1996; Waters, 1999). An example is the Kensington Welfare Rights Union, 'a membership organization of poor and homeless people with a program that encompasses neighborhood-based organizing to meet basic needs and national, even global, organizing to address the political and economic structures that produce those needs' (Baptist and Bricker-Jenkins, 2002: 204). It has organized direct action campaigns together with national and international marches and meetings and has generated a national Poor People's Economic Human Rights Campaign (see chapter 7). The assault on welfare rights in the US in the 1990s has also provoked a National Campaign for Jobs and Income Support, which aims to provide a direct voice for those in poverty so as to advance more progressive anti-poverty policies.

Sometimes the very factors that serve to constrain political participation can paradoxically themselves act as spurs to (individual or collective) action. Against the conventional wisdom, a New York study found that 'respondents in the most dire of economic circumstances were *more* likely to be political participants . . . Qualitative responses . . . illustrate how a brush with total destitution and the most desperate of circumstances may mobilize citizens' (Lawless and Fox, 2001: 372, emphasis in original). The very disrespect involved in the process of Othering may, according to Axel Honneth, 'become the motivational impetus for a struggle for recognition', provided 'the means of articulation of a social movement are available' (1995: 138–9; 2003). Even in the absence of a social movement, some people in poverty have seized the opportunity provided to them by voluntary organizations to speak out against disrespectful attitudes and treatment (Russell, 1996; ATD Fourth World, 2000a; CoPPP, 2000).

Gendered action   We saw in chapter 3 how poverty is a gendered phenomenon; so too typically are the kinds of collective action described here. Women initiated the campaigning that led to the NWRO, although men became more dominant once the organization was formalized (Naples, 1998). This is a fairly typical pattern in community action also (Chanan, 1992). Women have nevertheless continued to be at the heart of US welfare rights campaigning, increasingly framing 'welfare as a matter of gender as well as economics' (Abramovitz, 2002: 172).

It is, though, at community level that the gendered nature of collective action among people in poverty is most obvious. Studies in a range of countries consistently find that 'women are often a *driving force in local action*' (Chanan, 1992: 86, emphasis in original; McCoy, 2000). Nancy Naples's study of 'activist mothering' – in which the 'mothering role' is expanded to embrace community activism – has underlined how, as both paid and unpaid activists, women 'establish themselves as central figures in the ongoing survival of their embattled communities' (1998: 3). Susan Hyatt has coined the term 'accidental activism' to describe the process through which poor and working-class 'women who previously did not see themselves as in any way "political" are becoming advocates and agents for social change' (1992: 95). Such activism, she suggests, can be understood as a model of active citizenship (see also Lister, 2003).

Conclusion

The theme of citizenship will be explored further in the next chapter, as it frames the relationship between the agency of people in poverty and questions of voice and rights. The purpose of this chapter has been to argue the importance to the conceptualization of poverty of agency itself – from the everyday level of 'getting by' to the more strategic level of 'getting organized'. It has cited a range of empirical material to demonstrate how people experiencing poverty are actors in their own lives, but within the bounds of frequently formidable and oppressive structural and cultural constraints, which are themselves the product of others' agency. This relationship between agency and structure is pivotal to the contemporary conceptualization of poverty as a dynamic process rather than a fixed state. It can also serve to frame Sen's agency-focused capabilities approach.

A key policy lesson from dynamic poverty research has been greater emphasis on identifying the pivotal points for intervention to enable people to get out of poverty or to prevent them falling into it (Leisering and Walker, 1998; Leisering and Leibfried, 1999). However, where this approach is used to justify the withdrawal of financial support from those out of work, as in the US, the effects can be very damaging (Albelda and Withorn, 2002). Policy must still address structural determinants and their consequences, while it both helps individuals negotiate those pathways open to them and strengthens the various resources they draw on in the everyday struggle to get by (Hills, 2002; C. C. Williams and Windebank, 2003). Policy also has an important role in promoting the citizenship of people in poverty, to which we will now turn.

7
Poverty, Human Rights and Citizenship

Poverty is the principal cause of human rights violations in the world. It also prevents people from assuming not only their duties as individuals, but also their collective duties as citizens, parents, workers and electors.

OHCHR, 1999: para. 9

The World Conference on Human Rights affirms that extreme poverty and social exclusion constitute a violation of human dignity.

UN General Assembly, 1993: para. 25

Poverty is increasingly seen to be a denial of fundamental rights. This is how those affected experience it themselves ... The worse-off individuals and families are, the more of all their civil, political, economic, social and cultural rights they lose. These situations clearly show how indivisible and inter-dependent rights are in daily life.

EAPN, 1999: 3

The human rights framework contributes to the achievement of the objective of enabling all people to be active citizens with rights, expectations and responsibilities.

DfID, 2000b: 1

Poor people lack voice and power.

Narayan et al., 2000: 265

No-one asks our views ... But we are the real experts of our own hopes and aspirations ... We can contribute if you are

prepared to give up a little power to allow us to participate
as partners in our own future, and in the future of the country.
Moraene Roberts, National Poverty Hearing. Russell, 1996: 4

The nexus of (the lack of) human rights, citizenship, voice
and power, illustrated by these quotations, represents the
subject of this chapter. An understanding of poverty in these
terms is located firmly at the relational/symbolic rim of the
poverty wheel. Such an understanding provides a 'pro-poor'
perspective on relations between 'the poor' and the wider
society and political structures. While the implications can be
very concrete, there is also a symbolic resonance that is significant for the conceptualization and politics of poverty. So,
for example, a rights discourse may lay claim to concrete legal
entitlements; but even in the absence of such entitlements it
can generate a symbolic rhetorical force that appeals to the
imagination. An example is President Lula's cry that impoverished young people in Brazil 'are losing the right to dream'
(da Silva, 2003).

From the UN and the World Bank to anti-poverty campaigns, such as the US Poor People's Economic Human Rights
Campaign and the European Anti Poverty Network (EAPN),
the use of elements of this vocabulary – of rights, voice and
power – constitutes an alternative poverty discourse to that
discussed in chapter 5. While these various actors do not
always subscribe to a common interpretation of such terms,
anti-poverty campaigners are deploying them in a political
discourse that serves to link their struggles to wider concerns
about human rights, citizenship and democracy. The chapter
explores the ways in which our understanding of poverty
can be enlarged when it is conceptualized in terms of
diminished human rights and citizenship, lack of voice and
powerlessness.

Human Rights

The equation of extreme poverty with a denial of human
rights was formally affirmed in the 1993 UN Vienna

Declaration on Human Rights. Important influences on UN thinking have been the work of Sen and the 1987 Wresinski Report, adopted by the French Economic and Social Council. Joseph Wresinski was the founder of ATD Fourth World, 'a human rights organisation working in partnership with families experiencing long-term poverty, to develop their potential abilities and to enable them to participate fully in the life of their communities' (ATD Fourth World, 2000a: 56). In line with ATD's philosophy, the report was drafted in consultation with people living in persistent poverty (ATD Fourth World, 1991; Ochoa, 2001). One of its key arguments is that 'as the various insecurities – material, cultural, social and civic – accumulate, they reinforce each other and lead to the loss of fundamental rights' (cited in ATD Fourth World, 1991: 13).

Sen was responsible for providing the conceptual framework for the 2000 UNDP Human Development Report entitled *Human Rights and Human Development*. In the first chapter, he refers to the 'fundamental commitment to promoting the freedom, well-being and dignity of individuals in all societies' that inspires human rights thinking (UNDP, 2000: 19; see also Vizard, 2001). 'Human rights', he argues, are 'ultimately grounded in the importance of freedom for human lives' (UNDP, 2000: 20). Freedom, in this view, is not simply, as new right thinkers would argue, about freedom 'from' coercion and interference. It is a more positive and substantive capability 'to choose a life one has reason to value' (Sen, 1999: 74). Freedom 'to' is shackled by poverty.

Since the Vienna Declaration, the UN has published a number of expert reports on 'human rights and extreme poverty' and a set of draft guidelines on 'a human rights approach to poverty reduction strategies'.[1] The Committee on Economic, Social and Cultural Rights has expressed 'the firm view that poverty constitutes a denial of human rights' (CESCR, 2001: para. 1). According to the OHCHR, a human rights conceptualization of poverty

> leads to more adequate responses to the many facets of poverty . . . It gives due attention to the critical vulnerability and subjective daily assaults on human dignity that accom-

pany poverty. Importantly, it looks not just at resources but also at the capabilities, choices, security and power needed for enjoyment of an adequate standard of living and other fundamental civil, cultural, political and social rights. (www.unhchr.ch/development/pov-02.html)

Two key tenets underpin this statement. First is 'respect for the inherent dignity of all members of the human family which is the foundation of . . . all human rights' (OHCHR, 2002: 42; van Genugten and Perez-Bustillo, 2001). Article 22 of the Universal Declaration of Human Rights states that 'Everyone . . . is entitled to realisation . . . of the economic, social and cultural rights indispensable to his [*sic*] dignity'. It can be the everyday *in*dignities that make poverty so difficult to bear. For instance, poverty activist Willie Baptist tells how the main concern of a group of homeless people in the US was the indignity of having to line up daily to receive a ration of five pieces of toilet paper. 'That infuriated them', he writes; 'it took them beneath any level of dignity they might have' and it was around that indignity, rather than the wider issue of their homelessness, that they were prepared to organize (www.kwru.org/educat/orgmod2.html; see also Warah, 2000).

Second is the notion of the 'indivisibility' and 'interdependence' of human rights – 'the fact that the enjoyment of some rights may be dependent on or contribute to the enjoyment of others' (OHCHR, 2002: 2). Thus, for example, it is difficult to exercise political and civil rights to the full, if hungry or homeless. People do not experience the denial of their rights as bifurcated between civil and political rights on the one hand and socio-economic and cultural rights on the other (Nyamu-Musembi, 2002). The principle is enshrined in the 1976 UN International Covenant on Economic, Social and Cultural Rights. The Covenant's preamble declares that 'the ideal of free human beings enjoying freedom from fear and want can only be achieved if conditions are created whereby everyone may enjoy his [*sic*] economic, social and cultural rights, as well as his civil and political rights'. The principle was later endorsed in the UN Vienna and Copenhagen Declarations and also the report of the European Commission's Expert Group on Fundamental Rights (1999).

A number of other advantages are claimed for a human rights approach to poverty. It implies an 'ethical' or 'moral' claim that can be translated into the duties of others to help realize these rights (Sen, 1999: 229; Pogge, 2002: 46). It strengthens needs-based claims on resources (Ferguson, 1999). This means it can underpin and strengthen the livelihoods framework discussed in chapter 6 (Moser and Norton, 2001). A rights approach supports the demands of people in poverty for their voices to be heard (discussed below). It constructs people in poverty as active and 'legitimate claimants of entitlements' rather than as 'beneficiaries of government largesse' (UNDP, 1997: 96). Rights 'are shaped through actual struggle informed by people's own understandings of what they are entitled to' (Nyamu-Musembi, 2002: 1; Stammers, 1999). A human rights approach thus acknowledges and promotes the agency of people in poverty.

The language of indivisible human rights has proved a valuable mobilizing tool for some groups. In Europe it underpins the anti-poverty and social exclusion strategy propounded by the EAPN (www.eapn.org). More specifically with regard to children, Euronet and others frame their analysis and demands with reference to the UN Convention on the Rights of the Child, which includes 'the right of every child to a standard of living adequate for the child's physical, mental, spiritual, moral and social development' (Ruxton and Bennett, 2002).

Even in the US, where there is not a strong socio-economic rights tradition (despite the 1960s' welfare rights movement), people in poverty and homeless people have now come together in the Poor People's Economic Human Rights Campaign 'to raise the issue of poverty as a human rights violation' (www.kwru.org/ehrc/ehrcfaq.html; Baptist and Bricker-Jenkins, 2002). The campaign has: conducted a number of 'poor people's national marches for economic human rights'; held an 'economic human rights tribunal'; and filed a case against the US Government at the Inter-American Commission of Organization of American States to hold the Government 'accountable for economic human rights abuses being caused by downsizing, poverty and welfare reform' (www.kwru.org). In Canada, 'the human right to food and its application to issues of food poverty is now on the agenda of an emerging . . . food security movement' (Riches, 2002: 660). In the province of Quebec people in poverty were among those who mobilized to achieve 'Law 112', in which are enshrined 'respect of the dignity of human beings' and recognition of rights, creating the potential for a rights-based anti-poverty strategy (International Movement ATD Fourth World, 2003).

Proponents of a human rights perspective argue that its global resonance helps to legitimize claims made in its name (Ferguson, 1999; Moser and Norton, 2001).[2] In fact, with the notable exception of France (in principle at least), Western governments have not generally endorsed an indivisible human rights approach with regard to domestic poverty (Choffé, 2001; Dean, 2002); nor, at a global level, has the World Bank (Maxwell, 2000). Moreover, more sceptical observers highlight the gap between the promise of international human rights instruments and the reality of 'underfulfilment' particularly of socio-economic rights (Pogge, 2002: 91; Townsend and Gordon, 2002). While a human rights discourse performs an important symbolic and mobilizing function and throws new light on the meaning of poverty, the ultimate test of its effectiveness as a *political* tool will be the closing of that gap between promise and reality.

Citizenship

Citizenship rights

In the context of individual nation states, this moves us on to the terrain of citizenship rights, which can be understood as the specific interpretation and concretization of the more abstract and universalizable human rights. Thus, for example, the Poor People's Economic Human Rights Campaign has been described as a commitment to 'struggle to translate the concepts of economic human rights into real programs for real people' (Baptist and Bricker-Jenkins, 2002: 153). As with human rights, the triad of civil, political and social citizenship rights, identified by T. H. Marshall (1950), is indivisible and interdependent (Lister, 1990). These rights, too, can be understood as vital to human dignity and respect (Honneth, 1995, 2003). Poverty pay, for example, can represent an affront to human dignity (Toynbee, 2003). A low-paid worker, involved in a Living Wage Campaign in the UK, challenged a shareholders' meeting at the head office of the bank where he cleans: 'I am asking you for a living wage so that I and my colleagues can have the same dignity as ordinary people' (quoted by Rachel Stevenson in *The Independent*, 31 May 2003).[3] A concern with dignity and respect also animates the more recent notion of cultural citizenship rights, which include the rights to 'symbolic presence and visibility (vs. marginalisation)' and 'dignifying representation (vs. stigmatisation)' (Pakulski, 1997: 80). While such rights are rarely embodied in the form of legal entitlements, the discussion in chapter 5 underlined their potential symbolic significance for people in poverty. The articulation of new forms of citizenship rights, together with struggles to defend and extend existing rights through political action, underlines how claims-making around rights is an active process involving agency.

Although, as we saw in chapter 4, the denial of full citizenship rights is frequently identified as a signifier of social exclusion, it is also important to the conceptualization of poverty (Scott, 1994). This is reflected in how some people with firsthand experience talk about poverty (UKCAP, 1997; Beresford et al., 1999). Historically, in countries such as the UK, US and France, receipt of public assistance meant the forfeit of certain political and/or civil rights. Today, 'the poor' are no longer formally required to forfeit political and civil rights in exchange for social assistance. Nevertheless, poverty and welfare receipt can still mean that these rights are compromised in practice. Homeless people without a fixed address, for example, are unable to vote unless special measures are adopted, as is the case in France (Choffé, 2001; Dean, 1999). As noted earlier, for Ehrenreich the surrender of 'basic civil rights' was the most offensive characteristic of low-waged work, as workers were subject to 'routine indignities' such as handbag searches and drugs-testing (2001: 208–9). In Gilliom's US study of increasingly sophisticated and extensive welfare surveillance techniques, the women he talked to tended to concentrate on 'the degradation and hassle of constant scrutiny' (2001: 67).[4]

Gilliom comments that welfare investigations have generally been designed 'with little attention to the dignity of the client' (2001: 14). Dignified and respectful treatment of welfare state users has been identified as a 'procedural' citizenship right, which regulates 'process' rather than 'outcome'. Procedural rights represent something of 'a hybrid between civil and political rights' (Coote, 1992: 9). They also embrace the accessibility of services and the availability of comprehensible information, which can be crucial in bridging the gap between formal and *de facto* rights faced, in particular, by disadvantaged groups (Goetz and Gaventa, 2001). Forms to claim means-tested assistance, for instance, can be extraordinarily complicated, contributing to imperfect take-up, yet potential claimants are likely to be over-represented among those with a low reading age, lacking 'document literacy' (OECD, 2000). In the digital age, the inability to access information and communication technology also has implications for citizenship (Warschauer, 2003).

Citizenship participation

Citizenship rights derive from membership of a particular society. At the first European Meeting of Citizens Living in Poverty, in 2001, 'participants stressed that they were first and foremost *"citizens"* before being *"people experiencing poverty"*. Citizenship is something to which we all stake a claim and means *"being part of the mainstream of society"*' (EAPN, 2003: 4, emphasis in original). 'Being part of the mainstream of society' involves participation in the social, economic, political, civic and cultural spheres. Poverty inhibits such participation and can lead to second-class citizenship. The Amsterdam Declaration on the Social Quality of Europe, signed by over 800 social scientists, states that:

> to be able to participate, citizens must have access to an acceptable level of economic security and of social inclusion, live in cohesive communities, and be empowered to develop their full potential. In other words, social quality depends on

the extent to which economic, social and political citizenship is enjoyed by all residents of Europe (www.socialquality.nl/declaration.htm).

The Declaration continues with a list of enforceable citizenship rights essential to participation and the achievement of social quality. However, governmental discourses of citizenship today are more likely to emphasize obligations – in particular work obligations – than rights. 'No rights without responsibilities' is a central tenet of the politics of the 'third way' espoused most fervently by New Labour (Giddens, 1998: 65). Yet, as the Wresinski Report underlined, poverty can undermine people's capacity to fulfil their responsibilities as citizens (ATD Fourth World, 1991; Ochoa, 2001). Rights serve to underpin responsibilities (APPGP, 1999; ATD Fourth World, 2000a). In the words of a study of disabled people's citizenship, 'the ability to contribute to or participate in society as a full citizen requires a basic level of access to essential goods, services and facilities' (Knight et al., 2002: 10).

The centrality of participation to the meaning of citizenship indicates how citizenship represents a practice involving agency, as well as a status carrying rights and responsibilities. Political participation is of particular significance given that in the civic republican tradition it was political participation that represented the essence of citizenship. Participation and rights converge in the growing demands, in both North and South, for more accountable and democratic forms of welfare provision in which users have a right to 'a say'.

Voice

A number of political theorists have posited the idea of a basic 'right of participation in decision-making in social, economic, cultural and political life' (Gould, 1988: 212; Janoski, 1998). With regard specifically to poverty, draft UN guidelines declare that

> a human rights approach to poverty reduction . . . requires active and informed participation by the poor in the formulation, implementation and monitoring of poverty reduction

strategies. The international human rights normative framework includes the right to take part in the conduct of public affairs. This is a crucial and complex human right that is inextricably linked to fundamental democratic principles. (OHCHR, 2002: 2)

It is a crucial human and citizenship right because it explicitly recognizes the agency of rights-bearers and underpins the effective realisation of other rights (Gould, 1988; Ferguson, 1999). It goes to the heart of the voicelessness and powerlessness associated with poverty (CoPPP, 2000; Narayan et al., 2000). 'Voice' is about having a 'right to a say' (ATD Fourth World, 2000a: 32). It means being listened to and heard in democratic spaces, as encapsulated in the title of the Commission on Poverty, Participation and Power's report: *Listen Hear: The Right to be Heard* (2000). Listening to marginalized voices can, in turn, be understood as a responsibility of citizenship (Porter, 2000).

In both North and South people in poverty identify lack of voice as critical to understanding their situation (Beresford et al., 1999; Narayan, 2000). It reflects and reinforces the powerlessness of 'the poor', discussed below, and also the processes of objectification and Othering that were the subject of chapter 5 (Beresford and Croft, 1995). Calls for the voices of the marginalized to be heard in policy-making and campaigning are becoming more vocal. For example, the final text of the first European meeting of Citizens Living in Poverty demanded that 'a voice is given to us, citizens who are ourselves faced with poverty and social exclusion, in the whole policy-making process . . . [and that] there is a legal framework that enforces our right of participation' (www.eapn.org).[5] In the UK, a number of organizations that involve people in poverty attempt to promote their voices and place the right to a say at the heart of their campaigning work (Beresford et al., 1999; ATD Fourth World, 2000a). The US Poor People's Economic Human Rights Campaign emphasizes 'the leadership of the poor' in the struggle against poverty (www.kwru.org/educat/orgmod2.html).

In addition to the fundamental plank of participation as a human and citizenship right, the case typically draws on a number of arguments. As an element of social inclusion, participation represents an end in its own right. There is a contradiction when the development of policies to promote social inclusion does not include those who are affected (Howarth et al., 2001). Moreover, it belies attempts to promote more participatory democracy. As Young asserts, 'a democratic public should provide mechanisms for the effective recognition and representation of the distinct voices and perspectives of those of its constituent groups that are oppressed or disadvantaged' (1990: 184).

The process of participation strengthens democracy and the accountability of government. It also enhances people's capacity to act as effective citizens. Experience in the UK indicates that, with support, the experience of participation can enhance the confidence of people in poverty in their ability to speak out and become active citizens (APPGP, 1999; ATD Fourth World, 2000a). In the US, research suggests that involvement in participatory poverty programmes 'encourages more positive orientations toward political involvement' generally (Soss, 1999: 374).

'Insider expertise'

A further argument is that the involvement of people with experience of poverty enhances the effectiveness of anti-poverty campaigning and policy-making (Beresford and Croft, 1995; Robb, 2002). The political and policy-making process is strengthened when the standpoints, perspectives and experiences of affected groups are directly represented (Young, 2000; CEC, 2001). At issue here is a demand for recognition of and respect for the understanding and expertise born of experience alongside those forms of knowledge and expertise that have traditionally been privileged.[6] In the words of the statement from the European Meeting of Citizens Living in Poverty, 'poor citizens must be recognized as experts' (www.eapn.org). The demand reflects a frustration at being treated as 'objects of other people's knowledge, not as authors of their own development – as problems . . . but not as people with views and voices of their own' (Bennett, 1999: 16). As 'people with views' they do not simply want the space to tell their stories and describe what it is like to

be poor but they are also asking for their analysis and prescriptions to be heard.

Participatory research in the South is demonstrating 'poor
people's capacity to analyse and problematize their own experience' (McGee, 2002: 17). In the North, the work of ATD
Fourth World with people in long-term and extreme poverty
testifies to how they 'are capable of thinking for themselves
and have the best knowledge of their own difficulties and
dreams' (ATD Fourth World, 1996: 12). Particularly revealing was a two-year project in France, which aimed to
'produce a new kind of knowledge through the merging of
three different types of knowledge . . . gained through experience . . . action and academic knowledge'. The result was 'a
clearer picture of what constitutes poverty and [of] . . . progressive ways forward in the fight against it (ATD Fourth
World, n.d.: 1). It involved 'personal transformations' and
'letting the intelligence, thought, and points of view of people
living in poverty re-educate society from the inside' (n.d.: 26,
24; Bennett with Roberts, 2004). The Commission on
Poverty, Participation and Power, half of whose members had
direct experience of poverty, represents another attempt at
forging a new form of knowledge out of experiential, academic and professional sources of expertise. Again, through an
'extraordinary process', participants learned, with difficulty,
to respect one another's expertise. The result was a report
that was 'generally seen as offering different insights in a different tone [as] it speaks from the heart and "touches"
people' (del Tufo and Gaster, 2002: 6, 7).

Wresinski told a UNESCO meeting in 1980 that even 'the
best researchers can hardly imagine' the reality – and in particular the constant humiliation – of extreme poverty (cited
in Bennett with Roberts, 2004). Gradually, the need for a
new form of 'poverty knowledge', which incorporates the
'insider expertise' of people in poverty, is gaining acceptance
among some – though by no means all – poverty researchers
(O'Connor, 2001: 293–4; Richardson and Le Grand, 2002:
513). It has been identified as 'a trend within and beyond the
World Bank that is challenging personal, professional, and
institutional norms' (Robb, 2002: 1). The World Bank's
World Development Report 2000/2001 places considerable
emphasis on the need for participatory mechanisms that can

'provide voice to . . . those from poor and excluded segments of society'. It contends that 'the poor are the main actors in the fight against poverty. And they must be brought center stage in designing, implementing, and monitoring antipoverty strategies' (2001: 12).

Voice without influence?

Such 'professions of participatory intent' have become common currency in development discourse (Cornwall, 2000: 11). They are reflected in the UN Copenhagen Declaration, which states that 'people living in poverty and their organizations should be empowered by involving them fully in the setting of targets and in the design, implementation, monitoring and assessment of national strategies and programmes for poverty eradication and community-based development, and ensuring that such programmes reflect their priorities' (1995, para. 28). In the EU, this principle is supposed to inform member states' development of regular National Action Plans on Social Inclusion. The 2003 UK Plan claims that 'the recognition that people with a direct experience of poverty have much to offer a successful anti-poverty strategy is beginning to transform the UK's approach' (DWP, 2003c: 1). Progress is, nevertheless, slow.

The growing acceptance of the principle of participation does not, however, necessarily translate into 'voice with influence' (Gaventa, 2002: 2). There is often a reluctance to accept that 'a human rights perspective on participation means moving beyond and above local-level processes of consultation through to ensuring poor people's participation in broader formal and informal systems of decision-making' (DfID, 2000b: 19). More generally, the literature identifies two main forms of participation. The first creates genuinely democratic and participatory 'spaces for citizen action', in which the role of citizens is transformed from 'users and choosers to makers and shapers' (Cornwall and Gaventa, 2000: 59, 50; Cornwall, 2002). More common, though, are 'instrumental' or 'consumerist/managerialist' approaches, in which agendas are still set from above (Cornwall, 2000; Beresford, 2002). These can too easily become 'devices for managing rather than "hearing" the voices of the poor' (Rademacher and Patel, 2002: 180). One of the clear messages received by the Commission on Poverty, Participation and Power was that 'people experiencing poverty see consultation without commitment, and phoney participation without the power to bring about change, as the ultimate disrespect' (CoPPP, 2000: 18). Lack of feedback on consultation invalidates the process and can leave participants feeling as if they do not matter (Cook, 2002).

Such phoney participation serves to reinforce the distrust that many people in poverty have of the formal political system (Bennett, 1999; ATD Fourth World, 2000a). Not surprisingly, it can mean that people are reluctant to participate when offered the opportunity. It thus represents one of a number of institutional barriers to participation identified by the Commission and others (see also DWP 2003c: annexe F). Professional cultures and practices can mean that participation exercises are experienced as exclusionary (Scottish Executive, 1999). Jargonistic and complex language 'that doesn't connect can simply create another barrier' (CoPPP, 2000: 29). Professional norms of communication and 'articulateness' can intimidate and silence people who feel that they lack the necessary communication skills to participate (Young, 2000: 56; Charlesworth, 2000; Richardson and Le Grand, 2002).

Other barriers stem from the lack of material, personal, cultural and physical resources associated with poverty and from the processes of Othering described in earlier chapters. They include: not having the 'right' clothes; feeling out of place; low self-confidence; lack of information; inadequate access to affordable child-care or transport; poor health or exhaustion; the toll taken by the struggle to survive (Cars et al., 1998; ATD Fourth World, 2000a). Genuine and effective participation requires time, resources and 'capacity-building' for professionals as well as people in poverty (CoPPP, 2000). Participation is a process that has to be nurtured, not a 'quick fix solution' (Farrell, 2003: 1; Cook, 2002). Participation has also to be genuinely voluntary – not another demand that makes people feel even more inadequate if they cannot meet it (Henderson and Salmon, 2001; Toynbee, 2003).

'Power not Pity'

Demands for effective voice and participation are inextricably linked with the question of power. Oxfam conceptualizes poverty as 'a state of powerlessness in which people are unable to exercise their basic human rights or control virtually any aspect of their lives' (Hocking, 2003: 236). In the words of the UNDP, 'reducing poverty depends as much on whether poor people have political power as on their opportunities for economic progress' (2002). Lack of voice is both a symptom of the political powerlessness of people in poverty and a cause of their feelings of powerlessness (Beresford and Croft, 1995; Narayan et al., 2000). Participation takes place within 'policy spaces' that are shaped and permeated by dynamics of power (Cornwall, 2002: 51). Genuine and effective participation involves unsettling these power dynamics in favour of the less powerful (Beresford, 2002; OHCHR, 2002). In contrast, phoney participation can act as a fig-leaf to mask power dynamics, while intensifying the powerlessness experienced by people in poverty (Bachrach and Baratz, 1970; CoPPP, 2000).

Power is important too to understanding the nature of human and citizenship rights. Power relations mediate the construction and exercise of rights, yet rights can, at the same time, provide people in poverty with a weapon for challenging inequalities in power (Stammers, 1999; Cornwall, 2002). According to the UN Committee on Economic, Social and Cultural Rights, 'while the common theme underlying poor people's experiences is one of powerlessness, human rights . . . can help to equalize the distribution and exercise of power within and between societies' (CESCR, 2001: para. 6). Power also frames the other dimensions of poverty we have discussed. From the structural divisions and processes described in chapters 3 and 4, through the relational/symbolic process of Othering (chapter 5), to the various resources that people in poverty can draw on to exercise agency and the constraints they face (chapter 6), issues of power are pivotal. It is not surprising therefore that powerlessness and lack of control over the conditions of one's life are a recurrent theme in the narratives of people in poverty in both North and

South (Holman, 1998; Narayan, 2000; Mumford and Power, 2003).

'Poverty', writes Kincaid, 'involves a particular sort of powerlessness, an inability to control the circumstances of one's life in the face of more powerful groups in society' (1973: 171). Two interrelated aspects of power are at play in this 'particular sort of powerlessness': power 'to' and power 'over' (Kabeer, 2000a: 29–30). Power 'to' is about the 'generative' capacity to achieve desired outcomes; power 'over' represents the 'hierarchical' ability of a group or individual to exert their will over others (Giddens, 1991: 211–14). There is also a third aspect of power: the unspoken assumptions that legitimate the existing order through an invisible process of 'non-decision-making', which keeps challenges to that order off the political agenda (Bachrach and Baratz, 1970: 44; Lukes, 1974).

Hierarchical and unspoken processes of power sculpt the experience of poverty in both its material and relational/symbolic aspects (Stammers, 1999). They also constrain the ability of people in poverty to exercise the power 'to'. This is frequently manifest in psychological feelings of powerlessness (Narayan et al., 2000). The effects are insidious. Not only can powerlessness, in its various forms, circumscribe what people in poverty are able to *do* in all the dimensions portrayed in figure 6.1. It can also affect what they *think* and *feel* so as to cramp their worldview and stunt their aspirations for something better, individually and collectively (Lukes, 1974; Hoggett, 2001).

Empowerment

The answer to the powerlessness associated with poverty is commonly held to be 'empowerment'. The discourse of empowerment is particularly dominant in the development and community renewal fields. It is, though, a chameleon 'feel-good' term that means different things to different people in different contexts, reflecting, in part, which meaning(s) of power inflect its articulation (Mayo and Craig, 1995). 'Once redolent with the struggles of the oppressed for voice, rights and recognition, it is now used by some as a shorthand for an agenda of economic and institutional reform, largely instigated and driven by supranational institutions' (Cornwall, 2000: 73). In a context of widening inequality, such top-down approaches tend to be about empowering the powerless to adjust to the consequences of economic restructuring, without addressing underlying socio-economic and power structures (Mayo, 2004). The model is frequently one of consumer rather than citizen power in which choice masquerades as power.

At local community level, if empowerment is limited to strengthening the self-confidence and capacity for action of some individuals, it might not benefit the community as a whole or might even exacerbate community divisions at the expense of the most marginalized (Taylor et al., 2000; Henderson and Salmon, 2001). Nevertheless, individual empowerment can release the capacity 'to make strategic life choices and to participate in the processes of decision-making which help to frame such choices' (Kabeer, 2003: 3). In more transformative understandings, such individual empowerment opens up the potential for collective political/citizenship strategic agency, which in turn can further empower both individuals and groups. It is 'not something that can be done to people, but something people do by and for themselves', albeit often with the support of professionals, notably community development workers (Cornwall, 2000: 33; Mayo, 2004). Community development is, in part, 'about changing power structures to remove the barriers that prevent people from participating in the issues that affect their lives' (SCCD, 2001: 5). As a member of the Manchester and Salford participatory Community Pride Initiative observes, 'people may have been disempowered, but they are finding new ways of organising themselves – they're not sitting down, they're getting on' through involvement in local government decision-making (www.oxfamgb.org/ukpp/heard/compride.htm). In doing so, they are enhancing their power 'to' effect change. Nevertheless, ultimately, transformative change will require also a shift in hierarchical power relations.

Conclusion

The struggles of some individuals and groups in poverty to claim more power over their lives is illustrative of the demand for 'power not pity',[7] as articulated by the Poor People's Economic Human Rights Campaign. The conceptualization of poverty in terms of human rights, citizenship, voice and powerlessness strengthens the analysis of poverty. It also reinforces earlier arguments about the agency of people in poverty and the constraints that relative powerlessness places on that agency. It points to rights-based and participatory approaches to anti-poverty policies. But it also does more. By drawing on the narratives of people in poverty themselves, it opens up a new way of thinking about the politics of poverty. This will be a central focus of the concluding chapter.

Conclusion: From Concept to Politics

The focus of this book has been the *concept* of poverty. Its main purpose has been to deepen our understanding of what poverty means both for the millions who suffer its pain and indignities daily and for the wider society. This concluding chapter is divided into three main sections. The first reviews a number of key themes. The second considers some broad implications for research and policy that have been touched on in the previous chapters. The final section returns to the poverty wheel in figure 0.2 and argues for a reconceptualization of the politics of poverty that combines the material and the relational/symbolic in an integrated politics of redistribution and recognition&respect.

Key Themes

The relationship between concepts, definitions and measures was illustrated in figure 0.1. I have argued, on the one hand, for a fairly narrow, focused *definition* of poverty that distinguishes clearly between the states of poverty and non-poverty and, on the other, for a broad *conceptualization* that better captures the multifarious ways in which poverty is experienced. The kind of definition favoured in chapter 1 was a relative one, but in the context of a critical discussion of the traditional absolute–relative dichotomy. 'Absolute' and 'relative', I suggested, represent not two distinct kinds of poverty but alternative constructions of poverty rooted in different understandings of the nature of human needs. A fairly narrowly focused definition best underpins measures designed to estimate the incidence of poverty. However, on its own, it would represent but a thin portrayal of the reality of poverty. Hence the importance of a focus on broader conceptualizations. The conceptualization offered here has attempted to provide a richer understanding in two main ways. First, at its heart is a bi-focal understanding of poverty as a relational/symbolic as well as a material phenomenon. Second, it has located the study of poverty within a wider social scientific framework, using concepts such as 'well-being', 'human flourishing', 'social quality', 'capabilities', 'social divisions', 'human rights', 'citizenship' and 'democracy'.

Structure and agency

Definitions of poverty carry implicit explanations for its existence and incidence. These tend to locate the causes of poverty in either the individual or the wider society and to attribute it to individual or collective agency on the one hand or to luck or fate on the other (van Oorschot and Halman, 2000). Individual agency-based explanations focus on what people in poverty do or do not do; societal or structuralist explanations can turn the spotlight on what people in more powerful positions do or do not do and on the cumulative impact of their actions at a systemic level. Although the causes of poverty have not been discussed in depth here, the relationship between structure and agency has been a key theme in the exposition of various aspects of the meaning of poverty.

The structural perspective was central to the discussion of inequality and social divisions in chapter 3. Poverty and inequality are intertwined globally and within individual nation states, so that more unequal societies tend to be scarred by more widespread poverty. Poverty is also shaped by structured social divisions of social class, gender, 'race' and disability and by spatial divisions. These divisions, in turn, mediate individuals' passage through the life-course. Structural inequalities simultaneously reflect and are reflected in inequalities of power and agency. Chapter 7 described how people in poverty frequently describe their situation in terms of powerlessness and lack of control over the conditions of their lives. Inequalities of power manifest themselves at both the material and the relational/symbolic level. More powerful actors control the wages, benefits, services and opportunities available to people in poverty. They also have the power to construct 'the poor' as Other through words, images and deeds, as we saw in chapter 5.

Despite structural and cultural constraints, people in poverty do exercise agency as actors in their own lives – from the everyday struggle of 'getting by', through instances of 'getting (back) at' the more powerful or 'everyday resistance' and attempts to 'get out' and stay out of poverty, to more collective forms of 'getting organized' and demands for participation in decision-making that affects their lives. Those who subscribe to individualistic agency-based explanations of poverty draw the conclusion that individuals are responsible for the poverty they experience. The issue of the agency of 'the poor' has thus tended to be trapped in disputes about whether their own actions bring about and perpetuate their poverty. The alternative view, espoused here, is that, while the actions of individuals in poverty may on occasion be a contributory factor, the underlying causes of poverty are to be found in the wider society. We need to pay more attention to the positive exercise of agency by people in poverty. This cannot, though, be divorced from their severely disadvantaged structural position or from the exercise of agency by more powerful actors, which helps to perpetuate that structural position. The latter is highlighted in those formulations of the concept of social exclusion that problematize the agency implied by the active verb 'to exclude' from which the term stems.

Dynamics and process

One of the claims made for the concept of social exclusion is that it encourages a more dynamic analysis than do traditional formulations of poverty. In addition to the exercise of agency, a dynamic analysis is concerned with *processes*, in terms of both individual trajectories and wider societal forces.

This is contrasted with a traditional focus on *outcomes* as manifest in poverty and its effects. However, the study of poverty itself has, in recent years, adopted a more dynamic approach. There is increasing dissatisfaction with static snapshots of poverty and growing awareness of how time affects measurement (chapter 2). Many more people experience poverty over time than are in poverty at any one measurement point, as longitudinal studies are revealing. However, while some people may experience only one or two brief spells of poverty, others are trapped for years, if not a lifetime, or move frequently in and out of poverty over many years, without ever enjoying genuine security. Others remain unscathed throughout their lives.

As noted in chapter 6, this interest in poverty dynamics is underpinned by a theorization of poverty that emphasizes the interplay between agency and structure in shaping individual trajectories. The discussion of agency in that chapter deliberately used active terms, such as 'getting by' and 'getting out', in order to underline how coping with poverty is an active process. The discussion of rights in chapter 7 noted how a human rights approach constructs people in poverty as active claimants of rights, who increasingly are demanding a voice in shaping the way specific rights are forged. Such constructions contrast with the growing tendency, for example among British politicians, to depict those out of work as 'passive' recipients of welfare. This portrayal of welfare recipients as passive members of a 'dependency culture' or 'underclass' is one of the more damaging examples of how the 'non-poor' Other 'the poor', even though, over time, the two are not necessarily totally fixed or distinct groups. Those in severe and persistent poverty are most vulnerable to this process of Othering. Again, the notion of 'Other*ing*' conveys how the idea of 'the poor' as Other refers not to an inherent state but to an ongoing process of social construction, differentiation and demarcation.

Discourses

The underlying premise of the discussion of Othering in chapter 5 was the importance of dominant discourses of poverty. Their significance lies in the power of language and images to label and stigmatize marginalized social groups, with implications for how they are treated by officials, professionals, politicians and their fellow citizens. The way the 'non-poor' talk about 'the poor' is often demeaning and disrespectful. It is not only the more pejorative terms, such as the 'underclass', that are harmful, but the historical and contemporary connotations of the 'p' words of 'poor' and 'poverty' render them problematic also.

Social exclusion has emerged in recent years as a dominant poverty discourse. There is some disagreement as to whether it avoids the derogatory overtones of existing discourses. This is, in part, because, when deployed politically, it comprises a number of competing discourses with very different implications (Levitas, 1998, 2000). We also do not know what people in poverty themselves think of the term. The one piece of research hitherto to explore in depth the meaning of social exclusion with those who experience it did not ask them explicitly whether they considered it a helpful term (Richardson and Le Grand, 2002). Experience suggests it is not a label that people in poverty readily apply to themselves.

An alternative discourse is beginning to be deployed by a range of organizations – from organizations of people in poverty themselves to the UN. It is a language of human rights, citizenship, power and voice. Translated into positive demands, this discourse helps to link struggles against poverty to a wider politics around democracy, human rights and citizenship.

Firsthand perspectives and expertise

This alternative discourse is an example of how our understanding of poverty is enhanced, if we listen to what the people experiencing it have to say. This is a lesson that has been learned initially in the development context, but is beginning slowly to be taken on board in the North also. I have attempted to apply the lesson to the writing of this book, drawing, where I can, on more participatory forms of research and on the reports of organizations that actively involve people in poverty. Accounts by people in poverty of the contempt and disrespect with which they are treated and the sense of shame and worthlessness this can engender have helped me to understand better the relational/symbolic dimensions of poverty. Although, inevitably, writing a book about poverty from the perspective of affluence involves a degree of objectification of a group more objectified than most, the emphasis on the perspectives, expertise and agency of people in poverty represents an attempt to accord due recognition to their subjectivity. This, in turn, has implications for research, policy-making and the politics of poverty.

Research and Policy

Research

Participatory approaches to poverty research have been mentioned at a number of points in the preceding chapters. As noted in chapter 2, their influence has hitherto been greatest in the development context, although some examples can be found in the North (Bennett with Roberts, 2004). Participatory research comes in various forms, reflecting different degrees and kinds of participation. At one level it is about ensuring that the views of people in poverty as research subjects find expression in the writing up of research findings so that their perspectives are adequately reflected and can inform policy (Robb, 2002). At another level, it is about involving people in poverty in the research process itself. This implies varying degrees of control at various stages of the research process and varying degrees of influence over the analysis and writing up of findings. In both cases, it is about treating people in poverty as subjects rather than as objects from whom data or colourful quotes are simply extracted (Bennett with Roberts, 2004). The difficulties are not to be underestimated. Nevertheless, if it is accepted that people with experience of poverty have a particular 'insider expertise', then it is sensible, as well as consistent with a concern with social inclusion, to draw on that expertise in the research process. Moreover, the more general arguments around respect, citizenship and voice, articulated earlier, can also be applied to researching poverty (Lister and Beresford, 2000).

The treatment of people in poverty as the objects or sub-jects of research is, in part, an issue of research ethics. This was highlighted in Corden's account of a study of a deprived area, the local media reporting of which provoked an angry reaction from residents who did not want themselves or their neighbourhood to be labelled as 'poor' (see chapter 5). Corden (1996) writes of her ethical dilemma. On the one hand, she felt obliged to her funders and the wider society to draw attention to the deprivation and exclusion experienced in the area. On the other hand was her desire to respect the participants' wish to have the strengths of the area and its residents, rather than their weaknesses, highlighted.

Participatory research into poverty is typically (though not necessarily) qualitative, thereby enabling people to talk about what poverty means to them. However, much research into poverty is quantitative, aimed at measuring the extent and depth of poverty and changes over time, together with its prevalence among different groups, relationship with social divisions, geographical incidence and longer-term effects. Chapter 2 provided a brief account of the main debates around poverty measurement. The conclusion reached was that, as measurement techniques become ever more sophisti-cated, the limitations of any single measure have become more apparent and therefore 'triangulation' – the combina-tion of a range of methods – is preferable.

The main implication for research of the conceptualization of poverty developed here is that, essential as quantitative studies are, there needs to be a greater emphasis on comple-menting them with open-ended qualitative research, if we are to understand what poverty means to those experiencing it.[1] This would include exploration of the relational/symbolic as well as the material dimensions of poverty and of discourses of poverty from the perspectives of both people with experi-ence of poverty and those with no such experience.

Two specific examples of where macro-level quantitative research could usefully be complemented by micro-level qual-itative research were suggested earlier. One concerned the development of quantitative indicators of poverty and depri-vation (Bennett and Roche, 2000; Hacourt, 2003). The other was in the area of poverty dynamics, where it was argued that we need a better understanding of the ways in which individuals exercise agency in the attempt to 'get out' of poverty and the difficulties they may encounter. Indeed, the discussion of agency in chapter 6 suggests a rich research agenda (see also McKendrick et al., 2003a). One example would be more systematic research in the North into how people 'get by', using the sustainable livelihoods and resources/assets-management framework developed in the South (Long et al., 2002; Rakodi with Lloyd-Jones, 2002). The deployment of this framework has been recommended in an official UK review of the literature on low-income families (Millar and Ridge, 2001). Another example would be more research focused specifically on the ways in which people in poverty 'get organized' and the barriers they face.

Policy

Poverty research is one possible influence on policy, although it would be naïve to assume that research findings are necessarily translated into policy. Policy responses to poverty reflect wider political considerations. Within this broader political context, policy responses are shaped by the conceptualization, definition and measurement of poverty, together with the explanations implicit in them. It is not appropriate to spell out detailed policy lessons here, not least because these will differ according to national policy contexts.[2] Instead, I will sketch out some broad policy implications, alluded to in earlier chapters.

A common thread running through a number of my arguments has been the need to embed anti-poverty policy within wider policy debates. The rationale is not only to underline how poverty overlaps with other policy issues but also, more importantly, to engage the general population by combating the tendency to residualize the issue of poverty. A similar point was made in a major New Policy Institute/Fabian Society report, which argued for a 'positive vision . . . of a socially inclusive society' at the heart of its blueprint for a social inclusion strategy. 'One important advantage of this approach', the authors assert, 'is that the result is a social inclusion strategy for everyone, rather than just a means for dealing with the problems of some "other" group with whom the majority of the people do not identify' (Howarth et al., 2001: 21).

Their suggested vision is 'built around the notion of the citizen, and specifically, what exactly it is the citizen can expect from society' in terms of minimum income and service standards (Howarth et al., 2001: 21). This accords with a number of messages from previous chapters. Most obviously, chapter 7 pointed to the importance of rights-based policies that strengthen the citizenship of all members of society and, through more participatory approaches to policy-making and politics, reinvigorate democracy. A human rights perspective points to a right to a decent standard of living consistent with human dignity, as acknowledged in various EC statements (Veit-Wilson, 1998). Citizenship would also be strengthened by the integration of anti-poverty policies with gender, 'race', disability and age equality and anti-discrimination strategies, as argued for in chapter 3. Such social divisions cut across those of social class, creating possible coalitions of interest between 'poor' and 'non-poor'. Furthermore, the idea of a 'positive' vision resonates with the case made in chapter 1 for greater emphasis on the kind of life we want all members of society to be able to achieve, as encapsulated in notions such as 'well-being', 'human flourishing', 'quality of life' and 'social quality'.

We saw in chapter 1 how the work of capability theorists such as Sen and Nussbaum contributes to such an approach. It also fits well with the analysis, in chapter 6, of the ways in which people actively manage poverty and attempt to improve their situation, using the different kinds of resources available to them. Development policy increasingly is aimed at strengthening the capabilities of people in poverty to achieve a decent and sustainable livelihood, through the enhancement of a range of resources. Although it is not an approach that can be neatly translated into the context of industrialized welfare states, because of the very different institutional context, it is possible that there are, nevertheless, some useful lessons for policy-makers in these welfare states (Long et al., 2002).

The livelihoods framework suggests a rather different conceptualization of the notion of 'active' anti-poverty policies to those that have become fashionable recently among politicians. For them, the 'active–passive' dichotomy is shorthand for prioritizing 'welfare-to-work' type policies over improving the living standards of people not in paid work. While formal paid work has a crucial role to play in any anti-poverty strategy (provided that it is work at a decent wage), the notion of 'active' anti-poverty policies suggested by my approach would have a broader focus. It would aim at nourishing the agency of people in poverty through investment in the range of resources (particularly financial, personal and social) that they draw on to 'get by' and to 'get out' of poverty. It would aim to 'legitimize or improve the livelihoods options' of people in poverty (Hocking, 2003: 242). This would include, where appropriate, acknowledgement of the important role that unpaid work (caring, community action and voluntary work) and informal paid work can play in people's lives (Darton et al., 2003; C. C. Williams and Windebank, 2003). It would also place emphasis on *prevention* – the need for policies that secure the livelihoods and enhance the capabilities of those at risk of poverty so as to minimize the number who fall into poverty in the first place. Such an approach is consistent with some (though not all) of the policies pursued by the UK Government.[3] It could also be incorporated within a social exclusion framework of the kind elaborated in chapter 4 and within Sen's capability model (discussed in chapter 1).

In addition to broad policy frameworks, many of my earlier arguments have implications for *how* policy is developed and implemented. Chapter 5's analysis of the processes of Othering carries important lessons for how the media represent people in poverty. It also underlines the significance of respectful treatment of people in poverty by the officials and professionals who have considerable power over their lives (Buhaenko et al., 2003). At a more macro-policy level, the less that people in poverty are divided off from the wider society, for instance through the means-testing of benefits and services, the less policy will reinforce Othering processes. More positively, it will also 'furnish citizens with *basic capabilities* according to the principle of *equal concern and respect*, thereby placing them on a more or less equal footing in respect to their ability to act as autonomous citizens' (Rothstein, 1998: 157, emphasis in original). Finally, as argued in chapter 7, people in poverty, who want to, should be able to participate effectively in the development of policies that affect their lives, thereby enhancing their voice and political power. This brings us to the closely related question of the politics of poverty.

A Politics of Redistribution and of Recognition&Respect

At the outset I emphasized the political and moral claims that poverty makes – or should make – on the wider society and indeed, in a global context, on the international community. The conceptualization, definition and measurement of poverty all have political implications and reflect political positions. By 'political' I do not refer to party politics, although political parties do tend to be divided in their approaches to poverty. Instead, I am concerned with the more general 'capacity of social agents, agencies and institutions to maintain or transform their environment, social or physical . . . expressed in all the activities of cooperation, negotiation and struggle over the use and distribution of resources', and over symbolic representations (Held, 1987: 275, 277).

The poverty wheel in figure 0.2 provides a framework for re-conceptualizing the struggles that constitute the politics of poverty. I shall argue that the politics of poverty can be helpfully understood as a politics of *redistribution* at the material hub of the wheel and as a politics of *recognition&respect* at its relational/symbolic rim. Again, this is a way of integrating the issue of poverty into wider contemporary political and theoretical debates, associated, most notably, with the work of the political theorist Nancy Fraser. Fraser roots the politics of redistribution in the struggle against socio-economic injustice and the politics of recognition in the struggle against cultural or symbolic injustice. The former has long underpinned poverty politics, which has often been waged around whether, how and to what extent material resources should be redistributed to those in poverty. The application of the latter to poverty politics is more unusual but follows from the conceptualization developed here. It also reflects a central theme of Sennett's thesis on respect: 'the relation between respect and inequality' (Sennett, 2003: xvi).

In figure 0.2 the hub of the wheel is expressed as a material core of 'unacceptable hardship'. The extent and depth of that hardship, and the suffering it entails, represent a damning indictment of governments and the non-poor citizens who elect them in far too many affluent societies. Although poverty is not synonymous with inequality, it is, as argued in chapter 3, rooted in the same socio-economic structures and processes of polarization. It is not very fashionable to argue for the redistribution of resources from the better-off to those at the bottom of the socio-economic hierarchy. Nevertheless, the case for redistribution in savagely unequal societies such as the UK is as strong as, if not stronger than, ever. Inequality of such magnitude is not inevitable (T. Atkinson, 2002). The bottom line is that 'the poor' do not have enough money or other necessary resources. Paid work (in either the formal or informal economy) is not, as we have seen, a guaranteed passport out of hardship. It then follows that the only way to eradicate poverty is to redistribute resources from those who have much more than they need to those who have less than they need to live with dignity. Moreover, as notions of global justice and citizenship gain currency, the case for redistribution at the global level has also to be heard.

Moving out to the relational-symbolic rim of the wheel brings us to the politics of recognition&respect. Although the literature talks of a politics of 'recognition', I have added 'respect' to reflect the language used by people in poverty themselves. Indeed, Fraser mentions disrespect as one example of 'cultural or symbolic injustice': 'Nonrecognition (being rendered invisible via the authoritative representational, communicative, and interpretative practices of one's culture); and disrespect (being routinely maligned or disparaged in stereotypic public cultural representations and/or in everyday life interactions)' (Fraser, 1997: 14). This formulation encapsulates well the processes of Othering analysed in chapter 5. As we have seen, the politics of poverty is increasingly being couched in a non-materialist discourse of voice, respect, and rights in some quarters – in other words, a politics of recognition&respect. A politics of recognition is, however, typically identified with the assertion of group difference and identity – by women, lesbians and gays, racialized groups and disabled people. People in poverty do not want to be treated as different. Instead, their struggle is for recognition of their common humanity and citizenship and the equal worth that flows from that. This underpins what is also a struggle for recognition of agency and political voice (Phillips, 2003).

Although she does not write about poverty, Fraser's articulation of a politics of recognition is helpful here.[4] She dismisses as misleading its common equation with identity politics. The appropriate form of recognition claim depends on the nature of the misrecognition: 'in cases where misrecognition involves denying ... common humanity ... the remedy is universalist recognition' (2003: 46). She treats misrecognition as a question of social status subordination and injustice, rather than of identity: 'What requires recognition is not group-specific identity but rather the status of group members as full partners in social interaction' (2000: 113). This she terms 'participatory parity' (2003). The obstacles to parity of participation are both cultural and material.

In this model, recognition and redistribution do not relate to separate domains of the cultural and the economic but represent two dimensions of, and perspectives on, social justice that are applicable to both, interconnected, domains. Fraser (2003) contends that the struggle for social justice requires the integration of a politics of recognition and redistribution. The conceptualization of poverty developed here leads to the same conclusion. People in poverty are denied participatory parity because of material deprivation; processes of Othering; the infringement of their human and citizenship rights; lack of voice; and relative powerlessness. The struggle for social justice has to involve both redistribution and recognition&respect.

A dual politics of poverty of redistribution and recognition&respect flows from the conceptualization developed in this book. Our understanding of and attitude towards poverty, together with our determination to do something about it, reflect the ways in which we conceptualize it – implicitly or explicitly. My aim has been to provide a conceptualization which deepens our understanding of poverty and supports the struggles of both 'poor' and 'non-poor' against poverty and the suffering it causes.

Notes

Introduction

1 $2 a day is one of a number of international income poverty
   lines applied by the World Bank. The underlying methodology
   has been criticized as underestimating the extent of global
   poverty (Townsend and Gordon, 2002). The debate is summarized in UNDP (2003: 42). The EU and UK figures refer to
   those living below 60 per cent of national median income. Since
   the 2002 Barcelona Summit, the EU has described this as 'at risk
   from poverty'.
2 Some of these issues are dealt with more fully by Alcock (forthcoming) and Deacon (2002, 2003).

Chapter 1 Defining Poverty

1 Nevertheless, some of the indicators used to monitor progress
   in tackling poverty – for instance, educational attainment – are
   arguably measures of 'capability deprivation' rather than of
   poverty as such.
2 For a fuller account of the various explanations of poverty see:
   Holman (1978); Townsend (1979, 1993); George and Howards
   (1991); Alcock (forthcoming); Deacon (2002, 2003).

Chapter 2   Measuring Poverty

1   The following sources provide helpful overviews of measurement issues: *Journal of Social Policy* 16 (2), Nolan and Whelan (1996) and T. Atkinson et al. (2002). For a discussion of area-based indices of deprivation, which are not discussed here, see Tunstall and Lupton (2003).

Chapter 3   Inequality, Social Divisions and the Differential Experience of Poverty

1   The notion of gendered individualization, together with how it is addressed in policy debates in a number of European countries, is discussed in *Social Policy & Society* (2004).

Chapter 4   Poverty and Social Exclusion

1   Among key texts are: Room (1995, 1999); Levitas (1998); Byrne (1999); Gordon and Townsend (2000: chs. 15–17); Percy-Smith (2000); Hills et al. (2002).
2   See also Rodgers et al. (1995); Bhalla and Lapeyre (1999); *IDS Bulletin* (1998); Clert (1999); Kabeer (2000b); Room (2000); Sen (2000) and, for a more critical account, Jackson (1999).
3   A fourth, more critical, paradigm, which analyses social exclusion in the context of class relations within global capitalism, might also be identified (Allen, 1998; Byrne, 1999; Castells, 2000).
4   Although definitions vary, in this context social capital refers to the networks, relationships, norms and values that link people together.
5   The 'community experts' were 'residents of low-income social housing areas themselves, who have some experience of social exclusion', as well as 'wider community links and a representative role for people in their neighbourhoods' (Richardson and Le Grand, 2002: 497).
6   The empirical conflation of paid and unpaid work, as in the CASE study, while giving due value to the latter is not necessarily the answer, as it elides the different implications for economic status of the two activities. Arguably voluntary and care work might better be treated as indicators of integration into social networks.

Chapter 5 Discourses of Poverty: From Othering to Respect

1 See, for example, Ross's analysis of how the rhetoric deployed in US Supreme Court decisions 'conceptually segregates' 'the poor' as 'different and deviant' (1991: 1540–1). Veit-Wilson identifies a number of poverty discourses that, he argues, underlie the various policy positions adopted in different countries (1998, 2004).

2 Marx used similar language to describe the very lowest social strata or 'lumpen-proletariat' (Mann, 1994; Coole, 1996).

3 © *The Independent*. The author and publisher gratefully acknowledge permission to reproduce this copyright material.

4 Much of the UK evidence is summarized in Lister (1996); see also Marshall et al. (1996), Walker with Howard (2000) and, for a more agnostic assessment, MacDonald (1997), whose more recent work questions its appropriateness in relation to young people in a very deprived area (MacDonald and Marsh, 2001). Evidence regarding the US can be found in, for instance, Katz (1989) and Jencks (1992).

5 See Schram (1995); Handler and Hasenfeld (1997); O'Connor (2001); Goode and Maskovsky (2001); Schram and Soss (2002).

6 The World Bank *Voices of the Poor* study found that this is particularly the case in the former Soviet bloc where the shame associated with poverty is especially intense (Narayan, 2000).

7 Leisering and Leibfried (1999: ch. 7) also provide an account of the changing images of poverty in the post-war Federal Republic.

8 The *Big Issue* is a street magazine sold by people who are or have been homeless or vulnerably housed.

Chapter 6 Poverty and Agency: From Getting By to Getting Organized

1 Examples of the influence of this framework on thinking about poverty in the North can be found in Room (2000); Hill (2001); Piachaud (2002) and Steinert and Pilgram (2003). A narrower notion of (financial) assets underpins the fashionable idea of 'asset-based welfare'.

2 I am grateful to Jan Flaherty for this point.

3 A recurrent theme in an edited collection on begging is how it represents a 'sort of work' or 'informal economic activity' at the bottom of the hierarchy of survival strategies and one which carries considerable risk (H. Dean, 1999).

4 The everyday resistance of people in poverty within the legal system has similarly been identified by a number of critical socio-legal studies (summarized and critiqued in McCann and March, 1996).

5 See, for instance, Whelan et al. (2000); Bradbury et al. (2001); DWP (2003d); Kuchler and Goebel, (2003); Layte and Whelan (2003) and, in relation to 'severe' child poverty, Adelman et al. (2003).

6 See Shropshire and Middleton (1999); Layte et al. (2000); Ermisch et al. (2001); Ridge (2002); Adelman et al. (2003); Buhaenko et al. (2003); Vegeris and Perry (2003); Yeandle et al. (2003).

7 See Holloway et al. (1997); Daly and Leonard (2002); Jarrett and Jefferson (2003); McKendrick et al. (2003b); Mumford and Power (2003); Yeandle et al. (2003).

Chapter 7 Poverty, Human Rights and Citizenship

1 These and other relevant UN documents can be found at www.unhchr.ch.

2 It should, however, be noted that the legitimacy of the idea of *universal* human rights is not uncontested (see Sen, 1999, ch. 10; Lister 2003: 215 for a discussion).

3 © *The Independent*. The author and publisher gratefully acknowledge permission to reproduce this copyright material.

4 However, although their privacy rights were at stake, this group of women did not generally use a rights discourse to express their resentment. Gilliom is consequently sceptical of its value for welfare claimants. For a discussion of some of the arguments against rights-based approaches see H. Dean (2002).

5 Euronet also emphasizes the need specifically to listen to children in poverty (Ruxton and Bennett, 2002).

6 This demand echoes those of new social movements who have challenged traditional definitions of what counts as knowledge (Wainwright, 2003).

7 The phrase comes from Willie Baptist of the Kensington Welfare Rights Union and Poor People's Economic Human Rights Campaign. <www.kwru.org/educat/orgmod2.html>.

Conclusion: From Concept to Politics

1   Lupton (2003b) has also argued for better integration between quantitative and qualitative research into neighbourhood poverty and its effects on individuals.

2   UK readers might find the following sources helpful for discussions about possible future policy directions: Howarth et al. (2001); Darton et al. (2003); JRF (2004); Alcock (forthcoming).

3   For an exposition of these policies see the annual *Opportunity for All* reports published by the DWP and the biennial National Action Plans (Incl.) produced by all Member States for the European Commission.

4   Fraser's formulation involves rejection of an alternative 'identity model' of recognition propounded by recognition theorists such as Charles Taylor (1992) and Axel Honneth (1995). Although such a model is inappropriate for people in poverty, the emphasis placed by Taylor and Honneth on the psychological injury caused by misrecognition should not be lost sight of (see ch. 5). Moreover, Honneth (2003) argues that claims for respect are integral to demands for redistribution.

References

Abramovitz, M. 2002: Learning from the history of poor and working class women's activism. In Albelda and Withorn, 2002.

Adelman, L. 2000: Childhood poverty. *Benefits*, 29, 11–15.

Adelman, L., Middleton, S. and Ashworth, K. 2003: *Britain's Poorest Children*. London: Save the Children.

Adorno, T. W. 1973: *Negative Dialectics*. London/New York: Routledge.

Ahmad, W. and Craig, G. 2003: 'Race' and social welfare. In P. Alcock, A. Erskine and M. May (eds), *The Student's Companion to Social Policy*, 2nd edn. Oxford: Blackwell Publishers.

Albelda, R. and Withorn, A. (eds) 2002: *Lost Ground*, Cambridge, Mass.: South End Press.

Alcock, P. forthcoming: *Understanding Poverty*, 3rd edn. Basingstoke: Palgrave.

Allen, J. 1998: Europe of the neighbourhoods: class, citizenship and welfare regimes. In A. Madanipour et al., 1998.

Allen, J., Cars, G. and Madanipour, A. 1998: Introduction. In Madanipour et al., 1998.

Anderson, D. n.d.: *The Unmentionable Face of Poverty in the Nineties*. London: Social Affairs Unit.

Andress, H. J. and Schulte, K. 1998: Poverty risks and the life-cycle. In H. J. Andress (ed.), *Empirical Poverty Research in Comparative Perspective*. Aldershot: Ashgate.

Anthias, F. 2001: The concept of 'social division' and theorising social stratification. *Sociology* 35 (4), 835–54.

Apospori, E. and Millar, J. (eds) 2003: *The Dynamics of Social Exclusion in Europe*. Cheltenham/Northampton, Mass.: Edward Elgar.

APPGP 1999: *Policy, Poverty and Participation.* London: APPGP.

Askonas, P. and Stewart, A. (eds) 2000: *Social Inclusion.* Basingstoke: Macmillan.

ATD Fourth World 1991: *The Wresinski Approach: The Poorest – Partners in Democracy.* Paris: Fourth World Publications.

ATD Fourth World 1995: *This is How We Live: Listening to the Poorest Families.* Landover, Md.: Fourth World Publications.

ATD Fourth World 1996: *'Talk with Us, Not at Us'.* London: ATD Fourth World.

ATD Fourth World 2000a: *Participation Works.* London: ATD Fourth World.

ATD Fourth World 2000b: 'Art speaks' to the Secretary of State. *Fourth World Journal,* Autumn, 1–2.

ATD Fourth World. n.d.: *Introducing the Knowledge of People Living in Poverty into an Academic Environment.* London: ATD Fourth World.

Atkinson, A. B. 1989: *Poverty and Social Security.* Hemel Hempstead: Harvester Wheatsheaf.

Atkinson, A. B. 1990: *Comparing Poverty Rates Internationally.* Discussion Paper, WSP/53, London: STICERD.

Atkinson, A. B. 1998: Social exclusion, poverty and unemployment. In A. B. Atkinson and J. Hills (eds), *Exclusion, Employment and Opportunity.* CASEpaper 4. London: CASE.

Atkinson, R. and Davoudi, S. 2000: The concept of social exclusion in the EU. *Journal of Common Market Studies,* 38 (3), 427–48.

Atkinson, R. and Kintrea, K. 2001: Disentangling area effects evidence from deprived and non-deprived neighbourhoods. *Urban Studies,* 38 (12), 2277–98.

Atkinson, T. 2002: Is rising income inequality inevitable? In Townsend and Gordon, 2002.

Atkinson, T., Cantillon, B., Marlier, E. and Nolan, B. 2002: *Social Indicators: The EU and Social Exclusion.* Oxford: Oxford University Press.

Attwood, C., Singh, G., Prime, D. and Creasey, R. 2003: *2001 Home Office Citizenship Survey.* London: Home Office.

Baars, J., Knipscheer, K., Thomése, F. and Walker, A. 1997: Conclusion. In Beck et al., 1997.

Bachrach, P. and Baratz, M. S. 1970: *Power and Poverty.* New York/London: Oxford University Press.

Baptist, W. and Bricker-Jenkins, M. 2002: A view from the bottom: poor people and their allies respond to welfare reform. In Albelda and Withorn, 2002.

Barclay, P. 1996: Foreword to Kempson, 1996.

Barnes, H. and Baldwin, S. 1999: Social security, poverty and disability. In J. Ditch (ed.), *Introduction to Social Security*, London: Routledge.

Barnes, M., Heady, C., Middleton, S., Millar, J., Papadopoulos, F. and Tsakloglou, P. 2002: *Poverty and Social Exclusion in Europe.* Cheltenham/Northampton, Mass.: Edward Elgar.

Barry, B. 2002: Social exclusion, social isolation, and the distribution of income. In Hills et al., 2002.

Baulch, B. 1996a: The new poverty agenda. *IDS Bulletin*, 27 (1), 1–10.

Baulch, B. 1996b: Neglected trade-offs in poverty measurement. *IDS Bulletin*, 27 (1), 36–42.

Bauman, Z. 1998. *Work, Consumerism and the New Poor*, Buckingham/Philadelphia: Open University Press.

Beall, J. 2002: Living in the present, investing in the future. In Rakodi with Lloyd-Jones, 2002.

Bebbington, A. 1999: Capitals and Capabilities. *World Development*, 27 (12), 2021–44.

Beck, U. and Beck-Gernsheim, E. 2002: *Individualization.* London: Sage.

Beck, W., van der Maesen, L. and Walker, A. (eds) 1997: *The Social Quality of Europe.* The Hague/London/Boston: Kluwer Law International.

Beck, W., van der Maesen, L., Thomése, F. and Walker, A. (eds) 2001: *Social Quality: A Vision for Europe.* The Hague/London/ Boston: Kluwer Law International.

Becker, S. 1997: *Responding to Poverty.* London/New York: Longman.

Begg, I. and Berghman, J. 2002: EU social (exclusion) policy revisited. *Journal of European Social Policy*, 12 (3), 179–94.

Benefits 2002: *The Cycle of Deprivation*, 10 (3).

Bennett, F. 1999: *Influencing Policy in Partnership with the Poorest.* London: ATD Fourth World.

Bennett, F. with Roberts, M. 2004: *From Input to Influence: Participatory Approaches to Research and Inquiry into Poverty.* York: Joseph Rowntree Foundation.

Bennett, F. and Roche, C. 2000: The scope for participatory approaches. *New Economy*, 7 (1), 24–8.

Beresford, P. 1996: Poverty and disabled people. *Disability and Society*, 11 (4), 553–67.

Beresford, P. 2002: Participation and social policy. In R. Sykes, C. Bochel and N. Ellison (eds), *Social Policy Review 14*. Bristol: Policy Press.

Beresford, P. and Croft, S. 1995: 'It's our problem too': challenging the exclusion of poor people from poverty discourse. *Critical Social Policy*, 44/45, 75–95.

Beresford, P., Green, D., Lister, R. and Woodard, K. 1999: *Poverty First Hand*. London: CPAG.

Berghman, J. 1997: The resurgence of poverty and the struggle against social exclusion. *International Social Security Review*, 50 (1), 3–21.

Berting, J. and Villain-Gandossi, C. 2001: Urban transformations, the French debate and social quality. In Beck et al., 2001.

Bhalla, A. and Lapeyre, F. 1999: *Poverty and Exclusion in a Global World*. Basingstoke: Macmillan.

Blair, T. 1997. Speech at the Aylesbury Estate, Southwark, London, 2 June.

Bleiker, R. 2003: Discourse and human agency. *Contemporary Political Theory*, 2, 25–47.

Born, A. and Jensen, P. H. 2002: A second order reflection on the concept of inclusion and exclusion. In J. G. Andersen and P. H. Jensen (eds), *Changing Labour Markets, Welfare Policies and Citizenship*. Bristol: Policy Press.

Bourdieu, P. 1999: *The Weight of the World*. Cambridge: Polity.

Bowring, F. 2000: Social exclusion: limitations of the debate. *Critical Social Policy*, 20 (3), 307–30.

Bradbury, B. and Jäntti, M. 2001: Child poverty across the industrialised world. In Vleminckx and Smeeding, 2001.

Bradbury, B., Jenkins, S. P. and Micklewright, J. (eds) 2001: *The Dynamics of Child Poverty in Industrialised Countries*. Cambridge: Cambridge University Press.

Bradshaw, J. 1997: Why and how do we study poverty in industrialized countries? In N. Keilman, J. Lyngstad, H. Bojer and I. Thomsen (eds), *Poverty and Economic Inequality in Industrialized Western Societies*. Oslo: Scandinavian University Press.

Bradshaw, J. 2000a: Preface to Centennial Edition of Rowntree's *Poverty: A Study of Town Life*, Bristol: Policy Press.

Bradshaw, J. 2000b: Child poverty in comparative perspective. In Gordon and Townsend, 2000.

Bradshaw, J. 2000c: The Relationship between Poverty and Social Exclusion in Britain. Conference of the International Association for Research in Income and Wealth, Cracow, 27 August–2 September.

Bradshaw, J. (ed.) 2002: *The Well-Being of Children in the UK*. London: Save the Children.

Bradshaw, J. and Finch, N. 2003: Overlaps in dimensions of poverty. *Journal of Social Policy*, 32 (4), 513–25.

Bradshaw, J. and Holmes, H. 1989: *Living on the Edge*, London: CPAG.

Bradshaw, J., Finch, N., Kemp, P. A., Mayhew, E. and Williams, J. 2003: *Gender and Poverty in Britain*. Manchester: EOC.

Brock, K. and McGee, R. (eds) 2002: *Knowing Poverty. Critical Reflections on Participatory Research and Policy.* London: Earthscan.

Broughton, C. 2003: Reforming poor women. *Qualitative Sociology*, 26 (1), 35–51.

Buchanan, J. and Young, L. 2000: Examining the relationship between material conditions, long-term problematic drug misuse and social exclusion. In J. Bradshaw and R. Sainsbury (eds), *Experiencing Poverty*. Aldershot: Ashgate.

Buck, N. 2001: Identifying neighbourhood effects on social exclusion. *Urban Studies*, 38 (12), 2251–75.

Buck, N., Gordon, I., Hall, P., Harloe, M. and Kleinman, M. 2002: *Working Capital: Life and Labour in Contemporary London.* London/New York: Routledge.

Buhaenko, H., Flower, C. and Smith, S. 2003: *'Fifty Voices are Better than One': Combating Social Exclusion and Gender Stereotyping in Gellideg.* Cardiff: Gellideg Foundation Group/Oxfam GB.

Bullock, H. E., Wyche, K. F. and Williams, W. R. 2001: Media images of the poor. *Journal of Social Issues*, 57 (2), 229–46.

Burchardt, T. 2000a: *Enduring Economic Exclusion: Disabled People, Income and Work.* Findings 060, York: Joseph Rowntree Foundation.

Burchardt, T. 2000b: Social exclusion: concepts and evidence. In Gordon and Townsend, 2000.

Burchardt, T. 2003: *Being and Becoming: Social Exclusion and the Onset of Disability.* CASEreport 21. London: CASE.

Burchardt, T., Le Grand, J. and Piachaud, D. 1999: Social exclusion in Britain 1991–1995. *Social Policy & Administration*, 33 (3), 227–4.

Burchardt, T., Le Grand, J. and Piachaud, D. 2002a: Introduction. In Hills et al., 2002.

Burchardt, T., Le Grand, J. and Piachaud, D. 2002b: Degrees of exclusion. In Hills et al., 2002.

Burgoyne, C. 1990: Money in marriage. *Sociological Review*, 38, 634–65.

Burns, D. and Taylor, M. 1998. *Mutual Aid and Self-help.* Bristol: Policy Press.

Burns, T. R. 1994: Two conceptions of human agency. In P. Sztompka (ed.), *Agency and Structure*. Reading: Gordon and Breach.

Byrne, D. 1999: *Social Exclusion*. Buckingham/Philadelphia: Open University Press.

Cabannes, Y. 2000: Poor or excluded? Some lessons from Latin America and the Caribbean. *Habitat Debate*, 6 (4), 18–19.

Cantillon, S. and Nolan, B. 1998: Are married women more deprived than their husbands? *Journal of Social Policy*, 27 (2), 151–71.

Carabine, J. 2000: Constituting welfare subjects through poverty and sexuality. In G. Lewis, S. Gewirtz and J. Clarke (eds), *Rethinking Social Policy*. London: Sage.

Cars, G., Madanipour, A. and Allen, J. 1998: Social exclusion in European cities. In Madanipour et al., 1998.

Castells, M. 1997: *The Power of Identity*, Oxford: Blackwell Publishers.

Castells, M. 2000: *End of Millennium*, 2nd edn. Oxford: Blackwell Publishers.

CEC 1992: *Towards a Europe of Solidarity*. COM(92) 542. Brussels: CEC.

CEC 1998: *Non-monetary Indicators of Poverty and Social Exclusion*. Luxembourg: Office for Official Publications of the European Communities.

CEC 2001: *Draft Joint Report on Social Inclusion*. COM(01) 565 final. Brussels: CEC.

CESCR 2001: *Poverty and the International Covenant on Economic, Social and Cultural Rights*. E/C 12/2001/10. New York: UN Economic and Social Council.

Chamberlayne, P. and Rustin, M. 1999: *From Biography to Social Policy*. London: Centre for Biography in Social Policy.

Chambers, R. 1997: *Whose Reality Counts?* London: Intermediate Technology Publications.

Chambers, R. and Conway, G. 1992: *Sustainable Rural Livelihoods*. IDS Discussion Paper 296. Brighton: IDS.

Chanan, G. 1992: *Out of the Shadows: Local Community Action and the European Community*. Dublin: European Foundation for the Improvement of Living and Working Conditions.

Charlesworth, S. J. 2000: *A Phenomenology of Working Class Experience*. Cambridge: Cambridge University Press.

Choffé, T. 2001: Social exclusion: definition, public debate and empirical evidence in France. In Mayes et al., 2001.

Christie, I., Harrison, M., Hitchman, C. and Lang, T. 2002: *Inconvenience Food: The Struggle to Eat Well on a Low Income*. London: Demos.

Christopher, K. 2002: Welfare state regimes and mothers' poverty. *Social Politics*, 9 (1), 60–86.

Clarke, J. 1999: Coming to terms with culture. In H. Dean and R. Woods (eds), *Social Policy Review 11*. Luton: Social Policy Association.

Clarke, J. and Cochrane, A. 1998: The social construction of social problems. In E. Saraga (ed.), *Embodying the Social: Constructions of Difference*. London/New York: Routledge.

Clasen, J., Gould, A. and Vincent, J. 1998. *Voices Within and Without: Responding to Long-term Unemployment in Germany, Sweden and Britain*. Bristol: Policy Press.

Clert, C. 1999: Evaluating the concept of social exclusion in development discourse. *European Journal of Development Research*, 11 (2), 176–99.

Cloke, P. and Little, J. 1997: *Contested Countryside Cultures*. London/New York: Routledge.

Cohen, C. J. and Dawson, M. C. 1993: Neighbourhood poverty and African-American politics. *American Political Science Review*, 87 (2), 286–302.

Cohen, J. R. 1997: Poverty: talk, identity and action. *Qualitative Inquiry*, 3 (1), 71–92.

Cohen, R., Coxall, J., Craig, G. and Sadiq-Sangster, A. 1992: *Hardship Britain*. London: CPAG.

Community Development Journal 2003: special issue: *Sustainable Livelihoods and Community Development*. 38 (3).

Cook, D. 1997: *Poverty, Crime and Punishment*. London: CPAG.

Cook, D. 2002: Consultation, for a change? *Social Policy & Administration*, 36 (5), 516–31.

Coole, D. 1996: Is class a difference that makes a difference? *Radical Philosophy*, 77, 17–25.

Coote, A. 1992: Introduction. In A. Coote (ed.), *The Welfare of Citizens*. London: Rivers Oram Press.

CoPPP 2000: *Listen Hear: The Right to be Heard*. Bristol: Policy Press.

Corden, A. 1996: Writing about poverty: ethical dilemmas. In H. Dean (ed.), *Ethics and Social Policy Research*. Luton: University of Luton Press.

Cornwall, A. 2000: *Beneficiary, Consumer, Citizen: Perspectives on Participation for Poverty Reduction*. Stockholm: Swedish International Development Cooperation Agency.

Cornwall, A. 2002: Locating citizen participation. *IDS Bulletin*, 33 (2), 49–58.

Cornwall, A. and Gaventa, G. 2000: From users to choosers to makers and shapers. *IDS Bulletin*, 31 (4), 50–62.

Council of Europe 2001: *Promoting the Policy Debate on Social Exclusion from a Comparative Perspective*. Strasbourg: Council of Europe.

Craig, G. 2002: Ethnicity, racism and the labour market: a European perspective. In J. G. Andersen and P. H. Jensen (eds), *Changing Labour Markets, Welfare Policies and Citizenship*, Bristol: Policy Press.

Craine, S. 1997: The 'black magic roundabout': cyclical transitions, social exclusion and alternative careers. In MacDonald, 1997.

da Costa, A. B. 1997: Social exclusion and the new poor. In Gore and Figueiredo, 1997.

da Silva, L. 2003: Contribution to Leaders' Symposium, Progressive Governance Conference, London, 13 July.

Dahrendorf, R. 1987: The erosion of citizenship and its consequences for us all. *New Statesman*, 12 June, 12–15.

Daly, M. 1992: Europe's poor women? Gender in research on poverty. *European Sociological Review*, 8 (1), 1–12.

Daly, M. and Leonard, M. 2002: *Against All Odds: Family Life on a Low Income in Ireland*. Dublin: Institute of Public Administration/Combat Poverty Agency.

Daly, M. and Rake, K. 2003: *Gender and the Welfare State*, Cambridge: Polity.

Daly, M. and Saraceno, C. 2002: Social exclusion and gender relations. In B. Hobson, J. Lewis and B. Siim (eds), *Contested Concepts in Gender and Social Politics*, Cheltenham/Northampton, Mass.: Edward Elgar.

Darton, D., Hirsch, D. and Strelitz, J. 2003: *Tackling Disadvantage: A 20 Year Enterprise*. York: Joseph Rowntree Foundation.

Davies, N. 1998: *Dark Heart: The Shocking Truth about Hidden Britain*. London: Vintage.

Davis, A. and Hill, P. 2001: *Poverty, Social Exclusion and Mental Health*. London: Mental Health Foundation.

de Goede, M. 1996: Ideology in the US welfare debate: neoliberal representations of poverty. *Discourse and Society*, 7 (3), 317–57.

de Haan, A. 1998: Social exclusion. *IDS Bulletin*, 29 (1), 10–19.

de Haan, A. 1999: *Social Exclusion: Towards an Holistic Understanding of Deprivation*. London: DfID.

Deacon, A. 2002: *Perspectives on Welfare*. Buckingham/Philadelphia: Open University Press.

Deacon, A. 2003: Levelling the playing field, activating the players: New Labour and the cycle of disadvantage. *Policy & Politics*, 31 (2), 123–37.

Deacon, A. and Mann, K. 1999: Agency, modernity and social policy. In *Journal of Social Policy*, 28 (3), 413–35.

Dean, H. 1992: Poverty discourse and the disempowerment of the poor. *Critical Social Policy*, 35, 79–88.

Dean, H. 1998: Benefit fraud and citizenship. In P. Taylor-Gooby (ed.), *Choice and Public Policy*. Basingstoke: Macmillan.

Dean, H. (ed.) 1999: *Begging Questions*. Bristol: Policy Press.

Dean, H. 2002: *Welfare Rights and Social Policy*. Harlow: Prentice-Hall.

Dean, H. 2003a: Re-conceptualising welfare-to-work for people with multiple problems and needs. *Journal of Social Policy*, 32 (3), 441–59.

Dean, H. 2003b: The third way and social welfare. *Social Policy & Administration*, 37 (7), 695–708.

Dean, H. 2004: What are the implications of third way social policy for inequality, social cohesion and citizenship? In J. Lewis and R. Surender (eds), *Welfare State Change: Towards a Third Way?* Oxford: Oxford University Press.

Dean, H. and Melrose, M. 1996: Unravelling citizenship: the significance of social security benefit fraud. *Critical Social Policy*, 16 (3), 3–31.

Dean, H. and Melrose, M. 1997: Manageable discord: fraud and resistance in the social security system. *Social Policy & Administration*, 31 (2), 103–18.

Dean, H. with Melrose, M. 1999: *Poverty, Riches and Social Citizenship*. Basingstoke: Macmillan.

Dean, H. and Shah, A. 2002: Insecure families and low-paying labour markets. *Journal of Social Policy*, 31 (1), 61–80.

Dean, H. and Taylor-Gooby, P. 1992: *Dependency Culture*. Hemel Hempstead: Harvester Wheatsheaf.

Dean, J. and Hastings, A. 2000: *Challenging Images: Housing Estates, Stigma and Regeneration*. Bristol: Policy Press.

Dean, M. 1992. A genealogy of the government of poverty. *Economy and Society*, 21 (3), 215–51.

del Tufo, S. and Gaster, L. 2002: *Evaluation of the Commission on Poverty, Participation and Power*. York: Joseph Rowntree Foundation.

Dennis, N. 1997: *The Invention of Permanent Poverty*. London: IEA Health & Welfare Unit.

Devereux. E. 1998: *Devils and Angels: Television, Ideology and the Coverage of Poverty*. Luton: University of Luton Press.

Dewilde, C. 2003: A life-course perspective on social exclusion and poverty. *British Journal of Sociology*, 54 (1), 109–28.

DfID 2000a: *Disability, Poverty and Development*. London: DfID.

DfID 2000b: *Human Rights for Poor People*. London: DfID.

Dickens, R. and Ellwood, D. 2001: Welfare to work: poverty in Britain and the US, *New Economy*, 8 (2), 98–103.

Donnison, D. 1982: *The Politics of Poverty*. Oxford: Martin Robertson.

Douthitt, R. A. 1994: *'Time to Do the Chores?' Factoring Home-production Needs into Measures of Poverty*. Institute for Research on Poverty Discussion Paper 1030–94. www.ssc.wisc.edu/irp/pubs.htm.

Dowler, E. and Leather, S. 2000: 'Spare some change for a bite to eat?' In J. Bradshaw and R. Sainsbury (eds), *Experiencing Poverty*. Aldershot: Ashgate.

Dowler, E., Turner, S. with Dobson, B. 2001: *Poverty Bites*. London: CPAG.

Doyal, L. and Gough, I. 1991: *A Theory of Human Need*. Basingstoke: Macmillan.

DSS 1999: *Opportunity for All. First Annual Report*. London: Stationery Office.

Duncan, C. M. 1999: *Worlds Apart: Why Poverty Persists in Rural America*. New Haven/London: Yale University Press.

Duncan, S. and Edwards, R. 1999: *Lone Mothers, Paid Work and Gendered Moral Rationalities*. Basingstoke: Macmillan.

Dundee Anti-Poverty Forum 2003: *No Room for Dreams*. Dundee: DAPF.

DWP 2002: *Measuring Child Poverty: A Consultation Document*. London: DWP.

DWP 2003a: *Households Below Average Income 1994/95–2001/02*. London: DWP.

DWP 2003b: *Measuring Child Poverty Consultation: Preliminary Conclusions*. London: DWP.

DWP 2003c: *UK National Action Plan on Social Inclusion 2003–05*. London: DWP.

DWP 2003d: *Low-Income Dynamics 1991–2001*. London: DWP.

DWP 2003e: *Measuring Child Poverty*. London: DWP.

EAPN 1999: *A Europe for All*. Brussels: EAPN.

EAPN 2003: Becoming full 'citizens'. *EAPN Network News*, 101, 4.

Edelman, M. 1977: *Political Language*. New York/London: Academic Press.

Edin, K. and Lein, L. 1996: Work, welfare and single mothers' economic survival strategies. *American Sociological Review*, 61 (Feb.), 253–66.

Ehrenreich, B. 2001: *Nickel and Dimed*. New York: Henry Holt & Co.

Elam, G. and Thomas, A. 1997: *Stepping Stones to Employment*. London: DSS/Stationery Office.

End Child Poverty 2002: *Child Poverty and Education*. London: ECP/National Children's Bureau.

EOC 2003: *Gender and Poverty in Britain.* Manchester: EOC.

Erikson, R. 1993: Descriptions of inequality: the Swedish approach to welfare research. In Nussbaum and Sen, 1993.

Ermisch, E., Francesconi, M. and Pevalin, D. J. 2001: *Outcomes for Children of Poverty.* Leeds: DWP/Corporate Document Services.

Esping-Andersen, G. 2002: *Why we Need a New Welfare State.* Oxford: Oxford University Press.

Evans, M. 1998: Behind the rhetoric: the institutional basis of social exclusion and poverty. *IDS Bulletin,* 29 (1), 42–9.

Farrell, C. and O'Connor, W. 2003: *Low Income Families and Household Spending.* Leeds: DWP/Corporate Document Services.

Farrell, F. 2003: Participation is not a quick fix solution. *EAPN Network News,* 101 (July), 1.

Ferguson, C. 1999: *Global Social Policy Principles: Human Rights and Social Justice.* London: DfID.

Figueiredo, J. B. and de Hann, A. (eds) 1998: *Social Exclusion: An ILO Perspective.* Geneva: ILO.

Floro, M. S. 1995: Women's well-being, poverty, and work intensity. *Feminist Economics,* 1 (3), 1–25.

Forrest, R. and Kearns, A. 1999: *Joined-up Places? Social Cohesion and Neighbourhood Regeneration.* York: Joseph Rowntree Foundation.

Franklin, R. 1991: *Shadows of Race and Class.* Minneapolis: University of Minnesota Press.

Fraser, N. 1997: *Justice Interruptus.* New York/London: Routledge.

Fraser, N. 2000: Rethinking recognition. *New Left Review,* 3 (May/June): 107–20.

Fraser, N. 2003: Social justice in the age of identity politics. In N. Fraser and A. Honneth, *Redistribution or Recognition?* London/New York: Verso.

Fraser, N. and Gordon, L. 1994: 'Dependency' demystified. *Social Politics,* 1 (1), 4–31.

Friedrichs, J. 1998: Do poor neighbourhoods make their residents poorer? in H. J. Andress (ed.), *Empirical Poverty Research in Comparative Perspective.* Aldershot: Ashgate.

Furbey, R. 1999: Urban 'regeneration'. *Critical Social Policy,* 19 (4), 419–45.

Gallie, D. 1999: Unemployment and social exclusion in the EU. *European Societies,* 1 (2), 139–67.

Gallie, D. and Paugam, S. (eds) 2000: *Welfare Regimes and the Experience of Unemployment in Europe,* Oxford: Oxford University Press.

Gallie, D. and Paugam, S. 2002: *Social Precarity and Social Integration.* Brussels: CEC.

Gallie, D., Paugam, S. and Jacobs, S. 2003: Unemployment, poverty and social isolation. *European Societies*, 5 (1), 1–32.

Galloway, K. 2002: *A Scotland Where Everyone Matters*. Manchester: Church Action on Poverty.

Gans, H. J. 1995: *The War against the Poor*. New York: Basic Books.

Gaventa, J. 2002. Exploring citizenship, participation and accountability. *IDS Bulletin*, 33 (2), 1–11.

George, V. and Howards, I. 1991: *Poverty Amidst Affluence: Britain and the United States*. Aldershot: Edward Elgar.

Ghate, D. and Hazel, N. 2002: *Parenting in Poor Environments*. London: Jessica Kingsley.

Giddens, A. 1991: *Modernity and Self-Identity*, Cambridge: Polity.

Giddens, A. 1998: *The Third Way*. Cambridge: Polity.

Giddens, A. 2002: *Where Now for New Labour?* Cambridge: Polity.

Gilens, M. 1999: *Why Americans Hate Welfare: Race, Media and the Politics of Antipoverty Policy*. Chicago: University of Chicago Press.

Gilliat, S. 2001: *How the Poor Adapt to Poverty in Capitalism*. New York: Edwin Mellen Press.

Gilliom, J. 2001: *Overseers of the Poor*. Chicago/London: University of Chicago Press.

Gilroy, R. and Speak, S. 1998: Barriers, boxes and catapults: social exclusion and everyday life. In Madanipour et al., 1998.

Ginn, J., Street, D. and Arber, S. (eds) (2001) *Women, Work and Pensions. International Issues and Perspectives*. Buckingham/Philadelphia: Open University Press.

Glennerster, H., Lupton, R., Noden, P. and Power, A. 1999: *Poverty, Social Exclusion and Neighbourhood*. CASEpaper 22. London: CASE.

Goetz, A. M. and Gaventa, J. 2001: *Bringing Citizen Voice and Client Focus into Service Delivery*. IDS Working Paper 138, Brighton: IDS.

Goffman, E. 1968: *Stigma*. Englewood Cliffs, NJ: Prentice-Hall.

Golding, P. (ed.) 1986: *Excluding the Poor*. London: CPAG.

Golding, P. 1995: Public attitudes to social exclusion. In Room, 1995.

Golding, P. 1999: Thinking the unthinkable: welfare reform and the media. In B. Franklin (ed.), *Social Policy: The Media and Misrepresentation*. London/New York: Routledge.

Golding P. and Middleton, S. 1982. *Images of Welfare*. Oxford: Martin Robertson.

Goode, J. and Maskovsky, J. 2001: Introduction. In J. Goode and J. Maskovsky (eds), *The New Poverty Studies*. New York/ London: New York University Press.

Goode, J., Callender, C. and Lister, R. 1998: *Purse or Wallet? Gender Inequalities within Families on Benefits*, London: Policy Studies Institute.

Goodin, R. 1996: Inclusion and exclusion. *European Journal of Sociology*, 37 (2), 343–71.

Gordon, D. 2000: Measuring absolute and relative poverty. In Gordon and Townsend, 2000.

Gordon, D. and Spicker P. 1999: *The International Glossary on Poverty*. London/New York: Zed Books.

Gordon D. and Townsend, P. (eds) 2000: *Breadline Europe*, Bristol: Policy Press.

Gordon, D., Adelman, L., Ashworth, K., Bradshaw, J., Levitas, R., Middleton, S., Pantazis, C., Patsios, D., Payne, S., Townsend, P. and Williams, J. 2000a: *Poverty and Social Exclusion in Britain*. York: Joseph Rowntree Foundation.

Gordon, D., Pantazis, C. and Townsend, P. 2000b: Absolute and overall poverty. In Gordon and Townsend, 2000.

Gordon, D., Levitas, R. and Pantazis, C. (eds) 2004: *Poverty and Social Exclusion in Britain*. Bristol: Policy Press.

Gore, C. 1995: Social exclusion and social change. In Rodgers et al., 1995.

Gore, C. and Figueiredo, J. B. (eds) 1997: *Social Exclusion and Anti-Poverty Policy*. Geneva: ILO.

Gough, I. 1992: What are human needs? In J. Percy-Smith and I. Sanderson (eds), *Understanding Human Needs*. London: IPPR.

Gould, C. 1988. *Rethinking Democracy*. Cambridge: Cambridge University Press.

Graham, H. 1993: *Hardship and Health in Women's Lives*. Hemel Hempstead: Harvester Wheatsheaf.

Green, D. 1998: *Benefit Dependency*. London: IEA Health & Welfare Unit.

Greener, I. 2002: Agency, social theory and social policy. *Critical Social Policy*, 22 (4), 688–705.

Grewal, I., Joy, S., Lewis, J., Swales, K. and Woodfield, K. 2002: *'Disabled for Life?' Attitudes towards and Experiences of Disability in Britain*. Leeds: DWP/Corporate Document Services.

Gustafsson, B. and Lindblom, M. 1993: Poverty lines and poverty in seven European countries, Australia, Canada and the USA. *Journal of European Social Policy*, 3 (1), 21–38.

Hacourt, G. 2003: *European Project on Poverty Indicators starting from the Experience of People Living in Poverty*. www.eapn.org.

Hamilton, K. and Jenkins, L. 2000: A gender audit for public transport: a new policy tool in the tackling of social exclusion. *Urban Studies*, 37 (10), 1793–800.

Handler, J. 1992: Postmodernism, protest and the new social movements. *Law and Society Review*, 20 (4), 697–732.

Handler, J. and Hasenfeld, Y. 1997: *We the Poor People: Work, Poverty, and Welfare*. New Haven/London: Yale University Press.

Harrington, M. 1962: *The Other America*. New York: Macmillan.

Harvey, D. L. and Reed, M. H. 1996: The culture of poverty. *Sociological Perspectives*, 39 (4), 465–95.

Hastings, A. and Dean, J. 2003: Challenging images: tackling stigma through estate regeneration. *Policy and Politics*, 31 (2), 171–84.

Heady, C. 1997: Labour market transitions and social exclusion. *Journal of European Social Policy*, 7 (2), 119–28.

Heady, C. and Room, G. 2002: Patterns of social exclusion: implications for policy and research. In Barnes et al., 2002.

Healey, P. 1998: Institutionalist theory, social exclusion and governance. In Madanipour et al., 1998.

Held, D. 1987: *Models of Democracy*, Cambridge: Polity.

Henderson, P. and Salmon, H. 2001: *Social Exclusion and Community Development*. London: Community Development Foundation.

Heslop, M. 2000: *Poverty and Ageing*. London: HelpAge International.

Hill, R. P. 2001: *Surviving in a Material World*. Notre Dame, Ind.: University of Notre Dame Press.

Hills, J. 2001: Poverty and social security. In A. Park, J. Curtice, K. Thomson, L. Jarvis and C. Bromley (eds), *British Social Attitudes: The 18th Report*. London: Sage.

Hills, J. 2002: Does a focus on 'social exclusion' change the policy response? In Hills et al., 2002.

Hills, J., Le Grand, J. and Piachaud, D. (eds) 2002: *Understanding Social Exclusion*. Oxford: Oxford University Press.

Hillyard, P., Kelly, G., McLaughlin, E., Patsios, D. and Tomlinson, M. 2003: *Bare Necessities: Poverty and Social Exclusion in Northern Ireland*. Belfast: Democratic Dialogue.

Himmelfarb, G. 1984: *The Idea of Poverty: England in the Early Industrial Age*. London/Boston: Faber & Faber.

Himmelfarb, G. 1995: *The De-moralization of Society*. London: IEA Health & Welfare Unit.

Hobcraft, J. 2003: *Continuity and Change: Pathways to Young Adult Disadvantage*. CASEpaper 66, London: CASE.

Hocking, G. 2003: Oxfam Great Britain and sustainable livelihoods in the UK. *Community Development Journal*, 38 (3), 235–42.

Hoggett, P. 2001: Agency, rationality and social policy. *Journal of Social Policy*, 30 (1), 37–56.

Holloway, S. D., Fuller, B., Rambaud, M. F. and Eggers-Piérola, C. 1997: *Through my Own Eyes: Single Mothers and the Cultures of Poverty*. Cambridge, Mass./London: Harvard University Press.

Holman, B. 1998: *Faith in the Poor*. Oxford: Lion Publishing.

Holman, R. 1978: *Poverty: Explanations of Social Deprivation*. London: Martin Robertson.

Honneth, A. 1995: *The Struggle for Recognition*. Cambridge: Cambridge University Press.

Honneth, A. 2003: Redistribution as recognition. In N. Fraser and A. Honneth, *Redistribution or Recognition?* London/New York: Verso.

hooks, b. 1994: *Outlaw Culture: Resisting Representation*. New York/London: Routledge.

Howarth, C., Kenway, P. and Palmer, G. 2001: *Responsibility for All*. London: New Policy Institute/Fabian Society.

Hunter, S. 2003: A critical analysis of approaches to the concept of social identity in social policy. *Critical Social Policy*, 22 (3), 322–44.

Hyatt, S. B. 1992: Accidental activists. *Crosscurrents*, 5, 93–102.

Hyatt, S. B. 2001: From citizen to volunteer. In J. Goode and J. Maskovsky (eds), *The New Poverty Studies*. New York/London: New York University Press.

IDS Bulletin 1998: Poverty and Social Exclusion in North and South. 29 (1).

ILC 2001: *Old and Poor in America*. New York: International Longevity Centre.

Illouz, E. 1994: Defense or prosecution? The ideology of poverty in elite and popular press. *Journal of Communication Enquiry*, 18 (1), 45–62.

Institute for Research on Poverty 1998: Subjective assessments of economic well-being. *Focus*, 19 (2), 43–6.

International Movement ATD Fourth World 2003: Written contribution to 59th session of the UN Commission on Human Rights. France: ATD Fourth World.

Iyengar, S. 1991: *Is Anyone Responsible? How Television Frames Political Issues*. Chicago: University of Chicago Press.

Jackson, C. 1998: Women and poverty or gender and well-being? *Journal of International Affairs*, 52 (1), 67–81.

Jackson, C. 1999: Social exclusion and gender. *European Journal of Development Research*, 11 (1), 125–46.

James, S. 1992: The good-enough citizen. In G. Brock and S. James (eds), *Beyond Equality and Difference*. London/New York: Routledge.

Janoski, T. 1998: *Citizenship and Civil Society*. Cambridge: Cambridge University Press.

Jarrett, R. L. 2003: Worlds of development: the experience of low income, African-American youth. *Journal of Children & Poverty*, 9 (2), 157–88.

Jarrett, R. L. and Jefferson, S. R. 2003: A 'good mother got to fight for her kids': maternal management strategies in a high-risk African-American neighbourhood. *Journal of Children & Poverty*, 9 (1), 21–39.

Jencks, C. 1992: *Rethinking Social Policy: Race, Poverty and the Underclass*. Cambridge, Mass./London: Harvard University Press.

Jenkins, R. 1996: *Social Identity*. London/New York: Routledge.

Jenkins, S. P. 1991: Poverty measurement and the within-household distribution. *Journal of Social Policy*, 20 (4), 457–83.

Jenkins, S. P. 1994: *The Within-Household Distribution and Why It Matters*. Swansea: University College of Swansea, Dept. of Economics.

Jenkins, S. P. 2000: Dynamics of household income. In R. Berthoud and J. Gershuny (eds), *Seven Years in the Lives of British Families*. Bristol: Policy Press.

Jenkins, S. P. and Rigg, J. 2001: *The Dynamics of Poverty in Britain*. Leeds: DWP/Corporate Document Services.

Jennings, J. and Kushnick, L. 1999: Introduction. In Kushnick and Jennings, 1999.

John, K., Payne, S. and Land, H. 2001: *Providing Training and Support for Lone Parents*. Findings 821, York: Joseph Rowntree Foundation.

Johnston, L., MacDonald, R., Mason, P., Ridley, L. and Webster, C. 2000: *The Impact of Social Exclusion on Young People Moving into Adulthood*. Findings 030, York: Joseph Rowntree Foundation.

Jones, C. and Novak, T. 1999: *Poverty, Welfare and the Disciplinary State*, London/New York: Routledge.

Jordan, B. 1993: Framing claims and the weapons of the weak. In G. Drover and P. Kerans (eds), *New Approaches to Welfare Theory*. Aldershot: Edward Elgar.

Jordan, B. 1996: *A Theory of Poverty and Social Exclusion*. Cambridge: Polity.

Jordan, B. and Redley, M. 1994: Polarisation, underclass and the welfare state. *Work, Employment and Society*, 8 (2), 153–76.

Jordan, B., James, S., Kay, H. and Redley, M. 1992: *Trapped in Poverty*. London/New York: Routledge.

Joseph, K. and Sumption, J. 1979: *Equality*. London: John Murray.

Journal of Social Issues 2001: 57 (1), 1–14, 73–92.

JRF (2004) *Overcoming Disadvantage*. York: Joseph Rowntree Foundation.

Kabeer, N. 2000a: Resources, agency, achievement. In S. Razavi (ed.), *Gendered Poverty and Wellbeing*, Oxford: Blackwell Publishers.

Kabeer, N. 2000b: Social exclusion, poverty and discrimination. *IDS Bulletin*, 31 (4), 83–97.

Kabeer, N. 2003: *Making Rights Work for the Poor*. IDS Working Paper 200. Brighton: IDS.

Kasparova, D., Marsh, A., Vegeris, S. and Perry, J. 2003: *Families and Children 2001: Work and Childcare*. Leeds: DWP/Corporate Document Services.

Katz, M. B. 1989: *The Undeserving Poor*. New York: Pantheon Books.

Kaus, M. 1992: *The End of Equality*. New York: Basic Books.

Kemmer, D., Cunningham-Bewley, S. and Backett-Milburn, K. 2001: How does working work for lone mothers on low incomes? *Benefits*, 32, 10–14.

Kempson, E. 1996: *Life on a Low Income*. York: Joseph Rowntree Foundation.

Kempson, E., Bryson, A. and Rowlingson, K. 1994: *Hard Times?* London: Policy Studies Institute.

Kennedy, C. and Fitzpatrick, S. 1999: *Excluded Identities: Emerging Findings from Research on Begging, Rough Sleeping and the Big Issue*. Social Policy Association Annual Conference, Roehampton Institute. 20–22 July.

Kenyon, S., Rafferty, J. and Lyons, G. 2003: Social exclusion and transport in the UK. *Journal of Social Policy*, 32 (3), 317–38.

Kincaid, J. C. 1973: *Poverty and Equality in Britain*. Harmondsworth: Pelican.

Kingfisher, C. P. 1996: *Women in the American Welfare Trap*. Philadelphia: University of Pennsylvania Press.

Kingfisher, C. 2002: *Western Welfare in Decline*. Philadelphia: University of Pennsylvania Press.

Kleinman, M. 1999: There goes the neighbourhood. *New Economy*, 6 (4), 188–92.

Knight, J. and Brent, M. 1998: *Access Denied: Disabled People's Experience of Social Exclusion*. London: Leonard Cheshire.

Knight, J., Heaven, C. and Christie, I. 2002: *Inclusive Citizenship: Social Equality for Disabled People*. London: Leonard Cheshire.

Korpi, W. 2000: Faces of inequality: gender, class, and patterns of inequalities in different types of welfare state. *Social Politics*, 7 (2), 127–91.

Kronauer, M. 1998. 'Social exclusion' and 'underclass': new concepts for the analysis of poverty. In H. J. Andress (ed.), *Empirical Poverty Research in Comparative Perspective*. Aldershot: Ashgate.

Kuchler, B. and Goebel, J. 2003: Incidence and intensity of smoothed income poverty in European countries. *Journal of European Social Policy*, 13 (4), 356–69.

Kushnick, L. 1999: Responding to urban crisis: functions of white racism. In Kushnick and Jennings, 1999.

Kushnick, L. and Jennings, J. 1999: *A New Introduction to Poverty: The Role of Race, Power and Politics*. New York/London: New York University Press.

Land, H. and Rose, H. 1985: Compulsory altruism for some or an altruistic society for all? In P. Bean, J. Ferris and D. Whynes (eds), *In Defence of Welfare*. London: Tavistock.

Langmore, J. 2000: Reducing poverty: the implications of the 1995 Copenhagen Agreement. In Gordon and Townsend, 2000.

Lawless, J. L. and Fox, R. L. 2001: Political participation of the urban poor. *Social Problems*, 48 (3), 362–85.

Lawless, P., Martin, R. and Hardy S. (eds) 1998: *Unemployment and Social Exclusion*. London: Jessica Kingsley.

Layte, R. and Whelan, C. T. 2003: Moving in and out of poverty. *European Societies*, 5 (2), 167–91.

Layte, R., Nolan, B. and Whelan, C. T. 2000: Targeting poverty. *Journal of Social Policy*, 29 (4), 553–75.

Le Grand, J. 2003: *Individual Choice and Social Exclusion*. CASEpaper 75. London: CASE.

Leisering, L. and Leibfried, S. 1999: *Time and Poverty in Western Welfare States*. Cambridge: Cambridge University Press.

Leisering, L. and Walker, R. (eds) 1998: *The Dynamics of Modern Society*. Bristol: Policy Press.

Lens, V. 2002: Welfare reform, personal narratives and the media. *Journal of Poverty*, 6 (2), 1–20.

Leonard, P. 1997: *Postmodern Welfare*. London: Sage.

Levitas, R. 1998: *The Inclusive Society?* Basingstoke: Macmillan.

Levitas, R. 2000: What is social exclusion? In D. Gordon and P. Townsend (eds), *Breadline Europe*, Bristol: Policy Press.

Lewis, J. 2001: *The End of Marriage?* Cheltenham: Edward Elgar.

Lewis, O. 1967: *La Vida*. London: Secker and Warburg.

Lister, R. 1990: *The Exclusive Society: Citizenship and the Poor*. London: CPAG.

Lister, R. 1996: Introduction: in search of the 'underclass'. In R. Lister (ed.), *Charles Murray and the Underclass: The Developing Debate*. London: IEA Health & Welfare Unit.

Lister, R. 2000: Strategies for social inclusion. In Askonas and Stewart, 2000.

Lister, R. 2003: *Citizenship: Feminist Perspectives*, 2nd edn. Basingstoke: Palgrave.

Lister, R. and Beresford, P. 2000: Where are 'the poor' in the future of poverty research? In J. Bradshaw and R. Sainsbury (eds), *Researching Poverty*. Aldershot: Ashgate.

Long, G., Phillips, K. and Reynolds, B. 2002: *The Sustainable Livelihoods Framework*. Glasgow: Active Learning Centre/Oxfam.

Loumidis, J. and Middleton, S. 2000: *A Cycle of Disadvantage? Financial Exclusion in Childhood*. London: Financial Services Authority.

Lukes, S. 1974: *Power: A Radical View*. Basingstoke: Macmillan.

Lupton, R. 2003a: *Poverty Street*. Bristol: Policy Press.

Lupton, R. 2003b: *Neighbourhood Effects*. CASEpaper 73. London: CASE.

Lupton, R. and Power, A. 2002: Social exclusion and neighbourhoods. In Hills et al., 2002.

Lyon-Callo, V. 2001: Homelessness, employment, and structural violence. In J. Goode and J. Maskovsky (eds), *The New Poverty Studies*. New York/London: New York University Press.

McCann, M. and March, T. 1996: Law and everyday forms of resistance. In A. Sarat and S. Silbey (eds), *Studies in Law, Politics and Society 15*. Greenwich, Conn.: JAI Press.

McCormick, J. and Philo, C. 1995: Where is poverty? In C. Philo (ed.), *Off the Map: The Social Geography of Poverty in the UK*. London: CPAG.

McCoy, G. 2000: Women, community and politics in Northern Ireland. In C. Roulston and C. Davies (eds), *Gender, Democracy and Inclusion in Northern Ireland*. Basingstoke: Palgrave.

McCrone, D. 1994: Getting by and making out in Kirkcaldy. In M. Anderson, F. Bechhofer and J. Gershuny (eds), *The Social and Political Economy of the Household*. Oxford: Oxford University Press.

MacDonald, R. 1994: Fiddly jobs, undeclared working and the something for nothing society. *Work, Employment and Society*, 8 (4), 507–30.

MacDonald, R. 1996a: Labours of love: voluntary working in a depressed local economy. *Journal of Social Policy*, 25 (1), 19–38.

MacDonald, R. 1996b: Welfare dependency, the enterprise culture and self-employed survival. *Work, Employment and Society*, 10 (3), 431–47.

MacDonald, R. (ed.) 1997: *Youth, the 'Underclass' and Social Exclusion*. London/New York: Routledge.

MacDonald, R. and Marsh, J. 2001: Disconnected Youth? *Journal of Youth Studies*, 4 (4), 373–91.

MacDonald, R. and Marsh, J. 2002: Crossing the rubicon: youth transitions, poverty, drugs and social exclusion. *International Journal of Drugs Policy*, 13, 27–38.

McGee, R. 2002: The self in participatory poverty research. In Brock and McGee, 2002.

McGee, R. and Brock, K. 2001: *From Poverty Assessment to Policy Change*. Working Paper 133. Brighton: IDS.

Mack, J. and Lansley, S. 1985: *Poor Britain*. London: George Allen & Unwin.

McKendrick, J., Cunningham-Burley, S. and Backett-Milburn, K. 2003a: *Life in Low Income Families in Scotland: A Review of the Literature*. Edinburgh: Scottish Executive Social Research.

McKendrick, J., Cunningham-Burley, S. and Backett-Milburn, K. 2003b: *Life in Low Income Families in Scotland: Research Report*. Edinburgh: Scottish Executive Social Research.

Macnicol, J. 1987: In pursuit of the underclass. *Journal of Social Policy*, 16 (3), 293–318.

Madanipour, A. 1998: Social exclusion and space. In Madanipour et al., 1998.

Madanipour, A., Cars, G. and Allen J. (eds) 1998: *Social Exclusion in European Cities*. London: Jessica Kingsley.

Mann, K. 1994: *The Making of an English 'Underclass'?* Buckingham/Philadelphia: Open University Press.

Mann, K. 1999: Critical reflections on the 'underclass' and poverty. In I. Gough and G. Olofsson (eds), *Capitalism and Social Cohesion*. Basingstoke: Macmillan.

Mann, P. S. 1997: Musing as a feminist in a postfeminist era. In J. Dean (ed.), *Feminism and the New Democracy*. London: Sage.

Marcoux, A. 1998: The feminization of poverty. *Population and Development Review*, 24 (1), 131–9.

Marsh, A. and Perry, J. 2003: Ethnic minority families: poverty and disadvantage. In C. Kober, *Black and Ethnic Minority Children and Poverty*. London: End Child Poverty.

Marsh, A. and Rowlingson, K. 2002: *Low- and Moderate-Income Families in Britain*. Leeds: DWP/Corporate Document Services.

Marsh, A., McKay, S., Smith, A. and Stephenson, A. 2001: *Low Income Families in Britain*. Leeds: DSS/Corporate Document Services.

Marshall, G., Roberts, S. and Burgoyne, C. 1996: Social class and the underclass in Britain and the USA. *British Journal of Sociology*, 47 (1), 22–44.

Marshall, T. H. 1950: *Citizenship and Social Class*, Cambridge: Cambridge University Press.

Martin, C. 1996: The debate in France over 'social exclusion'. *Social Policy & Administration*, 30 (4), 382–92.

Marx, K. 1987: First draft of *A Contribution to the Critique of Political Economy*. In K. Marx and F. Engels, *Collected Works*, vol. 49. London: Lawrence and Wishart.

Mason, R. 2003: Listening to lone mothers: paid work, family life and child care in Canada. *Journal of Children & Poverty*, 9 (1), 41–54.

Massey, D. S. 1996: The age of extremes. *Demography*, 33 (4), 395–412.

Maxwell, S. 2000: Developing the consensus. *New Economy*, 7 (4), 210–13.

Mayes, D. G., Berghman, J. and Salais, R. (eds) 2001: *Social Exclusion and European Policy*. Cheltenham/Northampton, Mass.: Edward Elgar.

Mayo, M. 2004: Exclusion, inclusion and empowerment. In J. Anderson and B. Siim (eds), *Politics of Inclusion and Empowerment*, Basingstoke: Palgrave.

Mayo, M. and Craig, G. 1995: Community participation and empowerment. In G. Craig and M. Mayo (eds), *Community Empowerment*. London/New York: Zed Books.

Micklewright, J. 2002: *Social Exclusion and Children*. CASEpaper 51. London: CASE.

Middleton, S. 1998. Revising the Breadline Britain questions. In J. Bradshaw, D. Gordon, R. Levitas, S. Middleton, C. Pantazis, S. Payne and P. Townsend, *Perceptions of Poverty and Social Exclusion*. Bristol: Townsend Centre for International Poverty Research.

Middleton, S. 2000: Agreeing poverty lines. In J. Bradshaw and R. Sainsbury (eds), *Researching Poverty*. Aldershot: Ashgate.

Middleton, S. 2002: Coping for the children. In ESRC, *How People on Low Incomes Manage their Finances*. Swindon: Economic and Social Research Council.

Middleton, S. and Walker, R. 1994: Conclusions on the reality of childhood poverty in Britain. In Middleton et al., 1994.

Middleton, S., Ashworth, K. and Walker, R. (eds) 1994: *Family Fortunes*. London: CPAG.

Middleton, S., Ashworth, K. and Braithwaite, I. 1997: *Small Fortunes*. York: Joseph Rowntree Foundation.

Millar, J. 2003: Gender, poverty and social exclusion. *Social Policy and Society*, 2 (3), 181–8.

Millar, J. and Glendinning, C. 1989: Gender and poverty. *Journal of Social Policy* 18 (3): 363–81.

Millar, J. and Glendinning, C. 1992: 'It all really starts in the family': gender divisions and poverty. In C. Glendinning and

J. Millar (eds), *Women and Poverty in Britain: The 1990s.* Hemel Hempstead: Harvester Wheatsheaf.

Millar, J. and Ridge, T. 2001: *Families, Poverty, Work and Care.* Leeds: DWP/Corporate Document Services.

Misra, J., Moller, S. and Karides, M. 2003: Envisioning dependency: changing media depictions of welfare in the 20th century. *Social Problems.* 50 (4), 482–504.

Mooney, G. 1998: Remoralizing the poor? In G. Lewis (ed.), *Forming Nation, Framing Welfare.* London/New York: Routledge.

Mooney, G. 2000: Class and social policy. In G. Lewis, S. Gewirtz and J. Clarke (eds), *Rethinking Social Policy.* London: Sage.

Morris, J. 2001: Social exclusion and young disabled people with high levels of support needs. *Critical Social Policy*, 21 (2), 161–83.

Morris, L. 1994: *Dangerous Classes.* London/New York: Routledge.

Morris, L. 1996: Dangerous classes: neglected aspects of the underclass debate. In E. Mingione (ed.), *Urban Poverty and the Underclass: A Reader.* Oxford/Cambridge, Mass.: Blackwell Publishers.

Moser, C. 1998: The asset vulnerability framework. *World Development*, 26 (1), 1–19.

Moser, C. and Norton, A. 2001: *To Claim our Rights.* London: Overseas Development Institute.

Mumford, A. and Power, A. 2003: *East Enders. Family and Community in East London.* Bristol: Policy Press.

Murray, C. 1988: *In Pursuit of Happiness and Good Government.* New York/London: Simon & Schuster.

Murray, C. 1996: The emerging British underclass. In R. Lister (ed.), *Charles Murray and the Underclass: The Developing Debate.* London: IEA Health & Welfare Unit.

Murray, C. 2001: *Underclass +10.* London: Institute for the Study of Civil Society.

Naples, N. 1998: *Grassroots Warriors: Activist Mothering, Community Work, and the War on Poverty.* New York/London: Routledge.

Narayan, D. 2000: *Can Anyone Hear Us?* New York/Oxford: Oxford University Press/World Bank.

Narayan, D., Chambers, R., Shah, M. K. and Petesch, P. 2000: *Crying out for Change.* New York: Oxford University Press/World Bank.

Newman, K. and Chin, M. M. 2003: High stakes: time poverty, testing and the children of the working poor. *Qualitative Sociology*, 26 (1), 3–34.

Nolan, B. and Whelan, C. T. 1996: *Resources, Deprivation, and Poverty.* Oxford: Clarendon Press.

Novak, M. 1987: *The New Consensus on Family and Welfare.* Washington, DC: American Enterprise Institute.

Novak, T. 2001: What's in a name? Poverty, the underclass and social exclusion. In M. Lavalette and A. Pratt (eds), *Social Policy: A Conceptual and Theoretical Introduction,* 2nd edn. London: Sage.

Nussbaum, M. 1995: Emotions and women's capabilities. In M. Nussbaum and J. Glover (eds), *Women, Culture and Development.* Oxford: Clarendon Press.

Nussbaum, M. 2000: *Women and Human Development.* Cambridge: Cambridge University Press.

Nussbaum, M. and Sen, A. (eds) 1993: *The Quality of Life.* Oxford: Clarendon Press.

Nyamu-Musembi, C. 2002: *Towards an Actor-Oriented Perspective on Human Rights.* IDS Working Paper 169. Brighton: IDS.

Nyoni, S. interviewed by P. Wiles 1988/9: Images of poverty. *Poverty,* 71, 6–10.

O'Connor, A. 2001: *Poverty Knowledge.* Princeton/Oxford: Princeton University Press.

Ochoa, M. A. U. 2001: Poverty and human rights in the light of the philosophy and contributions of Father Joseph Wresinski. In van Genugten and Perez-Bustillo, 2001.

OECD 2000: *Literacy in the Age of Information.* Paris: OECD.

OHCHR 1999: *Human Rights and Extreme Poverty.* Report of the independent expert on human rights submitted to Commission on Human Rights. 55th Session. E/CN 4/1999/48. New York: UN Economic and Social Council.

OHCHR 2002: *Draft Guidelines: A Human Rights Approach to Poverty Reduction Strategies.* Geneva: OHCHR.

Oliver, K. 2001: *Witnessing.* Minneapolis/London: University of Minnesota Press.

Orloff, A. S. 2002: Explaining US welfare reform. *Critical Social Policy,* 22 (1), 96–118.

Osberg, L. 2002: *Trends in Poverty: The UK in International Perspective – How Rates Mislead and Intensity Matters.* Working Paper 2002–10. Colchester: Institute for Social and Economic Research, University of Essex.

Øyen, E. 1996: Poverty research rethought. In E. Øyen, S. M. Miller and S. A. Samad (eds), *Poverty: A Global Review.* Oslo: Scandinavian University Press.

Øyen, E. 1997: The contradictory concepts of social exclusion and social inclusion. In Gore and Figueiredo, 1997.

Page, D. 2000: *Communities in the Balance.* York: Joseph Rowntree Foundation.

Pahl, R. 1984: *Divisions of Labour.* Oxford/New York: Basil Blackwell.

Pahl, J. 1989: *Money and Marriage.* Basingstoke: Macmillan.

Pakulski, J. 1997: Cultural citizenship. *Citizenship Studies*, 1 (1), 73–86.

Parekh, B. 2000: *The Future of Multi-Ethnic Britain.* London: Profile Books/Runnymede Trust.

Parry, G., Moyser, G. and Day, N. 1992: *Political Participation and Democracy in Britain.* Cambridge: Cambridge University Press.

Paugam, S. 1996: Poverty and social disqualification: a comparative analysis of cumulative social disadvantage in Europe. *Journal of European Social Policy*, 6 (4), 287–303.

Pawson, H. and Kintrea, K. 2002: Part of the problem or part of the solution? Social housing allocation policies and social exclusion in Britain. *Journal of Social Policy*, 31 (4), 643–67.

Payne, S. 1991: *Women, Health and Poverty.* Hemel Hempstead: Harvester Wheatsheaf.

Payne, S. and Pantazis, C. 1997: Poverty and gender. In D. Gordon and C. Pantazis (eds), *Breadline Britain in the 1990s,* Aldershot: Ashgate.

Pearce, D. 1990: Welfare is not *for* women. In L. Gordon (ed.), *Women, the State, and Welfare,* Madison/London: University of Wisconsin Press.

Percy-Smith, J. (ed.) 2000: *Policy Responses to Social Exclusion.* Buckingham/Philadelphia: Open University Press.

Pettigrew, N. 2003: *Experiences of Lone Parents from Minority Ethnic Communities.* Leeds: DWP/Corporate Document Services.

Phillips, A. 1999: *Which Inequalities Matter?* Cambridge: Polity.

Phillips, A. 2001: Feminism and liberalism revisited: has Martha Nussbaum got it right? *Constellations*, 8 (2), 249–66.

Phillips, A. 2003: Recognition and the struggle for political voice. In B. Hobson (ed.), *Recognition Struggles and Social Movements.* Cambridge: Cambridge University Press.

Philo, C., McCormick, J. and CPAG 1995: 'Poor places' and beyond. In C. Philo (ed.), *Off the Map: The Social Geography of Poverty in the UK.* London: CPAG.

Piachaud, D. 1987: Problems in the definition and measurement of poverty. *Journal of Social Policy,* 16 (2), 147–64.

Piachaud, D. 2002: *Capital and the Determinants of Poverty and Social Exclusion,* CASEpaper 60. London: CASE.

Pickering, M. 2001: *Stereotyping.* Basingstoke: Palgrave.

Pilkington, A. 2003: *Racial Disadvantage and Ethnic Diversity in Britain.* Basingstoke: Palgrave.

PIU 2002: *Ethnic Minorities and the Labour Market*. London: Cabinet Office.

Platt, L. 2002: *Parallel Lives? Poverty among Ethnic Minority Groups in Britain*. London: CPAG.

Pogge, T. 2002: *World Poverty and Human Rights*. Cambridge: Polity.

Polakow, V. 1993: *Lives on the Edge: Single Mothers and their Children in the Other America*. Chicago/London: University of Chicago Press.

Policy Action Team 9 1999: *Report of the Policy Action Team on Community Self-Help*. London: Social Exclusion Unit.

Porter, E. 2000: Participatory democracy and the challenge of dialogue across difference. In C. Roulston and C. Davies (eds), *Gender, Democracy and Inclusion in Northern Ireland*. Basingstoke: Palgrave.

Powell, M., Boyne, G. and Ashworth, R. 2001: Towards a geography of people poverty and place poverty, *Policy and Politics*, 29 (3), 243–58.

Prest, L. (ed.) 2000: *Out of the Shadows: A Collection of Poems from the Fourth World*. London: ATD Fourth World.

Procacci, G. 2001: Poor citizens: social citizenship vs. individualization of welfare. In C. Crouch, K. Eder and D. Tambini (eds), *Citizenship, Markets, and the State*. Oxford: Oxford University Press.

Proctor, B. D. and Dalaker, J. 2003: *Poverty in the United States: 2002*. Washington, DC: US Census Bureau.

Rademacher, A. and Patel, R. 2002: Retelling worlds of poverty. In Brock and McGee, 2002.

Rainwater, L., Smeeding, T. M. and Coder, J. 2001: Poverty across states, nations, and continents. In Vleminckx and Smeeding, 2001.

Rake, K. 2000: *Women's Incomes over the Lifetime*. London: Stationery Office.

Rakodi, C. 2002: A livelihoods approach: conceptual issues and definitions. In Rakodi with Lloyd-Jones, 2002.

Rakodi, C. with Lloyd-Jones, T. (eds) 2002: *Urban Livelihoods*. London: Earthscan.

Raup, E. 1996: Politics, race and US penal strategies. *Soundings*, 2, 153–68.

Raveaud, G. and Salais, R. 2001: Fighting against social exclusion in a European knowledge-based society. In Mayes et al., 2001.

Rawls, J. 1973: *A Theory of Justice*. Oxford: Oxford University Press.

Razavi, S. 1997: From rags to riches: looking at poverty from a gender perspective, *IDS Bulletin*, 28 (3), 49–62.

Razavi, S. 2000: Introduction. In S. Razavi (ed.), *Gendered Poverty and Wellbeing*. Oxford: Blackwell Publishers.

Revenga, A., Ringold, D., Tracy, W. M. 2002: *Poverty and Ethnicity : A Cross-country Study of Roma Poverty in Central Europe*. Washington, DC: World Bank.

Richardson, L. and Le Grand, J. 2002: Outsider and insider expertise: the response of residents of deprived neighbourhoods to an academic definition of social exclusion. *Social Policy & Administration*, 36 (5), 496–515.

Richardson, L. and Mumford, K. 2002: Community, neighbourhood and social infrastructure. In Hills et al., 2002.

Riches, G. 2002: Food banks and food security: welfare reform, human rights and social policy: lessons from Canada? *Social Policy & Administration*, 38 (6), 648–63.

Ridge, T. 2002: *Childhood Poverty and Social Exclusion*. Bristol: Policy Press.

Riggins, S. H. 1997: The rhetoric of othering. In S. H. Riggins (ed.), *The Language and Politics of Exclusion*. Thousand Oaks, Calif.: Sage.

Rimstead, R. 1997: Subverting poor me: negative construction of identity in poor and working class women's biographies. In S. H. Riggins (ed.), *The Language and Politics of Exclusion: Others in Discourse*. Thousand Oaks, Calif.: Sage.

Ringen, S. 1987: *The Possibility of Politics*. Oxford: Clarendon Press.

Robb, C. M. 2002: *Can the Poor Influence Policy?*, 2nd edn. Washington, DC: IMF/World Bank.

Robeyns, I. 2000: *An Unworkable Idea or a Promising Alternative? Sen's Capability Approach Re-examined*. <www.ingridrobeyns. nl/downloads/unworkable.pdf>.

Roche, M. and van Berkel, R. (eds) 1997: *European Citizenship and Social Exclusion*. Aldershot: Ashgate.

Rodgers, G. 1995: What is special about a 'social exclusion' approach? In Rodgers et al., 1995.

Rodgers, G. 1997: Labour market exclusions and the roles of social actors. In Gore and Figueiredo, 1997.

Rodgers, G., Gore, C. and Figueiredo, J. B. (eds) 1995: *Social Exclusion, Rhetoric, Reality, Responses*. Geneva: ILO.

Rogers, R. 2002: Discourses of resistance and the 'hostile job-seeker'. *Benefits*, 10 (1), 19–23.

Rogers-Dillon, R. 1995: The dynamics of welfare stigma. *Qualitative Sociology*, 18 (4), 439–56.

Room, G. (ed.) 1995: *Beyond the Threshold: The Measurement and Analysis of Social Exclusion*. Bristol: Policy Press.

Room, G. 1999: Social exclusion, solidarity and the challenge of globalisation. *International Journal of Social Welfare*, 8, 166–74.

Room, G. 2000: Trajectories of social exclusion: the wider context for the third and first worlds. In Gordon and Townsend, 2000.

Rosanvallon, P. 2000: *The New Social Question*. Princeton: Princeton University Press.

Ross, T. 1991: The rhetoric of poverty: their immorality, our helplessness. *Georgetown Law Journal*, 79 (5), 1499–547.

Rothstein, B. 1998: *Just Institutions Matter*. Cambridge: Cambridge University Press.

Rowlingson, K., Whyley, C., Newburn, T. and Berthoud, R. 1997: *Social Security Fraud*. London: DSS/Stationery Office.

Rowntree, B. S. 1937: *The Human Needs of Labour*. London: Longmans Green.

Runciman, W. G. 1966: *Relative Deprivation and Social Justice*. London: Routledge & Kegan Paul.

Runciman, W. G. 1990: How many classes are there in contemporary British society? *Sociology*. 24 (3), 378–96.

Ruspini, E. 1998: Women and poverty dynamics. *Journal of European Social Policy*, 8 (4), 291–316.

Ruspini, E. 2001: The study of women's deprivation. *International Journal of Social Research Methodology*, 4 (2), 101–18.

Russell, H. (ed.) 1996: *Speaking from Experience*. Manchester: Church Action on Poverty.

Russell, H. 1999: Friends in low places: gender, unemployment and sociability. *Work, Employment & Society*, 13 (2), 205–24.

Ruxton, S. 2003: *Men, Masculinities and Poverty in the UK*. Oxford: Oxfam.

Ruxton, S. and Bennett, F. 2002: *Including Children?* Brussels: Euronet.

Saraceno, C. (ed.) 2002: *Social Assistance Dynamics in Europe*. Bristol: Policy Press.

Saunders, P., Bradshaw, J. and Hirst, M. 2002: Using household expenditure to develop an income poverty line. *Social Policy & Administration*, 36 (3), 217–34.

Savage, M. 2000: *Class Analysis and Social Transformation*. Buckingham/Philadelphia: Open University Press.

SCCD 2001: *Strategic Framework for Community Development*. Sheffield: Standing Conference for Community Development.

Scharf, T., Phillipson, C., Smith, A. E. and Kingston P. 2002: *Growing Older in Socially Deprived Areas*. London: Help the Aged.

Schram, S. F. 1995: *Words of Welfare*, Minneapolis/London: University of Minnesota Press.

Schram, S. F. and Soss, J. 2002: Success stories: welfare reform, policy discourse and the politics of research. In Albelda and Withorn, 2002.

Scott, G., McKay, A., Sawers, C. and Harris, R. 1999: *What Can We Afford? A Woman's Role*. Glasgow: Scottish Poverty Information Unit.

Scott, J. 1994: *Poverty and Wealth*. London/New York: Longman.

Scott, J. C. 1985: *Weapons of the Weak*. New Haven/London: Yale University Press.

Scottish Executive 1999: *Making it Happen*. Edinburgh: Scottish Executive.

Sen, A. 1983: Poor, relatively speaking. *Oxford Economic Papers*, 35, 153–69.

Sen, A. 1985a: *Commodities and Capabilities*. Amsterdam: Elsevier Science Publishers.

Sen, A. 1985b: A sociological approach to the measurement of poverty: a reply to Professor Peter Townsend. *Oxford Economic Papers*, 37, 669–76.

Sen, A. 1990: Justice: means versus freedoms. *Philosophy and Public Affairs*, 19 (2): 111–21.

Sen, A. 1992: *Inequality Reexamined*. Oxford: Clarendon Press.

Sen, A. 1993: Capability and well-being. In Nussbaum and Sen, 1993.

Sen, A. 1999: *Development as Freedom*. Oxford: Oxford University Press.

Sen, A. 2000: *Social Exclusion*. Manila: Asian Development Bank.

Sennett, R. 2003: *Respect*. London: Allen Lane.

Sennett, R. and Cobb, J. 1972: *The Hidden Injuries of Class*. Cambridge: Cambridge University Press.

SEU 2000: *Minority Ethnic Issues in Social Exclusion and Neighbourhood Renewal*, London: SEU.

SEU 2001: *Preventing Social Exclusion*. London: SEU.

SEU 2003: *Making the Connections*. London: SEU.

Shaffer, P. 1996: Beneath the poverty debate: some issues. *IDS Bulletin*, 27 (1), 23–35.

Shoukens, P. and Carmichael, L. 2001: Social exclusion in Europe. In Mayes et al., 2001.

Shropshire, J. and Middleton, S. 1999: *Small Expectations*. York: Joseph Rowntree Foundation.

Shucksmith, M. 2000: *Exclusive Countryside?* York: Joseph Rowntree Foundation.

Sibley, D. 1995: *Geographies of Exclusion*. London/New York: Routledge.

Silburn, R., Lucas, D., Page, R. and Hanna, L. 1999: *Neighbourhood Images in Nottingham*. York: Joseph Rowntree Foundation.

Silver, H. 1993: National conceptions of the new urban poverty. *International Journal of Urban and Regional Research*, 17 (1), 336–54.

Silver, H. 1994: Social exclusion and social solidarity. *International Labour Review*, 133 (5–6), 531–78.

Silver, H. 1996: Culture, politics and national discourses of the new urban poverty. In E. Mingione (ed.) *Urban Poverty and the Underclass: A Reader.* Oxford/Cambridge, Mass: Blackwell Publishers.

Simmons, M. 1997: *Landscapes of Poverty.* London: Lemos & Crane.

6, P. 1997: *Social Exclusion: Time to be Optimistic.* Demos Collection, 12, 3–9.

Skeggs, B. 1997: *Formations of Class and Gender.* London: Sage.

Smith, A. 1776: *An Inquiry into the Nature and Causes of the Wealth of Nations*, 1892 edn. London: Routledge.

Smith, J. R. 2002: Commitment to mothering and preference for employment: the view of women on public assistance with young children. *Journal of Children & Poverty*, 8 (1), 51–66.

Social Policy & Society 2004: Themed issue on gender and individualization. 3 (1).

Solomon, A. 2001: *The Noonday Demon: An Anatomy of Depression.* London: Chatto & Windus.

Soss, J. 1999: Lessons of welfare. *American Political Science Review*, 93 (2), 363–80.

SOSTRIS 1997: *Social Exclusion in Comparative Perspective*, London: Centre for Biography in Social Policy.

Spicker, P. 1997: Exclusion. *Journal of Common Market Studies*, 35 (1), 133–43.

Spicker, P. 1999: Definitions of poverty. In Gordon and Spicker, 1999.

Spicker, P. 2001: Poor areas and the ecological fallacy. *Radical Statistics*, 76, 38–79.

Squires, P. 1990: *Anti-Social Policy.* Hemel Hempstead: Harvester Wheatsheaf.

Stammers, N. 1999: Social movements and the social construction of human rights. *Human Rights Quarterly*, 21 (4), 980–1008.

Standing, K. 1999: Lone mothers and 'parental' involvement. *Journal of Social Policy*, 28 (3), 479–95.

Steinert, H. and Pilgram, A. (eds) 2003: *Welfare Policy from Below: Struggles against Social Exclusion in Europe.* Aldershot: Ashgate.

Stephenson, A. 2001: *Work and Welfare: Attitudes, Experiences and Behaviour of Nineteen Low Income Families.* London: DSS.

Stier, H. and Mandel, H. 2003: *Inequality in the Family*. Luxembourg Income Study Working Paper 359. www.lisproject. org/publications.htm.

Strobel, P. 1996: From poverty to social exclusion. *International Social Science Journal*, 48 (2), 173–89.

Tawney, R. H. 1913: *Inaugural Lecture on Poverty as an Industrial Problem*, reproduced in *Memorandum on the Problems of Poverty*, vol. 2. London: William Morris Press.

Taylor, C. 1992: The politics of recognition. In A. Gutmann (ed.), *Multiculturalism and the Politics of Recognition*. Princeton: Princeton University Press.

Taylor, D. 1998: Social identity and social policy. *Journal of Social Policy*, 27 (3), 329–50.

Taylor, M., Barr, A. and West, A. 2000: *Signposts to Community Development*. London: Community Development Foundation.

Taylor-Gooby, P. 1998: Choice and the new paradigm in policy. In P. Taylor-Gooby (ed.), *Choice and Public Policy*. Basingstoke: Macmillan.

Thekaekara, S. and Thekaekara, M. 1994: *Across the Geographical Divide*. London: Centre for Innovation in Voluntary Action.

Titterton, M. 1992: Managing threats to welfare: the search for a new paradigm of welfare. *Journal of Social Policy*, 21 (1), 1–23.

Tolman, R. M. and Raphael, J. 2000: A review of research on welfare and domestic violence. *Journal of Social Issues*, 56 (4), 655–82.

Townsend, P. 1979: *Poverty in the United Kingdom*. Harmondsworth: Penguin Books.

Townsend, P. 1987. *Poverty and Labour in London*. London: Low Pay Unit.

Townsend, P. 1993: *The International Analysis of Poverty*. Hemel Hempstead: Harvester Wheatsheaf.

Townsend, P. and Gordon, D. 2000: Introduction. In Gordon and Townsend, 2000.

Townsend, P. and Gordon, D. (eds) 2002: *World Poverty*. Bristol: Policy Press.

Toynbee, P. 2003: *Hard Work*. London: Bloomsbury.

Tunstall, R. and Lupton, R. 2003: *Is Targeting Deprived Areas an Effective Means for Reaching Poor People?* CASEpaper 71. London: CASE.

Turner, J. and Grieco, M. 2000: Gender and time poverty. *Time & Society*, 9 (1), 129–36.

UKCAP 1997: *Poverty & Participation*. London: UKCAP.

Ulshoefer, P. 1998: Gender and social exclusion. In Figueiredo and de Hann, 1998.

UN 1995: *The Copenhagen Declaration and Programme of Action*. New York: UN.

UN General Assembly 1993: *Vienna Declaration and Programme of Action*. New York: UN.

UNDP 1995: *Human Development Report 1995*: New York/ Oxford: Oxford University Press.

UNDP 1997: *Human Development Report 1997*. New York/ Oxford: Oxford University Press.

UNDP 2000: *Human Development Report 2000*: New York/Oxford: Oxford University Press.

UNDP 2002: *Human Development Report 2002*. New York/ Oxford: Oxford University Press.

UNDP 2003: *Human Development Report 2003*. New York/ Oxford: Oxford University Press.

UNICEF 2000: *A League Table of Child Poverty in Rich Nations*. Report Card, 1. Florence: Innocenti Research Centre.

Urban Studies 2001: special issue: *Urban Neighbourhoods*. 38 (12).

Vaitilingam, R. 2002: Executive summary. In ESRC, *How People on Low Incomes Manage their Finances*. Swindon: Economic and Social Research Council.

Valentine, C. 1968: *Culture and Poverty*. Chicago/London: University of Chicago Press.

Van den Bosch, K. 2001: *Identifying the Poor*. Aldershot: Ashgate.

van Genugten, W. and Perez-Bustillo, C. (eds) 2001: *The Poverty of Rights: Human Rights and the Eradication of Poverty*. London/New York: Zed Books.

van Oorschot, W. and Halman, L. 2000: Blame or fate, individual or society? An international comparison of popular explanations of poverty. *European Societies*, 2 (1), 1–28.

Vegeris, S. and Perry, J. 2003. *Families and Children 2001*. Leeds: DWP/Corporate Document Services.

Veit-Wilson, J. 1986: Paradigms of poverty: a rehabilitation of B. S. Rowntree. *Journal of Social Policy*, 15 (1), 69–99.

Veit-Wilson, J. 1987: Consensual approaches to poverty lines and social security. *Journal of Social Policy*, 183–211.

Veit-Wilson, J. 1994: Measuring the minimum. *Poverty*, 87, 14–15.

Veit-Wilson, J. 1998: *Setting Adequacy Standards*. Bristol: Policy Press.

Veit-Wilson, J. 1999: Poverty and the adequacy of social security. In J. Ditch (ed.), *Introduction to Social Security*. London/New York: Routledge.

Veit-Wilson, J. 2004: Understanding poverty. In J. Flaherty, J. Veit-Wilson and P. Dornan, *Poverty: The Facts*, 5th edn. London: CPAG.

Verba, S., Schlozman, K. L., Brady, H. E. and Nie, N. H. 1993: Citizen activity. *American Political Science Review*, 87 (2), 303–18.

Verba, S., Schlozman, K. L. and Brady, H. E. 1995: *Voice and Equality*. Cambridge, Mass./London: Harvard University Press.

Vickery, C. 1977: The time poor: a new look at poverty. *Journal of Human Resources*, 12 (1), 27–48.

Vincent, D. 1991: *Poor Citizens*, Harlow: Longman.

Vizard, P. 2001: *Economic Theory, Freedom and Human Rights: The Work of Amartya Sen*. ODI Briefing Paper. London: ODI.

Vleminckx, V. and Smeeding, T. M. (eds) 2001: *Child Well-being, Child Poverty and Child Policy in Modern Nations*. Bristol: Policy Press.

Vobruba, G. 2000: Actors in processes of inclusion and exclusion. *Social Policy & Administration*, 34 (5), 601–13.

Vogler, C. 1994: Money in the household. In M. Anderson, F. Bechhofer and J. Gershuny (eds), *The Social and Political Economy of the Household*, Oxford: Oxford University Press.

Wacquant, L. J. D. 1996: Red belt, black belt: racial divisions, class inequalities and the state in the French urban periphery and the American ghetto. In E. Mingione (ed.), *Urban Poverty and the Underclass: A Reader*. Oxford/Cambridge, Mass.: Blackwell Publishers.

Wainwright, H. 2003: *Reclaim the State*. London/New York: Verso.

Walker, R. with Ashworth, K. 1994: *Poverty Dynamics*. Aldershot: Avebury.

Walker, R. with Howard, M. 2000: *The Making of a Welfare Class?* Bristol: Policy Press.

Walker, R. and Middleton, S. 1995: Defining poverty lines. *Benefits*, 14, 20–1.

Walker, R. and Park, J. 1998: Unpicking poverty. In C. Oppenheim (ed.), *An Inclusive Society*. London: IPPR.

Walker, R. and Shaw, A. 1998: Escaping from social assistance in Britain. In Leisering and Walker, 1998.

Warah, R. 2000: 'All I wanted was a toilet': why voices of the poor matter. *Habitat Debate*, 6 (4), 24–5.

Ward, C., Dale, A. and Joshi, H. 1996: Income dependency within couples. In L. Morris and E. S. Lyon (eds), *Gender Relations In Public and Private*, Basingstoke: Macmillan.

Wardhaugh, J. and Jones, J. 1999: Begging in time and space. In Dean, 1999.

Warschauer, M. 2003: *Technology and Social Inclusion*. Cambridge, Mass./London: MIT Press.

Waters, T. 1999: Chesson's choice. *New Internationalist*, March, 15–17.

Waxman, C. I. 1977: *The Stigma of Poverty*. New York: Pergamon Press.

Welshman, J. 2002: The cycle of deprivation and the concept of the underclass. *Benefits*, 10 (3), 199–205.

Wessels, B. and Miedema, S. 2003: Participation and social exclusion. In Steinert and Pilgram, 2003.

Whelan, C. T., Layte, R., Maître, B. and Nolan, B. 2000: Poverty dynamics. *European Societies*. 2 (4), 505–31.

Whelan, C. T., Layte, R. and Maître, B. 2003: Persistent income poverty and deprivation in the European Union. *Journal of Social Policy*, 32 (1), 1–18.

Williams, C. C. 2002: Social exclusion in a consumer society. *Social Policy and Society*, 1 (3), 203–11.

Williams, C. C. and Windebank, J. 1998a: *Informal Employment in the Advanced Economies*. London/New York: Routledge.

Williams, C. C. and Windebank, J. 1998b: The unemployed and the paid informal sector in Europe's cities and regions. In Lawless et al., 1998.

Williams, C. C. and Windebank, J. 2000: Self-help and mutual aid in deprived neighbourhoods. *Urban Studies*, 37 (1), 127–47.

Williams, C. C. and Windebank, J. 2002: The uneven geographies of informal economic activities. *Work, Employment and Society*. 16 (2), 231–50.

Williams, C. C. and Windebank, J. 2003. *Poverty and the Third Way*. London/New York: Routledge.

Williams, F. 1998: Agency and structure revisited. In M. Barry and C. Hallett (eds), *Social Exclusion and Social Work*. Lyme Regis: Russell House Publishing.

Williams, F. and Popay J. 1999: Balancing polarities: developing a new framework for welfare research. In Williams et al., 1999a.

Williams, F., Popay, J. and Oakley, A. (eds) 1999a: *Welfare Research: A Critical Review*. London: UCL Press.

Williams, F., Popay, J. and Oakley, A. 1999b: Changing paradigms of welfare. In Williams et al., 1999a.

Williams, P. and Hubbard, P. 2001: Who is disadvantaged? Retail change and social exclusion. *International Review of Retail, Distribution and Consumer Research*, 11 (3), 267–86.

Willow, C. 2001: *Bread is Free: Children and Young People Talk about Poverty*. London: Children's Rights Alliance.

Wilson, H. and Herbert, G. W. 1978: *Parents and Children in the Inner City*. London: Routledge & Kegan Paul.

Wilson, W. J. 1987: *The Truly Disadvantaged*. Chicago/London: University of Chicago Press.

Witcher, S. 2003: *Renewing the Terms of Inclusion*. CASEpaper 67, London: CASE.

Wolfe, M. 1995: Globalization and social exclusion: some paradoxes. In Rodgers et al., 1995.

Wood, M. and Vamplew, C. 1999: *Neighbourhood Images in Teeside*. York: Joseph Rowntree Foundation.

World Bank, 2001: *World Development Report 2000/2001*. New York: Oxford University Press.

Yeandle, S. Escott, K., Grant, L. and Batty, E. 2003: *Women and Men Talking about Poverty*. Manchester: EOC.

Young, I. M. 1990: *Justice and the Politics of Difference*. Oxford: Princeton University Press.

Young, I. M. 1994. Gender as seriality. *Signs*. 19 (3), 713–38.

Young, I. M. 2000: *Inclusion and Democracy*. Oxford: Oxford University Press.

Young, J. 1999: *The Exclusive Society*. London: Sage.

Index